Sex, Sin, and Our Selves

Sex, Sin, and Our Selves

*Encounters in Feminist Theology
and Contemporary Women's Literature*

ANNA FISK

☞PICKWICK *Publications* · Eugene, Oregon

SEX, SIN, AND OUR SELVES
Encounters in Feminist Theology and Contemporary Women's Literature

Copyright © 2014 Anna Fisk. All rights reserved. Except for brief quotations in critical publications or reviews, no part of this book may be reproduced in any manner without prior written permission from the publisher. Write: Permissions, Wipf and Stock Publishers, 199 W. 8th Ave., Suite 3, Eugene, OR 97401.

Pickwick Publications
An Imprint of Wipf and Stock Publishers
199 W. 8th Ave., Suite 3
Eugene, OR 97401

www.wipfandstock.com

ISBN 13: 978-1-62564-068-0

Cataloging-in-Publication data:

Fisk, Anna.

Sex, sin, and our selves : encounters in feminist theology and contemporary women's literature / Anna Fisk.

xx + 200 pp. ; 23 cm—Includes bibliographical references.

ISBN 13: 978-1-62564-068-0

1. Feminist theology. 2. Feminist literature. 3. Roberts, Michèle—Criticism and interpretation. 4. Maitland, Sara—Criticism and interpretation. I. Title.

BT83.55 F57 2014

Manufactured in the USA

For Nanny and Papa,

"... for the growing good of the world is partly dependent on unhistoric acts; and that things are not so ill with you and me as they might have been, is half owing to the number who lived faithfully a hidden life ..."

—George Eliot, *Middlemarch*
(London: William Blackwood, 1874).

Contents

Acknowledgments ix

Abbreviations xi

Introduction: "The Beauty of Bones" xiii

1. Annunciation: Autobiographical Fictions 1
2. Visitation: Reading and Writing Encounters 38
3. Selves 74
4. Suffering, Sacrifice, and Sin 104
5. Sex and the Sacred 134
6. Sea 166

Bibliography 191

Acknowledgments

THIS BOOK OWES ITS existence to three remarkable women: Sara Maitland, Michèle Roberts, and my PhD supervisor Heather Walton. I am deeply grateful to Sara and Michèle for their writing, which has been such a fruitful area of research, and in which I still take great pleasure in reading. I would also like to thank Sara for her interest in my work, her hospitality, and conversation when I visited her in Galloway. I am indebted to Heather's groundbreaking work on literature, feminism, and theology, but I want to thank her most of all for overseeing my doctoral project: I could not have wished for a better student-supervisor relationship.

Special thanks also goes to David Jasper and Nicola Slee, my doctoral examiners, who provided insightful critique as well as support that has continued long after the viva.

Others to whom I owe my thanks are:

Conversation-partners, readers, and friends: Alana Vincent, Dawn Llewellyn, Elizabeth Anderson, Jennifer Reek, and Mark Godin.

Those who gave of their time and attention to proofread earlier versions of this text: Andrew Macdonell, Jamie Heit, Katie Nail, Michael Mooney, and Robert Viney.

My inspiring, infuriating, and much loved siblings: Bethan Fisk, Sam Fisk, and Thomas Fisk.

The family and friends whose love and generous financial and practical support this book could not have been written without: Pip Fisk, Colin and Ethel Hasler, Peter Fisk, Carol Fisk, and Chris Pout.

Those who over the years have been there during the hardest times: Andrea Baildon, Jaime Grier, Lauren Probert, Maddy Hughes, and Sequoia Taylor.

Those whose friendship during recent difficult months has enabled the completion of this text: Agnes Marszalek, Antje Karl, and Robin Davis.

With tongue only ever so slightly in cheek, the last shout-out goes to Alyosha.

Abbreviations

Works by Sara Maitland

3TT	*Three Times Table*. London: Virago, 1990.
AAM	*Angel and Me: Short Stories for Holy Week*. London: Mowbray, 1995.
ABS	*A Book of Silence*. London: Granta, 2008.
AM	"About Me." No pages. Online: http://saramaitland.com/about_me.html.
AT	with Michelene Wandor. *Arky Types*. London: Methuen, 1987.
BFG	*On Becoming a Fairy Godmother*. London: Maia, 2003.
BG	*A Big-Enough God: A Feminist's Search for a Joyful Theology*. New York: Riverhead, 1995.
BJ	*Brittle Joys*. London: Virago, 1999.
BSP	*A Book of Spells*. London: Methuen, 1987.
DJ	*Daughter of Jerusalem*. London: Pan, 1978.
FF	"The Future of Faith." *Cross Currents* (Spring-Summer 2000) 154–56.
FN	*Far North and Other Dark Tales*. London: Maia, 2008.
FWP	"A Feminist Writer's Progress." In *On Gender and Writing*, edited by Michelene Wandor, 17–23. London: Thorsons, 1983.
GI	with Peter Matthews. *Gardens of Illusion*. London: Cassell, 2000.
HT	*Home Truths*. London: Sceptre, 1993.
IBB	"Sara Maitland." In *The Way We Write: Interviews with Award-Winning Writers*, edited by Barbara Baker, 102–11. London: Continuum, 2006.
IJB	Interview with Joan Bakewell. *Belief*. Radio 3. March 20, 2010.
LMC	"Is There a Link Between Madness and Creativity?" *Intervoice*. No pages. Online: http://www.intervoiceonline.org/2181/voices/personal-experience/sara-maitland.html
MNC	*A Map of the New Country: Women and Christianity*. London: Routledge & Kegan Paul, 1983.
PP	"Passionate Prayer: Masochistic Images in Women's Experience." In *Sex and God: Some Varieties of Women's Religious Experience*, edited by Linda Hurcombe, 125–40. London: Routledge & Kegan Paul, 1987.
RL	"Rose of Lima: Some Thoughts on Purity and Penance." In *Through the Devil's Gateway*, edited by Alison Joseph, 60–70. London: SPCK, 1990.
RWB	Panel discussion with Michelene Wandor and Anna Fisk. Re-Writing the Bible symposium, University of Glasgow, June 14, 2010.
SC	with Chris Gollon. *Stations of the Cross*. London: Continuum, 2009.
TPO	"Two for the Price of One." In *Fathers: Reflections by Daughters*, edited by Ursula Owen, 32–42. London: Virago, 1986.
TT	*Telling Tales*. London: Journeyman, 1983.
VM	with Wendy Mulford. *Virtuous Magic: Women Saints and Their Meanings*. London: Continuum, 1998.
VT	*Virgin Territory*. London: Virago, 1984.

Abbreviations

WFMW   *Women Fly When Men Aren't Watching*. London: Virago, 1993.
WR   "Ways of Relating." In *Feminist Theology: A Reader*, edited by Ann Loades, 148–57. London: SPCK, 1990.

Works by Michèle Roberts

ASW   *All the Selves I Was: New and Selected Poems*. London: Virago, 1995.
BMN   *The Book of Mrs Noah*. London: Vintage, 1987.
DH   *Daughters of the House*. London: Virago, 1992.
ET   "Epilogue." In *Tales I Tell My Mother: A Collection of Feminist Short Stories*, by Zoë Fairbairns et al. London: Journeyman, 1978.
FB   *Flesh and Blood*. London: Virago, 1994.
FE   *Fair Exchange*. London: Virago, 1999.
FSG   *Food, Sex and God: On Inspiration and Writing*. London: Virago, 1998.
GCG   with Dawn Llewellyn and Deborah F. Sawyer, "'Getting A/cross God': An Interview with Michèle Roberts." In *Reading Spiritualities: Constructing and Representing the Sacred*, edited by Dawn Llewellyn and Deborah F. Sawyer, 15–25. Aldershot: Ashgate, 2008.
IBR   with Patricia Bastida Rodríguez. "On Women, Christianity and History: An Interview with Michèle Roberts." *Atlantis* 25/1 (2003) 93–107.
IGS   with María Soraya García Sánchez. "Talking About Women, History and Writing with Michèle Roberts." *Atlantis* 27/2 (2005) 137–47.
IJN   with Jenny Newman. "An Interview with Michèle Roberts." *Cercles*, 2003. No pages. Online: http://www.cercles.com/interviews/roberts.html
IS   *Impossible Saints*. London: Virago, 1997.
LG   *The Looking Glass*. London: Virago, 2000.
MC   *The Mistressclass*. London: Virago, 2004.
MMT   "Martha and Mary Raise Consciousness from the Dead." In *Tales I Tell My Mother: A Collection of Feminist Short Stories*, by Zoë Fairbairns et al, 71–79. London: Journeyman, 1978.
MSL   *Mud: Stories of Sex and Love*. London: Virago, 2010.
PH   *Paper Houses: A Memoir of the '70s and Beyond*. London: Virago, 2008.
PN   *A Piece of the Night*. London: The Women's Press, 1978.
PS   *Playing Sardines*. London: Virago, 2001.
RMH   *Reader, I Married Him*. London: Virago, 2006.
RK   *In the Red Kitchen*. London: Minerva, 1990.
TV   *The Visitation*. London: The Women's Press, 1983.
UG   "Une Glossaire/A Glossary." In *More Tales I Tell My Mother*, by Zoë Fairbairns et al, 41–80. London: Journeyman, 1987.
WG   *The Secret Gospel of Mary Magdalene*. Original edition: *The Wild Girl*, 1984. London: Vintage, 2007.
WWH   "The Woman Who Wanted to Be a Hero." In *Walking on the Water: Women Talk About Spirituality*, edited by Jo Garcia and Sara Maitland, 50–65. London: Virago, 1983.

Introduction

"The Beauty of the Bones"

Nobody knew to whom these scrap bones belonged. They had been sorted and classified simply according to shape and appearance, then made into a mosaic... constructed of square wooden frames, each packed tight with a particular arrangement of bones, that, placed together formed a precise and repeated abstract pattern of straight lines, rosette, and mandalas. Only on a second glance did you realise that what you were looking at were massed tibias, fibulas, and femurs, with here and there a skull and crossbones for added decoration, or a prayer superimposed in bone letters in a language nobody could understand.

Isabel brought her granddaughter to see it. The child, frowning and black-haired, imagined the architects of this place as busy cooks inventing recipes, sorting and arranging, putting certain bones into the gold cupboards as you'd put joints of meat into larders, and setting some aside, to be boiled down for other uses, soup, perhaps, or glue. They were artists, surely. Sitting cross-legged on the floor, each with a lapful of bones, braiding them together like crochet, rearticulating them into fantastic shapes, making them speak like poetry. Fitting them into the square trays, according to the designs they'd worked out...

Bones pictures, arranged row on row, so that your eye could travel over them vertically or horizontally or both at once. You could see all the layers of bones, and you could see each individual bone; the part and the whole. The patterns were severe and mysterious. No one could say what they meant. What you saw was the overall dance of shapes. The beauty of the bones.[1]

1. *IS*, 2–3.

Introduction

PERHAPS DUE TO FEMINISM'S emphasis on theory that is practical and embodied, feminist engagement with literature and with theology has often envisioned its work in terms of material objects. When Adrienne Rich defined "feminist revisioning" as "the act of looking back" in order "not to pass on a tradition but to break its hold over us,"[2] this was given poetic form in "Diving into the Wreck." The feminist artist becomes an underwater explorer, seeking to find amongst the debris of patriarchy "the damage that was done / and the treasures that prevail."[3] Alicia Ostriker reads in women's poetry a "shared plundering" of the jewels that are worth keeping from patriarchy's treasure trove of symbols and stories.[4] Ann Loades uses the metaphor of "searching for lost coins," from the parable of Luke 15:8–10, in which God's care for sinners is likened to a woman sweeping the house, diligently seeking the one drachma she has lost.[5] Feminist theologians find few whole and untarnished objects amidst the fundamentally androcentric Christian tradition, and thus a large part of their work is to remodel into new shapes the symbols and stories from which that tradition is made.[6] The task of feminist critique and reinvention of a cultural heritage that is fundamentally patriarchal is not just a matter of scavenging and rebuilding; first there has to be the dismantling and deconstructing.

Both the constructive and reconstructive task of feminist critique are represented in the image of quilting. Drawn to material metaphors that pertain to the domestic arts, "women's work," feminist theology has often described itself in terms of spinning and weaving,[7] but it is the image of quilting that encapsulates the feminist project of seeking "to articulate new patterns from bits of contemporary experiences and ancient sources."[8] As an often communal activity that makes a new object from scraps of old cloth, quilting provides a symbol of women constructing together something new from fragments of experience and scraps of doctrinal and textual traditions. Rebecca Chopp writes that metaphors of quilting "underscore the history

---

2. Rich, "When We Dead Awaken," 91.
3. Rich, *Poetry and Prose*, 54.
4. Ostriker, *Stealing the Language*, 211.
5. Loades, *Searching for Lost Coins*.
6. See Christ, "Why Women Need the Goddess"; Jantzen, "Feminism and Flourishing"; McFague, *Metaphorical Theology*; Morley, "I Desire Her"; and Soskice, "Turning the Symbols," for feminist theological thought on symbol and metaphor.
7. See for example Christ and Plaskow, *Weaving the Visions*.
8. Johnson, *She Who Is*, 12.

"The Beauty of the Bones"

of women's lives in western culture, but also . . . locate the very identity of theology in the context of functional warmth, of common beauty, of daily practices."[9] Quilting can serve as a symbol for feminist piecing together of the religious symbols that it has torn apart, but also of the process of tearing apart itself. There is pleasure to be had in playing with the pieces, in making something new from the old. In the metaphor of quilting there is an appropriate violence to the cutting up and stitching together of fabric, and it is an act of re-creation that does not try to conceal the origins of its constituent parts, nor the differences between them, when in the early days of feminist theology there seemed to be the hope that feminist theology could rebuild patriarchal religious tradition into a new and systematized construction.[10]

The general emphasis of more recent feminist theological discourse has not been a rebuilding of a systematic theology. I myself do not believe that it is possible, or desirable, for feminist theology to rearrange the torn-apart symbols of Christian theology into a new harmonious whole. It has to go too far in the work of deconstruction for reconstruction to be achievable. The image of the quilt may hold this: the necessary destruction, the incongruity. But for me, as a metaphor it is too cozy and comfortable: worn-out clothing is altogether too pleasant to represent the harmful symbols of patriarchal religion. The finished object, a quilt, is one that symbolizes safety and solidity, and thus the use of this metaphor also represents a tendency for which feminist theology has been critiqued. In their groundbreaking, dedicated, meticulous, and profoundly valuable work, the more well-known voices of feminist theology resound with hope and certainty. While they may be conscientious in self-critique and honest about moments of doubt, they hold fast to a faith that goodness and justice are the essential truth and reality and will ultimately prevail.[11] I do not share this faith. In my feminist theological reflection, the finished products of feminist repatterning of symbol and story are more strange and discomforting than a quilt.

The feminist theology of this book is envisioned in terms of an image from Michèle Roberts's novel *Impossible Saints*. It is a macabre image which preserves a sense of the horror of women's existence within patriarchy, that the revisioning of old symbols and stories is not safe, soft, warm, or

---

9. Chopp, *Saving Work*, 74–75.

10. For example Ruether, *Sexism and God-Talk*, can be read as a systematic feminist theology.

11. See Sands, *Escape from Paradise*; Walton, *Imagining Theology*; and Walton, *Literature, Theology and Feminism*.

Introduction

comfortable. The image is based on the Golden Chamber attached to the Basilica of St. Ursula in Cologne, said to hold the remains of Ursula and eleven thousand virgin martyrs. As well as containing the relics of named women saints in wooden cupboards and gilded statues, the bones of the nameless saints, whose bones have got mixed up together, are formed into a mosaic, "constructed of square wooden frames, each packed tight with a particular arrangement of bones" around the upper part of the chapel's wall, reaching up to the vault's arches.[12] In *Impossible Saints*, this bizarre piece of interior design is imagined in terms of the domestic work of women, "busy cooks inventing recipes, sorting and arranging," their piecing together of a bone collage a "braiding," "like crochet." As a symbol for feminism and literature, the goods of women's communal work and creative endeavor are combined with the horrific and the tragic. The end result is not a complete and harmonious composition that can be easily assimilated and understood: "[t]he patterns were severe and mysterious. No one could say what they meant. What you saw was the overall dance of shapes. The beauty of the bones."[13]

As a feminist theological bone collage, this book pieces together fragments of feminist discourse and the broken shards of Christian theology. The violence inherent in the image of human bones is apt: in my engagement with the tradition of feminist theology I have simplified a diverse movement and body of work; I have made things fit to my own design, and not always fairly acknowledged the complexity and fluidity of the thought of the feminist theologians that I critique. To shift the metaphor from one of collage to painting, my brush strokes are broad ones. Perhaps all academic writing involves an appropriation of the work of others that can be described as violent, but it is important for me to acknowledge that I have made a composition from the pieces of my own reading of feminist theology, and that it should not foreclose other meanings held by other authors and readers. As this is my own composition, the issues often so central to feminist discourse today—such as intersecting oppressions gender, race and socioeconomics, differences between feminisms, and critique of gender-essentialism and assertion that the category 'woman' is not an unproblematic given—have been barely touched on. In part, this is due to the particular authors I have chosen to work on; I have also simplified in order to ensure that the discussion does not become unwieldy. Despite this,

12. *IS*, 2.
13. Ibid., 3.

as a, white, Western, middle-class, able-bodied, and cisgendered woman, I am uncomfortable when I notice which particular issues I have neglected to discuss, and hope to redress this in future work.

This book is a work of "literature and theology," in which my feminist theological bone collage is created not only from my reading of theological texts but also the literature of the British feminist novelists Michèle Roberts and Sara Maitland. My method of doing literature and theology follows the thought of David Jasper and Heather Walton, which emphasizes not theology *through* literature, or literature as the handmaid of theology, but the ways in which literature forms a renewing challenge to theological certainties.[14] Yet I cannot claim to be taking the literature on its own terms, as if such a thing were possible; my readings of Roberts and Maitland's work are my own. Both writers have a large and complex body of work, and there is perhaps a certain violence in the way I have chosen some elements to focus on at the exclusion of others. The image of a collage made from women's bones to represent my theological engagement with literature is particularly unsettling when the authors I work on are still alive and still writing.

As well as the image of the golden bone collage, this book is also envisioned in terms of a phrase Kathleen Sands uses to describe her own theological method: "[r]eading these stories beside my own, I find no answers to be believed in, but challenge and insight, delight and strength, that are fragile and finite but real."[15] This describes not only my sense of producing a "fragile and finite" theological composition rather than a solid and harmonious construction, my resistance to an eschatological optimism that lacks reality for me, and that this theology comes through engaging with the "stories" of women's literature, but also the importance of "reading these stories beside my own." In this book, the pieces of my readings in theology and literature are placed alongside fragments of autobiography, of my own experience rendered into narrative form. As with my use of theology and literature, my plundering of my own stories does not result in a satisfying and complete composition, and there is no more authenticity or integrity to my reading of the texts of personal experience than there is to my reading of the texts of others.

This book is based on my doctoral dissertation; it has its origins at the beginning of my twenties and is in the stages of completion in the months

---

14. See Jasper, "Study of Literature and Theology"; Walton, *Literature, Theology and Feminism*; and the essays collected in Walton, *Literature and Theology*.

15. Sands, *Escape From Paradise*, 167.

Introduction

before I turn thirty. As such, the book is something of a *Bildungsroman*, or a coming of age theology: I draw a lot on the experience of my teenage years and the earlier part of my twenties, and some of the particular issues that I chose to focus on no longer feel as personally or theologically resonant as they once did. Perhaps this is a result of having written about them; these beliefs, concept, words, and images that I spent so much time grappling with are now fixed down into a mosaic of bones. While it may not inscribe certainties or a narrative that works as a successive whole (there is no satisfying conclusion to this book), just having these things set out in a distinct form has lent a sense of closure.

The theological themes that form the core of this book are intimated in the title, *Sex, Sin, and Our Selves*, a nod to the classic feminist texts *Sex, Sin and Grace* by Judith Plaskow, and *Our Bodies, Ourselves* by the Boston Women's Health Book Collective. This book discusses the gendered issues of selfhood, redemptive suffering, theologies of sin, and sexuality inherent in spirituality.

Chapters 1 and 2 are concerned with what it means to do theology through reading Roberts and Maitland's "stories beside my own." Chapter 1 explores the practice of bringing one's autobiography into theological reading, contextualized with a critical survey of the use of the personal voice in recent academic discourse. I explore the issue of 'narrative selfhood' as it pertains to women's life-writing and the telling of my own stories. I then give an overview and discussion of the 'narrated selves'—as disclosed in their writing and interviews—of the novelists Michèle Roberts and Sara Maitland, utilizing the image of self-narration as 'annunciation.' Chapter 2 turns to the biblical visitation of Mary and Elizabeth as representative of the creative power of encounter with other women. My theological reading of Roberts and Maitland's writing is a 'visitation'; in turn their writing is generated from multiple and interrelated visitations. I consider this in terms of the communal context of feminist writing practice, feminist revisioning of women encountered in myth and history, and the relationships that readers have with books. The following four chapters put into practice the method of theological reflection envisioned in section 1 as 'annunciation' and 'visitation.' In chapter 3 I explore the tension between women's need for autonomous selfhood and feminist emphasis on connectedness and relationality. I then turn to psychoanalytic accounts of subjectivity as explanatory narratives of the conflicting human desires for separation and connection. Chapter 4 considers how the themes of sin and self-sacrifice in the Christian tradition have been radically critiqued in feminist theology, whilst arguing that feminism tends to privilege ideals above reality in its contention with issues of suffering. In chapter 5, I revisit the discussion of eros and loss of self taken up in chapter 3, via the interplay of sexuality and religious experience in 'erotic asceticism.' The final chapter brings together these theological fragments, looking to the sea for a metaphorical way of thinking about the divine that does not reinscribe idealized notions of purity and certainty.

1

Annunciation
Autobiographical Fictions

WRITING THE SELF

"The Waltz of the 'As A's": Autobiography in Academic Writing

FEMINIST THEOLOGY'S (NOT UNTROUBLED) faith in the authority of women's experience is far from alone in feminist discourse in asserting that what we see depends on where we stand. A central aspect of academic feminist theory—be it in philosophy, sociology, political science, literary criticism, and so on—is the argument that abstract and universalized accounts of knowledge serve to obscure the perspective and interests of those of the dominant social classes. Early feminist theorists such as Carol Gilligan and Nancy Hartsock (who coined the term "standpoint epistemology") claimed that women's social circumstances entail that they see and know differently from men.[1] This, in light of postmodern thought and the critiques of black and postcolonial criticism, led to an emphasis on the particular situation of the critic, researcher, or theorist. This is neatly summarized in the words of Margaretta Jolly: "[i]n today's pluralist culture, individuals assert that knowledge is by definition conditioned by its context, embodied and relative to its speaker. For them, the job of an academic is not to argue until we arrive at some final objectivity, but to find ways of understanding and living with our differences."[2]

---

1. Hartsock, *Feminist Standpoint*.
2. Jolly, "Speaking Personally," 214.

Thus in the last three decades it has become standard, at least in certain academic discourses, for an author to open a piece of work with a statement of their own social location; for example "as a white, western, middle-class woman." This convention, which Nancy Miller terms "the waltz of the 'as a's; the obligatory dance cards of representivity"[3] does not always entail that the academic writer will continue throughout their work to discuss the ways in which their own circumstances have influenced its production. More often than not, it is a way of paying tribute to the "anxiety over speaking *as* and speaking *for*,"[4] while avoiding full consideration of that very anxiety. Yet the academic culture of 'as a ___' has enabled the emergence of 'personal criticism,' in which the academic writer self-consciously reflects on their own experience.

Personal criticism—variously termed "engaged," "autobiographical," "confessional," "testimonial," "reflexive," and so on—is a form that deliberately transgresses normative conventions of academic objectivity.[5] It may highlight the process of the production of academic work, thus catching "intellectual authority . . . in the act of its own construction."[6] When scholarship is "self-conscious" about its own process, it points to "the fictional strategies inherent in all theory."[7] It is a move away from the academic culture of "books written by someone who, though appearing by name on the cover, endeavors with delight to argue for the unreality of his own existence."[8] In personal criticism the unique, embodied reality of the writer is not bracketed off, but given a central role in the text, with reference to their experiences, interests and desires. Personal criticism may use detailed or lengthy autobiographical material, but more significantly it involves "a certain intensity in the lending of oneself," in the words of Mary Ann Caws.[9] Anecdotes employed to illustrate a concept or argument are not necessarily personal in the same sense, even if drawn from real life experience, whereas personally engaged academic writing expresses a real sense of care towards the subject matter, saying 'this is important to me, and here is why.'

---

3. Miller, *Getting Personal*, 121.
4. Ibid., 20.
5. Henderson, "Introduction," 13.
6. Harbord, "Platitudes," 24.
7. Miller, *Getting Personal*, xii.
8. Cavarero, *Relating Narratives*, 76.
9. Miller, *Getting Personal*, 1.

Autobiography in Feminist Theology

The use of the personal voice has not been as widespread in feminist theology as one might have expected, with its emphasis on 'women's experience' often not going hand in hand with detailed autobiographical reflection. It is more common for feminist theologians to give a perfunctory statement of their social location—ethnicity, nationality, class, and so on—and perhaps give some mention of their experience within the church or university, or involvement in a particular political struggle. There are some exceptions to this generalization, for example Carol Christ has written from an increasingly personal standpoint—something she considers in the preface to the second edition of *Diving Deep and Surfacing*—and in *Rebirth of the Goddess* she entwines her systematic thealogy with autobiographical reflection. Carter Heyward's *When Boundaries Betray Us* explores issues of intimacy and integrity in friendship and love through an account of her troubled relationship with her therapist. Rita Nakashima Brock and Rebecca Parker wrote together *Proverbs of Ashes*, which relates their experience of suffering and how this has affected their theology. They claim that "[o]ur theological questions emerged in our daily struggles to teach, minister, and work for social change, and from personal grappling with how violence had affected us. The mask of objectivity, with its academic, distanced tone, hid the lived character of our theological questions and our theological affirmations."[10]

I have found *Proverbs of Ashes* somewhat disappointing as a representation of "the lived character of theological questions and affirmations." This is partly a matter of taste—the writing style, as with Christ and Heyward, is sometimes akin to that of the popular books categorized in bookshops as either "self-help" or "painful lives"—but, more importantly, because it is not always successful at striking a balance between theology and life-writing. Rebecca Parker's harrowing descriptions of recovered memories of child abuse do have much to say in addressing profound theological questions. Yet Rita Nakashima Brock does not fully develop how her experience of fragmented identity, growing up in the US with a Japanese mother, discovering late in life that her biological father was a Puerto Rican soldier, has affected her theology.

The same criticism can also be applied to a pseudonymous article in the journal *Theology and Sexuality*, "Anonymity Desirable, Bibliography Not Required," published under the name Nema McCallum. She writes

---

10. Brock and Parker, *Proverbs of Ashes*, 6.

vividly and powerfully of her experience of psychiatric institutions as a young woman, asserting at the close of the article that her theology is thus "terminally post-psychiatric."[11] She suggests that the contextual theologies of the contemporary academy run along lines of "metacontextual variables, such as gender, race, sexuality and class," but lack "the insider-theologies of experience which involve the personal and private unsaids of which it rarely seems safe to speak."[12] McCallum's argument is that "each of our experiences, perhaps more than our contextual identities, influence our theologies more than we know"; in her case, "[m]y experience of psychiatry, not my identity as a woman, is far more potent in affecting my sense of justice, style of theology, understanding of other people and thinking about God."[13] It is a shame that McCallum does not go on to explain further the ways in which her theology is molded by her experience of psychiatry. This is not the only aspect I find problematic: while I agree that our unique life experiences will shape our theology to a great extent—especially deep traumas such as those narrated by McCallum or Rebecca Parker—I am uncomfortable with the placing of individual, personal "experience" over and above the social contexts of race, gender and class. Like Christ, Brock and Parker, and Heyward, McCallum's theological life-writing seems to ascribe a certain authority to the experiences of the individual, and upon their ability to directly recall and recreate those experiences in narrative.

There are some instances of autobiographical theological writing that do not suffer from these same weaknesses. Marcella Althaus-Reid reflects on her own experience throughout her work in liberation and queer theology.[14] For example, in *The Queer God* her childhood memory of being reprimanded at her first confession for kneeling in front of the priest, imitating her male cousins rather than follow the convention for girls and kneel at the priest's right-hand side, is related to "the liturgical symbolic geography relating to gender and sexual positions in the church's structures."[15] The practical theologian Stephen Pattison draws on his own experience of child abuse and neglect in his analysis of how theological doctrine compounds the sense of shame common to victims of abuse, but his discussion is more

---

11. McCallum, "Anonymity Desirable," 51.
12. Ibid.
13. Ibid.
14. Althaus-Reid, *Indecent Theology*; *Queer God*; *From Feminist Theology to Indecent Theology*.
15. Althaus-Reid, *Queer God*, 10.

theologically-focused than is Rebecca Parker's on the same theme.[16] The feminist biblical scholar Ingrid Rosa Kitzberger has led the way in autobiographical criticism in biblical studies.[17] Much feminist theological thinking has taken place outside of traditional academic discourse, in poetry, liturgy and preaching, and these forms often draw on personal experience: for example, the poems and prayers of Nicola Slee.[18]

Apart from certain exceptions, including those mentioned above, the use of the personal voice in academic writing has been more sophisticated and skilful in literary criticism than in theology. This is perhaps unsurprising, as literature scholars are concerned on a daily basis with choice of words and sentence structure in a way that theologians are not; they will also be more attuned to the conceits of narrative, and the artifice of "the autobiographical I."

Out of the Shadows: Autobiography in Literary Criticism

The emotions that literary scholars feel about the books they study, but have traditionally set aside in academic discourse on literature, is captured in Sandra Gilbert's distinction between "the Critic" and "the Reader," in an early example of personal criticism in the wake of feminist literary theory:

> The Critic . . . sounds like someone who has so perfectly mastered his reading that he can criticize it, both in the ordinary (evaluative) and the extraordinary (analytic) sense of the term. Moving grandly among those long-established monuments, he is cool, superior, a godlike museum guide discoursing on the virtues and defects of each chiseled sonnet, each well-wrought novella. . . .
>
> The Reader, on the other hand, is hot and human—and therefore somehow imperfect. Afflicted by texts, she or he struggles to understand them . . . Enclosed in contexts, embarrassed by pretexts, the Reader devours poems, inhales syntax, exhales codes, and is in fact assaulted by so many and such various messages that she or he may eventually come to feel that they are inscribed on her or his skin.[19]

---

16. Pattison, "Suffer Little Children"; *Shame*.

17. Kitzberger, *Personal Voice in Biblical Interpretation*; *Autobiographical Biblical Criticism*.

18. Slee, *Praying Like a Woman*.

19. Gilbert, "Life Studies," 853.

Gilbert's expression of the desire to write as a Reader—"hot and human," "[a]fflicted by texts," "[e]nclosed in contexts, embarrassed by pretexts"— within an academy characterized by the disembodied (yet male), objective Critic, is an example of the *perceived* personal tone of feminist criticism. In 1981, Jean Kennard noted the general impression "that large numbers of feminist critics employ an overtly personal tone and that this in some significant way separates feminist criticism stylistically, if not methodologically, from other literary criticism."[20]

Despite this general impression, Kennard's detailed study of feminist literary criticism published in journals in the previous few years revealed only seven (including Gilbert's) that employ an overtly personal voice. Kennard also notes that the personal material is usually positioned at the beginning of the article and then it returns to a more traditional, detached critical style; a tendency Elspeth Probyn identifies as "a general pattern within feminist criticism of merely using the personal at the outset" before "plodding off into the usual disembodied type of argument."[21]

If the use of the personal voice is not actually as common in feminist criticism as she and others had thought, why, wonders Kennard, is it perceived to be so? One conclusion she makes is that the few examples that there are of personal criticism leave such a strong impression that they are thought to be more numerous than they are in actuality.[22] I would think that this is due to the deeply felt need, as expressed in Gilbert's article, for making explicit one's personal engagement with texts—thus instances of personal criticism occupy a significant place in the memory of those who read them. It is also a simple result of feminist theory's criticism of the dualistic, rational accounts of knowledge and modes of speaking. Yet however much feminists may think that they *ought* to write from a personal standpoint, it is not easy to actually do so.

An instance of writing in a personal voice, while simultaneously considering the difficulties of that process, is Jane Tompkins's "Me and My Shadow," an essay of virtually iconic status in discussions of personal criticism. It opens with the words "[t]here are two voices inside me . . . One is the voice of a critic who wants to correct a mistake in the essay's view of epistemology. The other is the voice of a person who wants to write about her feelings . . . These beings exist separately but not apart. One writes for

---

20. Kennard, "Personally Speaking," 141.
21. Probyn, *Sexing the Self*, 13.
22. Kennard, "Personally Speaking," 143.

professional journals, the other in diaries, late at night."[23] What follows is a phenomenological consideration of how she might go about reconciling those two voices, how to "move away from academic conventions that segregate intellectual concerns from meditations on what is happening outside my window or inside my heart."[24] It is difficult for Tompkins to integrate these voices: firstly because she is embarrassed to be writing about her "feelings," because it seems self-indulgent, yet her feminist convictions require her to resist this sense of shame.

In Tompkins's piece her emotional voice, struggling with the nature of academic discourse, is then joined by a resolutely embodied voice, with the sentences which provoked the most comment in response to the piece: "[m]ost of all I don't know how to enter the debate without leaving everything else behind—the birds outside my window, my grief over Janice, just myself as a person sitting here in stockinged feet, a little bit chilly because the windows are open, and thinking about going to the bathroom. But not going yet."[25] This collapsing of the public/private dichotomy to such an extent—making reference to a friend's suicide as well as needing to go to the toilet—marked a shift in the use of the personal voice in literary studies. The academic writer's personal testimony became truly engaged rather than anecdotal or rhetorical.

The personal criticism of which Jane Tompkins's "Me and My Shadow" is exemplary is routinely attacked for being emotional, uncontrolled, 'too much information,' 'gossipy.' There is, as Nancy Miller notes, a gendered element to this: "[b]y going/not going to the bathroom in public, Tompkins crosses the line into the dangerous zone of feminine excess."[26] This "calling attention to oneself" will more often than not embarrass the academic audience or reader; exhibitionism that leads to social discomfort may be regarded as 'impolite.' Miller asserts that the reader's embarrassment provoked by the appearance of the personal voice in academic discourse is not a reason to avoid it; rather, it is "a sign that it is working."[27] Miller also notes—as does Tompkins—that she herself gains enjoyment from autobiographical detail in an academic piece of writing, preferring "the gossipy

---

23. Tompkins, "Me and My Shadow," 169.
24. Ibid.
25. Ibid., 173.
26. Miller, *Getting Personal*, 23.
27. Ibid., 25.

grain of situated writing."[28] Those who are discomforted by the immensely revelatory tone of Tompkins's essay, Miller suggests, may be bothered more by her display of feminist anger, than by her reference to her bladder: "[i]t is her anger, that is 'not supposed' to show, but it does. 'She' is making a spectacle of herself. 'She,' as has often been said of me, is 'being emotional.'"[29]

The use of the personal voice in academic writing makes one vulnerable to attack that goes deeper than the intellectual. More unpleasant than a male audience member's comment on Elspeth Probyn's paper on eating disorders—that her speaking of her personal experience of anorexia made him "nervous"—was a feminist's response to the printed version, that Probyn's "weighty words" of confession "lacked sweat and blood" in their invocation of the female body.[30] This insensitivity to the point of cruelty in choice of vocabulary is a reminder why so many choose not to write from a personal perspective. The use of the impersonal tone in academic discourse serves to distance oneself from one's own intellectual positions, a distance that ensures that—however violent the assault—no one will get hurt.

Autobiography and Selfhood

While objections to personal criticism on the grounds that it is 'embarrassing' may rightly be dismissed, there are more profound problems with the presence of the personal voice in academic writing. Tompkins acknowledges her anxiety over the use of the personal voice: "[t]he voice in which I write about epistemology is familiar. I know how it ought to sound. This voice, though, I hardly know. I don't even know if it has anything to say. But if I never write in it, it never will."[31] These words are inspiring, but what is troubling is the notion of a distinct "voice," a unified essence that has been obscured by the conventions of patriarchal scholarship, struggling to break through. Here the turn to autobiographical criticism runs the risk of implying that the personal voice is invested with inherent authority, because it is implicitly associated with a 'person' in a way that 'objective' writing is not. In the words of H. Aram Veeser, it can be argued that personal criticism "builds on the hypothesis of liberal authenticity: 'I felt it, therefore it

---

28. Ibid., xi.
29. Ibid., 23.
30. Probyn, "This Body Which is Not One," 113.
31. Tompkins, "Me and My Shadow," 173.

is true."[32] Aside from questions of validity or truth, privileging one's own voice in this way may lead to a silencing of, or failure to listen to, the voices of others. This begs the question, "[c]an stories be told through selves and through emotions without being at the expense of other stories and selves?"[33] Probyn writes in the engaged, autobiographical mode, but in the hope that it is possible "to construct ways of thinking that are marked by 'me' but that do not efface actively or through omission the ways in which 'she' may see differently."[34] This requires resistance to "a simple reification of either experience or the experiencer,"[35] acknowledging that there is no "unmediated innocence"[36] to the self and to experience.

Feminist theology has a methodological commitment to the authority of "women's experience," but problems inherent in this were apparent from its earliest days, and extended and profound critiques are in no short supply.[37] The two main criticisms are the philosophical naivety of its notion of 'experience,' and its failure to account for difference in grouping together the experience of white middle-class westerners with that of women from different social contexts. Taking on the criticisms of womanist theologians, in 1989 Carol Christ and Judith Plaskow admitted that "[t]he notion of women's experience must be taken as an invitation to explore particularity rather than to homogenize significant differences."[38] Therein lies the enduring significance of feminist theological method: that particularities matter; that theological truths do not necessarily hold for everyone, and that theology is always done with an agenda, whether or not it is acknowledged. Emphasis on women's 'stories,' rather than 'experience,' could underscore that experience is never unmediated; rather it is constructed and interpreted. The communal nature of 'story' may guard against the charge of solipsism, and the accusation that liberal belief in the authority of experience rests on Enlightenment notions of the autonomous individual. At the same time, the particularity of 'story' can prevent white, middle-class feminist

---

32. Veeser, "Case for Confessional Criticism," x.
33. Probyn, *Sexing the Self*, 84.
34. Ibid., 4.
35. Ibid., 20.
36. Ibid., 4.
37. See, for example, Fulkerson, *Changing the Subject*; Graham, *Making the Difference*; Jantzen, *Becoming Divine*; Thistlethwaite, *Sex, Race and God*; West, *Deadly Innocence*.
38. Christ and Plaskow, *Weaving the Visions*, 3.

theologians from committing the error of confusing their own experience for 'women's experience.'

We do not look inside ourselves and find our stories there, submerged and waiting to be brought out into the light. The stories we tell about ourselves are produced—albeit from the 'stuff' of experience, however fragmented and unreliable our memory of it—within particular contexts and for particular purposes. This is especially the case with academic life-writing; for example, Probyn's story of her experience of anorexia, given as part of a conference paper, "was, of necessity, a representation forged for my argument," and this is confirmed by her family's reaction: "my mother's conclusion in reading the article was that I had a happy childhood, whereas my sister's was closer to the point as she gently mentioned the poetic, or academic, license involved in my description."[39] This is a reminder that our stories are never just our own: they are also part of the stories of those others whose lives intersect with ours. In putting experience into the public domain of academic discourse, respect for the feelings and privacy of partners, family, and friends will often require that only certain stories are told, in a very certain way. Furthermore, how one chooses to present oneself, in academic life-writing as anywhere else, is shaped by how one wishes to appear; thus behavior and motivations of which one is not proud are likely to be omitted or drastically altered in the telling.

These are issues that apply not only to academic life-writing, but, as "the process and the product of assigning meaning to a series of experiences, after they have taken place, by means of emphasis, juxtaposition, commentary, omission,"[40] to autobiography in general. In postmodern critical theory, autobiography does not disclose a life and its historical moments, or a unique individual self.[41] Rather, autobiography is "a narrative artifice, privileging a presence, or identity, that does not exist outside language";[42] indeed "[t]here is no essential, original, coherent autobiographical self before the moment of self-narrating."[43]

---

39. Probyn, "This Body Which is Not One," 113.

40. Smith, *Poetics of Women's Autobiography*, 45.

41. See Cavarero, *Relating Narratives*; Smith, *Poetics of Women's Autobiography*; Stanley, *Auto/Biographical I*.

42. Smith, *Poetics of Women's Autobiography*, 5.

43. Smith, "Performativity," 108.

The recollection of life events in the form of a coherent story is constitutive of a "narrative identity."[44] According to Paul Ricoeur, "life cannot be understood other than through stories we tell about it," thus "a life examined, in the sense borrowed from Socrates, is a life narrated."[45] Richard Kearney takes this rephrasing of Socrates as far as to say that "the unnarrated life is not worth living."[46] Writing of the human desire for narration, Adriana Cavarero describes how, in *The Odyssey*, Odysseus weeps for the first time when he hears his story told by another, "[n]ot only because the narrated events are painful, but because when he had lived them directly he had not understood their meaning . . . By fully realizing the meaning of his narrated story, he also gains a notion of who is its protagonist."[47] He weeps because he has encountered "the unexpected realization of his own desire for narration," the desire shared by all human beings, "narratable selves."[48]

The narrative identity produced in autobiography is ascribed a redemptive role by thinkers such as Kearney, who claims that "[a] model of narrative selfhood can . . . respond to anti-humanist suspicions of subjectivity while preserving a significant notion of the ethical-political subject."[49] I agree to an extent, but am suspicious of Kearney's emphasis on narrative "unity."[50] The sense of wholeness upon which rest rationalist accounts of the human subject, undermined by modernist literature and postmodern theory, have, it is argued, long been taken for granted by men, but proved harder to come by for women. As feminist theorists of autobiography have noted, "[n]o mirror of her era, the female autobiographer takes as a given that selfhood is mediated; her invisibility results from her lack of a tradition, her marginality in male-dominated culture, her fragmentation—social and political as well as psychic."[51]

Academic life-writing would do better not to reproduce, in terms of narrative, a stable and authoritative identity, "a postmodern, self-help driven subject who coheres around any story she is able to cobble together."[52]

44. Ricoeur, *Ricoeur Reader*, 436.
45. Ibid., 435.
46. Kearney, *On Stories*, 14.
47. Cavarero, *Relating Narratives*, 18.
48. Ibid., 32.
49. Kearney, *On Stories*, 152.
50. Ibid., 4.
51. Brodzki and Schenck, *Life/Lines*, 1.
52. Rudy, "Subjectivity and Belief," 40.

As Kathy Rudy writes of her experience of telling her story of leaving the Christian faith because of conflicts about her sexuality,

> [t]he "all-or-nothing" problem of unified subjectivity . . . is that it does not accurately reflect the way I feel in losing my faith. It was and is a much more jagged process, an uneven development. I find myself longing for things I no longer believe in, believing in things that seem patently absurd . . . What I need is a theory of subjectivity that would allow me to be two contradictory things at the same time, that would allow me to say "I believe" and "I don't" in a way that does not require coherent explanation. I need a theory that will allow me to be fragmented . . .[53]

The recognition that the 'personal voice' is neither unified or preexistent may guard against the temptation to invoke it as authoritative, thus silencing the voices of others. Speaking in a personal voice, but with an awareness that this voice is not natural or innocent, but deliberately adopted for a particular purpose, is preferable to an 'impersonal' voice—equally as unified, but denying its own existence. To write 'in *the* personal voice' is actually to employ one of many personal voices—in reading or writing engaged criticism it is usual for several voices to appear in one piece of work. As most of us are not gifted in impressionism, perhaps slightly shifting the metaphor to one of 'key' or 'pitch,' rather than 'voice,' would be helpful. Veeser writes of confessional criticism as "performance"[54]—we could conceive of this in terms of theatre as well as music. Sidonie Smith describes autobiography as "a kind of masquerade," and I find helpful the image of the life story as a mask—"an iconic representation of continuous identity that stands for, or rather before, her subjectivity as she tells of this 'I' rather than of that 'I'"[55]—representative of the self in the moment of performance, but not identical to it. Even more so than 'story,' performance is not individuated and solipsistic, but communal, dependent on the audience. It depends upon the forming of a relationship between the self in autobiographical narrative, and "the 'fictive reader' created by the autobiographer to help bring that self into existence."[56] In terms of autobiographical criticism, in the words of Nancy Miller, "[b]y the risks of its writing, personal criticism embodies a pact . . . binding writer to reader in the fabulation of self-truth,

---

53. Rudy, "Subjectivity and Belief," 42-3.
54. Veeser, "Case for Confessional Criticism," xiii.
55. Smith, *Poetics of Women's Autobiography*, 47.
56. Ibid., 6.

that what is at stake matters also to others: somewhere in the self-fiction of the personal voice is a belief that the writing is worth the risk."[57]

The Trouble with Narrative

The research that underpins this chapter thus far was originally undertaken to support my own choice of a methodology of autobiographical reflection. The period of my initial research into life-writing in academic scholarship coincided with the long summer vacation, the first six weeks of my giving up smoking, and living alone for the first time. I came to consider whether these factors had a considerable effect on my reading: without the sense of routine provided by cigarettes, flatmates or term-time activities, my sense of self became rather hazy, and this was exacerbated by reading about the theory and practice of writing the self. At the time I wrote, *I've been wandering around my flat, bearing sticking plasters. I forget that they are seeping in nicotine; instead I feel that they are patching up leaking holes.*

I was looking for theoretical support and precedence for bringing my self (a self that seemed to be dissolving into the haze of the smoke of the cigarettes that I was *not* smoking) into my scholarship. What I found instead was that it was more complicated than simply being brave and preparing myself for some of my academic colleagues finding my writing embarrassing, or inappropriate, or—even worse—boring. The above discussions of the personal voice in academic criticism underscored what I was already beginning to sense—that the attempt to write oneself into one's academic work can seem just as artificial as the attempt to make oneself invisible. Thinking about whether or not I wanted to write in this way, whether bringing my own story into my theological writing would be essentially pornographic—staged and false, while pretending to be revealing to the point of obscenity—also led me to think more deeply about the problems of a redemptive view of narrative.

Beneath the over-arching narrative of modernity, "we are encouraged to think of our lives as coherent stories of success, progress and movement."[58] Even in tragic stories, the narrative form still inclines to closure, to resolution. In the narrative structure of the popular imagination there is often little difference between epiphany and catharsis, and perhaps the anguish of the distance between the narrative of our hopes, and how our lives actu-

57. Miller, *Getting Personal*, 24.
58. Stacey, "Heroes," 83.

ally turn out, is not that the drama did not pan out as we would have liked, but that it did not follow a satisfying dramatic structure; events have not unfolded in a successive whole. Or, if we are able to tell our life stories as emplotted narratives in which there is a distinct pattern to events, we have to be extremely selective about which elements of experience to draw on. Janet Stacey, writing as someone in remission from cancer, but attempting to avoid "[t]he dangers of the success story"[59] and working with the recognition that "the accounts that we produce are structured by the formations of memory and the conventions of narrative,"[60] argues that "conventional narrative structure cannot necessarily contain the demands of a changing world."[61]

I have had a significant—albeit shifting—sense of my own 'story' for a large part of my life. I grew up in an evangelical context in which it is not only believed that the history of the world is the unfolding of God's perfect plan, but that one's own life as an individual is also a story penned by God's hand. Having been treated for depression from the age of thirteen, from an early age my self-understanding was shaped by a therapeutic paradigm in which the patient relates their emotions and experiences in order to arrive at a pattern of cause and effect, facilitating healing by making present distress explicable. I had lost interest in religion in the years leading up to my teens, which were characterized by stereotypically dysfunctional and rebellious behavior until I was 'born again' (*again*) aged fifteen. The severe depression did not lift, but it took on a different aspect, vacillating between elation and misery. The latter was dominated by religious guilt; this was compounded by the discord between my 'testimony'—the narrative of how I had gone wrong but was now saved, and well, and happy—and how I actually felt a lot of the time. In my final year of school I had a breakdown and became agoraphobic for several months: this was after a school year in which I had been happier than ever before, thus undermining a model of gradual recovery and also my ability to assess my own mental health.

I did get through it, however, and left home for university, studied theology and philosophy, felt my dogmatic certainties gradually crumble and fall away—a narrative common to so many who come to the academic study of theology from a strict religious background. The left-wing and feminist values that I had always cherished, though they sat somewhat

59. Ibid., 90.
60. Ibid., 99.
61. Ibid., 83.

uncomfortably with evangelicalism, were able to flourish; I also felt able for the first time since I was fifteen to accept that I was not heterosexual, and nor did I want to be. So I also had a 'coming out story'—a story of liberation from heteronormativity that would push aside my evangelical story of liberation from bondage to sin. Academically, I was for a while quite taken with canonical narrative theology,[62] more attractive than the abstractions of systematic theology or analytic philosophy, and it seemed like a way of holding together my feminist beliefs with my resistance to theological study emptied of divine stories and symbols.

After graduating, I wanted to give my mind a rest, get healthy spiritually and physically, and live in the countryside, before commencing a PhD program. So I spent a year living and working at a liberal Christian retreat center in the Dales National Park in North Yorkshire. That particular story did not work out as planned—in the course of my time there the charity ran out of money and the center had to close, despite the extreme hard work and fierce idealism of those involved. I felt like the whole experience—of living in a small, often troubled community in the middle of nowhere, and being part of a religious institution that has failed—had stripped me bare of all the stories and words that had previously defined me. Living in such a beautiful and isolated place, where the powers and cycles of nature are so manifest, my spirituality became oriented more towards the world around me than to the canonical Christian narratives. I also lost the idealism that enabled me to believe that feminist theology can follow the same pattern of the Christian story; that it can tear down and then rebuild the monoliths of Christian doctrine, as I had once hoped.

In the early stages of my PhD study, I was encouraged to foreground my personal narratives in my theological engagement with literature. But this was colored by a nagging sense that in my autobiographical writing I was selecting certain parts of myself, certain 'versions,' presenting confessional writing as a mirror when it is more like a mask—something displayed for performance, rather than a slightly distorted reflection of reality. More troublingly, I started to suspect that throughout my life the narrating of my own stories had kept me trapped rather than set me free, that my identity had been so tied up with certain narratives that other possibilities were closed off. It seems that my belief in the worthiness of my self and my life is dependent upon the realization of certain narrative outcomes. It also

---

62. See Frei, *Eclipse of Biblical Narrative*; Hauerwas, *Peaceable Kingdom*; Loughlin, *Telling God's Story*.

seems that deep and long-lasting anguish results from people having conflicting narrative versions of the same events. Having lost faith in the grand religious narratives, I had also come to doubt the good of the smaller-scale life narratives—especially my own.

I have told a story of how I came to distrust story. It is, in a sense, fiction, in that I made it, though over time, and not always consciously. I looked back over memory and chose certain experiences and interpretations (often remembering the interpretation rather than any direct recollection of the experience), I wrought them into sentences and I laid them out in a certain shape. Yet I still would not want to say that that I made it up. Rather, a multitude of different stories could be told in a survey of the same young life; a multitude of different voices adopted, different masks worn. In writing about myself, I am creating certain versions of myself. It is not pretense, but it is artifice. The trouble with narrative is when its artfulness is confused for the natural, not that the artfulness is bad in itself. These recognitions about narrative and selfhood have been helpful, in both personal and academic terms, to my understanding of certain things. But it is important that I wear this particular story lightly, that I do not give it a unity that becomes prescriptive.

Writing an entire book on feminist theology and literature without mentioning my own stories, adopting an impersonal voice, is not an option for me. But I am making golden bone collages, rather than weaving tapestries. In this book I read the stories of Michèle Roberts and Sara Maitland beside my own, but in the recognition that this is not an appeal to direct and unmediated experience, and that my writing is, in a sense, just as much a fiction as theirs. I read these stories beside my own because admitting the instability of one's standpoint does not imply that it is better to try to speak from nowhere. I read these stories beside my own because that is the best way I know to continually remind myself that I do not speak for everybody, that my reading and theology can only ever be that of a British, middle-class, well-educated white woman—but that acknowledgement should not be a rushed apology, placed at the beginning of a piece of academic work, and not referred to again.

Writing the Self in Sara Maitland and Michèle Roberts

In the second section of this chapter, I discuss the life-(or self-)writing of Michèle Roberts and Sara Maitland. I consider the ways in which the authorial self is composed and transmitted in their writing and interviews, and how they engage with the process of self-narration.

Sara Maitland: Voice and Silence

Sara Maitland was born in 1950, the second of six children, and grew up in London and then a mansion in south-west Scotland, her father's childhood home. Maitland describes her parents as encouraging their children—who they viewed "in a slightly collectivized way"—to be "highly articulate, contentious, witty, and to hold all authority except theirs in a certain degree of contempt."[63] While introspection was discouraged, "[w]ithin the magical space they had created for us . . . we were given an enormous amount of physical freedom—to play, to roam, to have fights and adventures."[64] A large family in an ancestral home in Scotland is the setting of the novel *Home Truths*, but perhaps the most significant influence family life has had on Sara Maitland as a writer is the witty, bantering style of her authorial voice.

Maitland was "excessively well-educated at expensive girls' schools in London and Wiltshire."[65] Her education would provide her with a love and sense of ownership of classical myth, so important in her short stories.[66] Maitland describes boarding school as "a damaging, brutal experience, made worse by the fact that in my parents' world not to enjoy your schooldays was proof that you were an inferior human being—you were supposed to be 'a good mixer,' to 'take the rough with the smooth.'"[67] The high expectations that Maitland grew up with, both at home and at school, perhaps feed into the explorations of religious guilt in her writing:

---

63. *ABS*, 4.
64. Ibid.
65. *TPO*, 32.
66. See ibid., 17.
67. *ABS*, 6.

> At home we were supposed to get into Cambridge, and wear long white gloves, a tartan silk sash and our deceased grandmother's pearls, and dance at Highland Balls. I was expected to have my own political opinions, and have them turn out the same as my parents. We were expected to be sociable, active and witty, and hard-working, industrious and calm. We were meant to be sociable and popular and bizarrely chaste. At school we were meant to be educated, independent, self-assured and totally innocent.[68]

In a 1986 essay Maitland compares the demands her father made of his children—his "tribe"—to those of Yahweh in the Hebrew Bible: "his devotion and loyalty in exchange for keeping their law."[69] As an adolescent she was "a father-identified daughter" who "wanted to be Pallas Athene to his Zeus."[70] The protagonists of Maitland's novels *Daughter of Jerusalem*, *Virgin Territory* and *Three Times Table* are women who have adoring relationships with demanding fathers. In "Two for the Price of One," Maitland conceptualizes the oppressive ideal 'Father' that she has internalized as a being separate from her real father, who died of cancer in 1982: "[i]n my late teens I fled away from my father's house; it has taken me a long time to realise that I carried with me the Father from whom I could not escape by escaping childhood, from whom I have not yet escaped, and from whom I have had, and still have, to wrest my loves, my voice, my feminism and my freedom."[71]

Maitland's upbringing in the Presbyterian Church of Scotland lent her "a great love of the Bible and a generally warm feeling about Christianity," but she had no "sense of 'personal conversion,' of passion or commitment"; thus "[a]s a teenager the mantle of Christianity simply slipped off."[72] The Christianity she encountered at Oxford in the 1970s was not to her at odds with her new-found socialism and feminism amidst those heady days: "[i]t was this conviction of enormous possibility that brought me back to thinking about God . . . made brave by hope and anger, I was tough enough for the enormous God whom I met."[73] In 1972, Maitland converted to Anglicanism; the same year she married an American training to be a vicar. They were Anglo-Catholic, a culture Maitland enjoyed as "colourful, gossipy,

---

68. Ibid., 7.
69. *TPO*, 37.
70. Ibid., 39.
71. Ibid., 33.
72. *BG*, 4.
73. Ibid., 5.

close-knit, extravagant and deeply-ironic," while believing that "the strongly sacramental constructions of high-church liturgical practice balanced the rationalist and individualist tendencies of much feminist theory."[74]

Maitland had her first child, a daughter, in 1973, and living in London as a mother and vicar's wife she became more involved with the feminist movement, and started to refer to herself as a writer. She wrote and published with the Women Writers Collective of Michelene Wandor, Zoe Fairbairns, Valerie Miner and Michèle Roberts; her 1978 novel *Daughter of Jerusalem*—a contemporary feminist's ambivalent struggle with infertility, interspersed with the stories of biblical women—won the Somerset Maugham Award. In 1982 her son Adam was born; 1983 saw the publication of a non-fiction book about Christian feminism, *A Map of the New Country*, and a collection of short stories, *Telling Tales*. At this time she also wrote a third-person narrative of her experience as a feminist writer, "A Feminist Writer's Progress," with a fairy-tale structure, explaining her move from social realism to revisioning of myth.[75] Her second novel, *Virgin Territory*, was published in 1984; a further book of short stories, *A Book of Spells*, and an epistolary novel, *Arky Types*, written with Michelene Wandor, would appear in 1987. As a feminist writer, mother and vicar's wife, she would both play up to and feel awkward about her "eccentric" image.[76] In an autobiographical essay at the end of *A Book of Spells*, she describes being a writer and a mother:

> This morning I was meant to be upstairs, drafting a short story. It is not their demandingness that keeps me from this sterner pleasure, but their loveliness. I have written before about how their dailiness and iron will for my attention balance and protect me against the dangerous voyages of the imagination—they ballast me safely with normality and connectedness, and ensure my return to sanity and to home. I have not written about the reverse: how the rigour and excitement and challenge of writing fiction weights me against their enchantment, against maternal romanticism and the isolated womb life in the garden.[77]

---

74. Ibid., 5.
75. *FWP*, 86–87, 95.
76. *BSP*, 165–66.
77. Ibid., 168.

Maitland describes her life in the 1970s and 80s as an immensely happy time, "a marvelous life."[78] But at the end of the 1980s, this disintegrated: her marriage was ending, amidst the depressing contexts of Thatcherism and the increasing right-wing misogyny of Anglo-Catholicism. Thus in the early 1990s she underwent a period of profound life changes. Her theological interests, enriched by her interest in science, focused on "a huge, wild, dangerous God . . . a God of almost manic creativity, ingenuity and enthusiasm; a Big-Enough God";[79] a theme of her novels *Three Times Table* and *Home Truths*, and some of the short stories of *Women Fly When Men Aren't Watching*. In 1993 she converted to Roman Catholicism: "there has been no doctrinal or liturgical change for me, merely a repositioning of my relationship to authority; a reaffirmation, despite its many sillinesses (and I must say wrongnesses) that a church can, and must, be universal, can be large scale through time and space—can indeed be big enough."[80]

Maitland moved to a house in a small Northamptonshire village, in which she was "suddenly, and without exactly planning it, living on my own for the first time in my life."[81] Maitland found that she loved the solitude and silence, and wanted more of it. She associates the experience of change and a renewed sense of self with her age—not only the changing circumstances of a marriage ending and children leaving home—but also by the physiological "change" of the menopause. This is something that is little discussed in western culture, "terrified of the process of ageing, and in which women are encouraged to take artificial hormones so that they do not enter this magical condition."[82] Maitland's collection of short stories written during this time, *On Becoming a Fairy Godmother*, retells old and invents new tales about menopausal women, "making unexpected changes in their lives, opening up their imaginations and finding a new self-sufficiency."[83]

Maitland's solitary lifestyle and increasing interest in silence meant that she became more attuned to the natural world: "I would go out into the garden at night or in the early morning and just look and listen: there

---

78. *ABS*, 13.
79. *BG*, 150.
80. Ibid., 6.
81. *ABS*, 15.
82. Ibid., 18.
83. Ibid., 19.

Annunciation

were stars, weather, seasons, growth and repetition."[84] For the first time in her life she tended her own garden, finding sacramentality in its silent joy:

> Gardening puts me in contact with all this silent energy; gardeners become active partners in all that silent growth. I do not make it happen, but I share in its happening. The earth works its way under my nails and into my fingerprints, and a gardener has to pay attention to the immediate now of things . . . In Warkton for the first time a garden became precious to me—it became an occupation, a resource and also my first glimpse that there might be art forms that I could practise that might not be made out of words.[85]

She became interested in "how gardens might reflect ideas, thoughts and desires, just as literature or painting does"[86] and wrote a book about such gardens, along with the garden designer Peter Matthews, called *Gardens of Illusion*. Researching the book, she travelled around the UK, and, observing "the wild and desolate places that still . . . occupy a great deal of space in our supposedly overcrowded land," such as the Pennines, the Lake District and the Highlands. In this she found that "it was not peace and contentment that I craved, but that awed response to certain phenomena of the 'natural' world . . . I discovered in myself a longing for the sublime, for an environment that, rather than soothing me, offered some raw, challenging demands in exchange for grandeur and ineffability."[87]

Maitland became more interested in silence itself and contemplative prayer, and in 2000 decided to move to "the Huge Nothing of the high moorlands" of Weardale, in pursuit of "not just a greater quantity of silence, but also a more intense and focused experience of it."[88] Shortly after moving to the moors, she spent six weeks in isolation on the Isle of Skye: "[f]ascinated by silence, drawn joyfully into the void, I wanted to experience a total version."[89] Her commitment to silent living deepened, and her historical, literary, and theological research, as well as her own thought on the experience of silence, was published in 2008's *A Book of Silence*. The book opens with Maitland "sitting on the front doorstep of my little house with a cup of coffee, looking down the valley at my extraordinary view of

84. Ibid., 16.
85. Ibid., 21.
86. Ibid., 22.
87. Ibid., 23.
88. Ibid., 29.
89. Ibid., 37.

nothing,"⁹⁰ feeling particularly satisfied because the previous day she had received the completion certificate for this house, that she had built on the moors of Galloway. On her website, she says, "[h]ere I write and pray and walk and am happy."⁹¹

Maitland's writing of her self is more prominent in non-fiction than in her novels or short stories; it is in Michèle Roberts's fiction that I read a lot of fictionalizing of the author's own life experience (hence this chapter's section on Roberts is considerably longer than that on Maitland). However, one aspect of Maitland's life that is employed in her novels and short stories is her voice hearing: from the 1980s onwards she experienced auditory hallucinations: voices which she knows are internal and "something to do with my imagination," to which she gives descriptive names: "the Dwarf, the Angel, the Little Girl."⁹² In *A Book of Silence* she writes, "I found the content of these voices more absorbing and engaging than tormenting, and they certainly never urged hideous actions upon me."⁹³ She does not believe in the existence of schizophrenia, thinking that "there must be something wrong, when people are unable to distinguish between Peter Sutcliffe (the Yorkshire Ripper) and William Blake (who as a boy saw angels sitting in a tree on Peckham Rye, 'bright wings bespangling every bough like stars')."⁹⁴ The voice of Angel is heard by characters in the novel *Brittle Joys* and in some of the stories of *Angel and Me: Short Stories for Holy Week*. The "collective voice I called the Godfathers and who seemed to represent a kind of internalised patriarchy"⁹⁵ are put to direct use in *Virgin Territory*.

It is in another kind of voice that Maitland's self is present in her fiction: her authorial voice, the writerly 'I,' is sometimes inserted into the story, particularly when she is engaging with the story of an other; for example "Triptych" in *A Book of Spells* or "Requiem" in *Women Fly When Men Aren't Watching*. This is part of a practice of bringing the process of writing the story into the text itself; at the end of *The Book of Spells* is a non-fiction piece which begins with her discussing her feelings about the brief for the essay, and whether to write it or not.⁹⁶ This device is also used in *Arky Types*,

90. Ibid., 1.
91. *AM*.
92. *LMC*.
93. *ABS*, 14.
94. *LMC*.
95. *ABS*, 14.
96. *BSP*, 165–66.

in which the 'characters' Sara and Michelene write to each other debating how to write a novel together. In Maitland's writing in the first person, the boundaries between fiction and non-fiction are blurred: "A Feminist Writer's Progress" describes in story form her experience as a feminist writer, with a footnote that reads "[w]hether, and in what ways, you believe any of this is, of course, entirely up to you, but remember always that the writer is a writer of fictions and too literal or chronological a belief may prove dangerous to your health."[97] In the theological book, *A Big-Enough God*, she says of her account of becoming a feminist and a Christian, "I at least am convinced by my own narrative."[98]

Although Maitland's distinctive voice—witty, passionate, eccentric—is what makes her self so present in her writing, the personal narrative that has come to define her in recent years is her embracing of that which may seem antithetical to 'voice': silence. This is not just because her most extended work of life-writing, *A Book of Silence*, is a book about silence which interweaves her story with her thought and research on silence, rather than a straightforward autobiography, nor even because that book and Maitland's discussion of it have proved so popular with the wider public. Rather, it is because Maitland has come to understand herself as a seeker of silence; the story of her life flowing towards silence. This has had interesting implications for her consideration of herself as a writer. During the last decade, she found that she was not writing fiction any more:

> When I had come north it had been with a sense that the stories were not enough—I wanted to dig deeper into them, to pull more out of them. It had not occurred to me that I would abandon them, nor they me. The desire to write, to tell stories that pull my thoughts and emotions together, has been something that I have lived with and felt integral to my sense of well-being, even identity, for as long as I can remember. Now quite simply stories did not spring to mind; my imagination did not take a narrative form. I had in a peculiarly literal way "lost the plot."[99]

Although Maitland has written a number of acclaimed short stories since embarking on a predominately silent lifestyle, she doubts that she will write another novel. Considering why this is, she notes that, historically, silent living has given rise to great poetry and non-fiction, but not to fiction,

---

97. *FWP*, 23
98. *BG*, 5.
99. *ABS*, 189.

especially novels: "[p]erhaps it is because fiction involves creating whole new worlds and this requires a greater assertion of the ego than recording what comes, as a gift, into your own silent life."[100] On the other hand, the sense of self that comes across so clearly in Maitland's writing and interviews has perhaps been strengthened by silence; she comments that writers who live silently, even those "who build in a rhetoric of self-abnegation . . . end up writing autobiographically."[101] Maitland's love of silence has led her to consider deeply the nature of language and narrative—these things that structure human experience and yet are opposite to the silence she finds so profoundly fulfilling. Novels (at least the kind of novels that Maitland once wrote) involve "narrative, plot and resolution or closure, all of which are linear or time-bound and therefore deeply alien to silence."[102] Maitland's account of silence, repeatedly retold in articles, interviews and speaking engagements, is both a narrative she has constructed, and a way of being that is resistant to narrative, especially narrative closure. This is something that comes to the fore in the final paragraph of *A Book of Silence*:

> I am finding it hard to finish this book, because I don't feel that I am at the end of anything. Back in Warkton, at the very beginning, I tried to design a garden that would open out into infinity; that would forgo the satisfaction of closure, in the hope of finding the jouissance of the unresolved, the open-ended. Now I am trying to design a whole life that will do that. For me silence is both the instrument and content of that life.[103]

Michèle Roberts's Life Story

If Sara Maitland's writing of her self comes to be defined by silence, Michèle Roberts's is in some ways the very opposite: being a writer is absolutely essential to her sense of self, and is a theme of nearly all her fiction. Roberts is a particularly interesting writer to consider in terms of autobiography, because her self-writing is entwined with her theorization of the process of doing so. The self that Michèle Roberts discloses—or narrates—in her writing and interviews is projected clearly, and in bright colors. This

---

100. Ibid., 259.
101. Ibid.
102. Ibid., 260.
103. Ibid., 287.

autobiographical fiction is not stable, and flickers in and out of her novels, taking a different guise when read in the light of her memoirs, but it is indisputably there, throughout all her work.

Michèle Roberts was born in 1949 to a French mother and an English father. She has a brother and two sisters, one of which is her twin. Roberts's childhood was divided between Edgware in Surrey and summers in rural Normandy, and her potted biographies usually open with the information that she is "half-French," making this detail significant to her identity as a writer, despite the fact that all her published works are in English. Her fiction is sometimes set in France, but usually involves a character that is in some way both French and English, or else an English person living in France or vice-versa. In an interview with Jenny Newman, Roberts describes how growing up with the feeling of "having two families and two homes, and [having] to move back and forth across the sea to join them up" was an important impetus for becoming a writer.[104] The awkwardness of growing up not-quite English and not-quite French—the dual identity that results from being raised in two places, two cultures, divided by language and by the sea—is given to Roberts's protagonists Julie in *A Piece of the Night* and Léonie in *Daughters of the House*, and explored autobiographically in "Une Glossaire/A Glossary." In the latter, the division is represented linguistically—with each section headed by a French word and its English meaning—by the oblique between the two languages. Roberts's repeated recreation of a childhood in rural Normandy—particularly evocative of the material and domestic—represents the attempt to restore a sense of closeness to her mother. Childhood is also an important aspect of Roberts's writing because "[w]hen you're young, you're very open to the world, you're vulnerable, you're soft-shelled. I think your childhood stamps you, wounds you, shapes you . . . you struggle to turn it into language and make something of it."[105]

The childhood "wound" that opens again and again in Roberts's writing is the Roman Catholicism she inherited from her mother and from convent school. She describes its influence as all-pervasive: "as integral as the blood in my veins, passed on to me by my mother like milk. Catholicism was a language itself: a complete system of images, and such a rich one, within which to live and name the world."[106] Roberts had been devout-

104. *IJN*.
105. Ibid.
106. *WWH*, 52.

ly religious as a child, and believed she had a vocation to become a nun, but lost her faith once leaving home and going to university.[107] Looking back—in anger—on her religious childhood and adolescence, she came to regard church teaching on women, sexuality, sin, and judgment as a cause of great harm: "the Catholic split between body and soul . . . damaged me almost irreparably, I would say, as a young woman growing up, because it made me feel so bad about desire, sex, pleasure, myself, my own body. Part of what my work's been trying to do is to repair damage."[108]

Thus a devout young girl's struggle with Catholicism and sexuality appears again and again in Roberts's fiction, and in an especially autobiographical way in the characters of Julie in *A Piece of the Night*, Helen in *The Visitation* and Thérèse in *Daughters of the House*. Thirteen-year-old Thérèse, who wants to be a nun, copes with her mother's terminal cancer by focusing on the purity of piety: "she lay on the floor in the shape of a cross, and prayed. . .What comforted her, when from time to time she opened her eyes and squinted upwards, was the sight of her statue of Our Lady of Lourdes. The Madonna with a heavenly look, a light veil over her fair hair, blue sash about her girlish waist."[109] Yet this is disturbed by her developing body: "[s]he hated her stomach which stuck out as though she were pregnant however hard she tried to suck it in. She hated her breasts."[110] This echoes Roberts's own experience of adolescence and the onset of menstruation,[111] of seeing herself as female within a church whose symbolism denies the physicality of womanhood. For Julie at convent school on the feast day of Joseph the worker, dedicated to the Virgin: "[t]his is our day, the little girls' day, when we sing of pearls, of lilies, of bleeding hearts, of secret soft places visited by God. Only my hands are slimy with heat and perspiration, there is a sanitary towel strapped like a dead rabbit between my legs."[112] In *The Visitation* the conflict between the church and teenage sexuality is played out in Helen's guilt at kissing a boy at the church youth club dance; her twin brother and her friend caught having sex in her father's car headlights, the priest calling them whores. That night she thinks of how "[t]he nuns teach her how to compose herself for sleep: lie on your back, arms folded across

107. *GCG*, 15.
108. *IJN*.
109. *DH*, 76.
110. Ibid., 73.
111. *WWH*, 54.
112. *PN*, 146.

your breast, and think of the four last things. Death, judgment, heaven and hell."[113]

Having moved away from religious faith, Roberts's teenage spiritual fervor was channeled into the desire to be a writer; a parallel she draws explicitly: "I lost my religious vocation easily, in my first term at Somerville [College, Oxford], standing on the staircase outside the college library cradling copies of *Paradise Lost* and *Beowulf* . . . I realised that nuns were not allowed to stay up all night reading. Very well, then. Don't be a nun. That was that."[114] This narrative of having exchanged God for books would be told in terms of swapping one vocation for another: from being a nun to being a writer. Yet Roberts acknowledges the relationship between her Catholic heritage and the desire to write, because of the images and stories integral to the Catholic tradition, the women saints she learnt about at convent school, and the medieval mystics she studied at university. The image of saint as writer and writer as saint is a significant motif throughout her work.

The sense of vocation—including a willed poverty—took her to London after university, to write and train to be a librarian at the British Museum. Her experience working in the Department of Printed Books feeds into the image at the heart of *The Book of Mrs Noah*, of the Ark as a great library for women; her relationship to the physical presence of ancient printed books is echoed in the mystical heretical scrolls of *Impossible Saints*.[115] She remembers "[s]preading my hands over the thick paper of the pages, I knew that knowledge was physical . . . Books were material; like beloved bodies; provided not only intellectual but also sensual delight. I could touch them, open them, caress them, feed from them."[116] Roberts portrays her wanderings around London with an equal sense of physical intimacy: "[t]he city was like one of the manuscripts I studied at the British Museum. Layer upon layer of history lay quietly underneath the current written surface; not gone but just forgotten; biding its time. The city held memory in its very stones and bricks."[117]

Although Roberts had been witness to radical politics and the spirit of 1968 while an undergraduate at Oxford, it was in London in the early 1970s

113. *TV*, 33.
114. *PH*, 11.
115. *IS*, 188
116. *PH*, 22.
117. Ibid., 43.

that her commitment to socialism and feminism was to flourish. Through her friend Alison Fell, she became part of a feminist street theatre group, whose acts of protest were "carnivalesque and amusing"[118] and went to consciousness-raising group meetings. The development of feminist identity, and friendship, is an important aspect of *A Piece of the Night*, Roberts's first novel. It describes a rural French childhood and Oxford university education, and the fermenting of feminist consciousness, against the backdrop of a troubled mother-daughter relationship, couched in psychoanalytic terms.

A Piece of the Night also relates the tensions and difficulties of experiments in communal living, which Roberts experienced in a collective household headed by Alison Fell's husband. The guilt she felt at her inability to live this way, without possessions or even a room of her own, led her to draw parallels between this politically idealistic lifestyle and her childhood religious vocation: "[l]ooking back, I think I was like a young nun making up her mind to leave the convent: how difficult to go against a community you have chosen, ferociously loved and supported and now criticise. You feel you are betraying them."[119] Shortly after leaving and renting a flat, the unease caused by not having the safe and conventional lifestyle expected by her middle-class family led her to go and work at the British Council in Bangkok for a period, which features in *The Visitation*. On her return to London, Roberts worked for the Pregnancy Advisory Board, and was a clerk for a sociological research unit. At the same time she was deeply involved with the feminist literary community, publishing poetry with Judith Kazantzis and Alison Fell, and short fiction as part of the Women Writers Collective. Roberts was the poetry editor of *Spare Rib*, the magazine of the women's liberation movement in the UK. *A Piece of the Night* was the first novel to be published by The Women's Press.

The Visitation, Roberts's second novel, contends with being a writer, a twin (as Roberts is), the death of her beloved English grandmother, the joys and struggles of female friendship and the possibility of heterosexual love. Both *A Piece of the Night* and *The Visitation* are saturated with Jungian ideas on archetypes and the search for integration and wholeness. Jungian thought was to be even more prevalent in *The Wild Girl*, which Roberts has explained as her altered view of herself once she got married in 1983: "[t]he novel had been sparked off by my transition from being single to being married. The Catholic Church taught that a single woman could not

---

118. Ibid., 48.
119. Ibid., 69.

be both holy and sexual. Why not? Why did a woman have to be split in two? I began to re-imagine Christianity, to imagine a Christ who loved and listened to women."[120]

Roberts had married an older man, a scholar of Renaissance architecture she had met at one of her poetry readings. The time spent immersed in Italy's art, architecture and cuisine—and the loneliness and unease caused her by this marriage—are reflected in *The Book of Mrs Noah* and some of the short stories of *Playing Sardines*. *The Book of Mrs Noah*—which, like so many of Roberts's works, is made up of lots of different stories—is threaded together by the voice of Mrs Noah, a woman staying in Venice while her husband researches architectural history, who has nothing to do except dive into her imagination. This novel explores the relationship between writing and motherhood, utilizing the Ark-library as an image of pregnancy—which Roberts relates to her experience of infertility.[121] She accompanied her husband to Harvard, but at the end of the first academic year there she decided to leave him, and returned to London in time for the publication of *The Book of Mrs Noah*. Having achieved success as a writer, especially with *The Wild Girl*, she took up the post of Theatre Writer in Residence at Essex University.

At Essex, while working on an original play called *The Journeywoman*, she met the artist Jim Latter, who would become her second husband. Her happiness with him formed part of *In the Red Kitchen*, in which the character Hattie speaks in the second person to her lover, with whom she is making a home. As Hattie decorates their house, it becomes the embodiment of the contentment she has achieved, wrapped up with her love for the man her narrative is addressed to: "[y]our cufflinks and loose change share a big yellow Pernod ashtray with my watch and brooches."[122] The house in which Roberts first lived with Jim was divided between him and his ex-wife, so their sons could live with both of them; ideas of "the house as repaired body, as metamorphosing body" also inspired *In the Red Kitchen*, "which circled around haunting, breakages and secrets."[123] These themes—and the importance of the house—were carried over into *Daughters of the House*, written "out of a sudden need to think about where I came from (parents

---

120. Ibid., 248.
121. *GCG*, 18.
122. *RK*, 25.
123. *PH*, 308.

and politics), about the Second World War's impact on civilians in occupied France, about collaboration."[124]

Daughters of the House—with its clearer storytelling that Roberts attributes to her relationship with Jim—was shortlisted for the Booker Prize and won the WH Smith Literary Award. With the resulting increased sales and prize money, Roberts could afford to buy her own home, and she opted for a house in France, in order to reconnect with her French side, associated with her mother. Roberts's mother had reacted angrily to her fiction, and their relationship had been difficult for many years, but around this time they "reached an oasis. We felt able to express our love for each other. We forgave each other. A miracle in the desert."[125]

Roberts would come to terms with the trauma of another familial relationship—that with her father—staying in the childhood home in France after the death of her aunt, haunted by "a projection of old childhood fears and desires."[126] She explains,

> What came up for me, the ghoul that haunted me . . . was the strong feelings I'd had in this house for my father. At puberty, aged ten, I was madly in love with him, flirted with him, competed with my mother for his attention. I didn't know this was normal, that little girls routinely fall in love with their dads. Catholicism taught that sex before marriage was wicked. Sexual feelings in a child of ten were therefore of course very wicked indeed, and sexual feelings for my father were wickedest of all.[127]

Impossible Saints, written shortly before her father died, was the novel through which Roberts grappled with the complexities of the father-daughter relationship, and its guise in patriarchal religion. The main narrative, of Josephine, features a father-daughter relationship with hints of incestuous desires, but it is in the short narratives of a multitude of women saints that "we get various ways in which the daughter fights her father, loves him, flirts with him, gets raped by him."[128] Roberts felt that *Impossible Saints* was a "breakthrough novel"[129] not only in terms of her father, but also as regards religion. Her works of fiction that followed—*Fair Exchange*,

124. Ibid., 313.
125. Ibid., 325.
126. Ibid., 330.
127. Ibid.
128. *IBR*, 99.
129. Ibid., 106.

The Looking Glass, Playing Sardines, The Mistressclass and *Reader I Married Him*—circled around her interests in the importance of the material—of sex, food and place—and women as writers and historical agents, but in a lighter way than in her earlier work.

This neat narrative of Michèle Roberts's life story is based mostly on her memoir *Paper Houses*, but could also have been pieced together by information from her interviews and non-fiction writing, which augment the tale told in *Paper Houses*. It ends at a certain point—around the writing of *Impossible Saints*—although a little information about the years since are given on the last page, on which Roberts reveals that, after seventeen years together, her marriage to Jim had ended. Even though I already knew that, as the reader of this memoir I encountered the ending of this story with a jolt of sadness for its narrator.

Yet the narrator is not Michèle Roberts the partner, friend, daughter, sibling, step-mother, aunt—at least not the one known by her lovers, friends or family—it is Michèle-Roberts-the-writer, as disclosed to her readers. It is a fiction, but Roberts is well aware of that. She recognizes the "human need to make a shape for the story that we all have . . . autobiography and biography are not very different from fiction: similar impulses and similar stylistic devices are there to make a beautiful or truthful shape."[130] Roberts is also aware of the dangers of unified narratives told in one, omniscient voice. She had deliberately chosen to write novels that experimented with multiple perspectives and fragmented narratives—"plaiting, . . . interweaving down-to-earth voices rather than up-in-the sky ones"—associating omniscient narrators with God, fathers, the Pope. As such, *Paper Houses* is her only novel-length work which employs a single, 'reliable' narrator telling a straightforward narrative.

In the introduction, Roberts reflects on the process of writing her memoir, a fictionalized account of a person and a life, pieced together from the notebooks she wrote at the time: "[w]hen I spread them out on the floor of the room where I write they look like the multi-colored pavement of a piazza. This memoir is like fiction, in as much as I have shaped and edited it, but it is as truthful as I can make it, honouring both facts and the way I saw them at the time."[131] As the editor and shaper of the narrative, she chose, "[o]ut of consideration for others' privacy," to omit some

---

130. Ibid., 97.
131. *PH*, 7.

"characters" and to "censor some episodes"[132]—but she recognizes that this is not the only sense in which she is "in charge" of the narrative: "[w]riting this memoir joins up all the scattered bits of me, makes them continuous, gives me a conscious self existing in history . . . Out of what often felt at the time like muddle and mess I subsequently make this memoir, this story."[133] Roberts images the artifice of memoir in terms of her enjoyment of exploring and wandering a city's streets (of which *Paper Houses* contains many vivid descriptions): "[m]y narrative in one sense goes in a straight line, chronologically, charting my rake's progress, but in another sense is a *flâneur*. It circles around recurrent images and themes, runs back and forth between inner and outer worlds."[134] Thus Roberts's being "in charge" of the narrative is not the same as having complete control over it: "[y]ou become part of a flow and dance of words. You forget yourself and just get on with writing, just as, walking in the city, you can dissolve into the crowd, simply float, listen, look."[135]

Writing her autobiography, "the *flâneur* enjoys being enticed down side streets,"[136] both figuratively and literally. This relates to the importance of place, materiality and home in Roberts's life-writing (indeed, all her work). The house is a symbol of redemption, but it is not the physical house her memoir is named after, but that which gave her security, meaning and identity during the years of wandering: "[m]y diary was a room of my own in which I could speak and act as I liked. Reading created me a temporary house, spun a cocoon around me."[137] This is carried forward into the future; the final sentence of *Paper Houses*: "[w]riting goes on too: I keep on building my paper house; my chrysalis."[138]

Michèle Roberts's Life-Writing as Redemptive

For Michèle Roberts writing is home; it is also an alternative vocation. She frequently draws an analogy between her childhood desire to become a nun, and her vocation as a writer, which entails discipline and sacrifice, but

132. Ibid.
133. *PH*, 6.
134. Ibid.
135. Ibid., 6–7.
136. Ibid., 6.
137. Ibid., 250.
138. Ibid., 337.

has great spiritual reward: "writing is a bit like waiting on God ... trusting in the darkness, opening yourself up to what comes, being empty ... I've invented my own version of the convent, becoming a writer."[139] This, the connection between writers and saints and Roberts's interest in medieval literature, means that "spiritual autobiography" as a genre is important in her work. The piece of life-writing, "The Woman Who Wanted to Be a Hero," reads like a feminist Jungian version of a medieval saint's spiritual autobiography, describing Roberts's "journey" to "wholeness."[140] The childhood mystical experiences of interconnection attested to here may also be read in *The Wild Girl*: "suddenly, with no warning, the world was utterly transformed ... [t]he universe breathed in and out and I dissolved in it, no longer I ... This world shimmered and danced and changed constantly, and I, the not-I, was part of it, and understood it, and was it."[141]

Although the novel draws on patristic and gnostic texts, Mary's narration is more akin to that of spiritual autobiography than a gospel. *The Book of Mrs Noah* features the spiritual autobiography of a nun awaiting the results of a trial for heresy, relating her movement from a guilt-ridden, self-hating religion to a creation and birth-centered spirituality, influenced by (a fictionalized) Marguerite de Porete and the Heresy of the Free Spirit. The struggles of historical women mystics to transmit their ideas, sometimes directly defying the religious authorities, at other times employing cunning strategies of collaboration, are celebrated by Roberts,[142] especially in *Impossible Saints*. Yet this novel, and *Daughters of the House*, also suggest that women's spiritual autobiographies are not innocent. In *Impossible Saints*, Sister Josephine (Roberts's reimagining of Teresa of Avila) writes a version of her *Life* that coheres with approved dogma, in order to escape the suspicion of the Inquisition: "[s]he had danced their prescribed dance and performed their set gestures, had sung their recommended song, and received their polite applause."[143] The character of Thérèse in *Daughters of the House* is inspired by Thérèse of Lisieux, whose posthumous spiritual autobiography *The Story of a Soul* was exceptionally popular and ensured her canonization in 1925. Roberts's Thérèse, the pious child who became a nun in the wake of family trauma and secrets, writes her autobiography,

139. *FSG*, 199.
140. *WWH*, 51.
141. *WG*, 29.
142. *IGS*, 140–41.
143. *IS*, 130.

"the story of a soul"[144] twenty years after leaving home: "I thought if I wrote what happened when we were children it would help me to decide what it is I've got to do."[145] Léonie reacts thus: "if you tell any more lies about the past I'll kill you... You always were good at making things up... in your version I was the sinner and you were the saint... Yours will be the Authorised Version of what happened won't it."[146] Roberts's exploration of "a woman's dodgy desire to control a story"[147] in the characters of Léonie and Thérèse, perhaps expresses in fiction an ambivalence about life-writing that does not come across in her interviews and non-fiction. In *Daughters of the House* there is a sense that the healing and redemption that Roberts elsewhere ascribes to writing is not achieved easily, or without cost.

A sense of redemption through writing comes across in Roberts's words in 1983: "I became a writer through sheer necessity. I desperately needed to describe experience in order not to be overwhelmed by it, to name the conflicts inside myself, to imagine solutions to them."[148] She often describes her novels as attempts at solving a particular problem, for example *A Piece of the Night* asks "what is a woman?" and *The Visitation*, "[h]ow do men and women love each other?"[149] This is couched in terms of her relationships—for example *Impossible Saints* is concerned with her father; *A Piece of the Night* and *Flesh and Blood* are about the mother-daughter relationship. Writing about conflicts in relationships may bring further division rather than healing, because, as for Léonie and Thérèse, "versions clash."[150] Roberts's mother hated *A Piece of the Night*, "finding it ugly, cruel and disgusting, and believed I had written it deliberately wanting to hurt her."[151] Novels cannot bring ultimate healing or redemption, and so for Roberts similar themes are brought up again and again; the "sense of constant failure, of not getting something good enough or beautiful enough" results in the writing of "another novel and another and another."[152] Psychoanalytic ideas about artistic creation as the attempt to make reparation

144. *DH*, 19.
145. Ibid., 23.
146. Ibid.
147. *PH*, 313.
148. *WWH*, 51.
149. *IJN*.
150. *PH*, 313.
151. Ibid., 183.
152. *IJN*.

for the loss of connection with the mother's body have an important role in Roberts's conception of writing. But there can be no final restoration to the primordial paradise, only the repeated attempt to cope with the anger and emptiness felt at its loss: "[w]e re-create the mother inside ourselves, over and over again."[153] Thus the healing, or redemption, brought about by writing one's life or self is not final or complete, but nonetheless deeply valuable.

Annunciation: Writing the Self as Birthing the Self

Speaking about the lack of finality and need for multiple attempts in writing novels to solve problems, Roberts comments, "I'm not saying I'm finding earth-shattering solutions, but I am interested in making the novel different every time," for the same reasons that people have more than one child, and enjoy the differences between their children.[154] Continuing the novel-as-child motif, she sees the way that each of her novels has been provoked, inspired or enabled in some way by another person in her life, as that person engendering a child with her: "a very problematic image to use—that making a book is like making a baby . . . but I think you could use pregnancy as an image, as a womanly creation . . . I haven't had children myself—I was infertile—but I think I've had ten children by different people."[155]

One of the reasons why this image is "problematic" for a woman novelist is related to the relationship between autobiography and fiction, what Domna Stanton refers to as "the age-old, pervasive decoding of all female writing as autobiographical."[156] Roberts has said that she is defensive when hers and other women novelists' work is designated as "autobiographical," as if to undermine the skill and artfulness of constructing a piece of writing.[157] As Sidonie Smith suggests, men's autobiography is viewed as "crafted," whereas writing by women that is classified as "autobiographical" is "spontaneous" or "natural."[158] The conflation of women's biology with their writing is satirized by Roberts in *The Book of Mrs Noah* in the character of the Gaffer, "Author of the Word of God":

153. *FSG*, 21.
154. *IJN*.
155. *IBR*, 97.
156. *FSG*, 132.
157. Ibid., 4.
158. Smith, *Poetics of Women's Autobiography*, 16.

> Women writers, well, they're like leaky wombs, aren't they, letting out the odd stream of verbiage, the odd undisciplined shriek. They don't create. They just spill things out of that great empty space inside ... It's the male who represents humanity, creativity, spiritual quest, after all. How could a woman possibly do that? How could a mother know anything about human growth? Any fool can give birth. Writing a book is *labour*.[159]

Although there are troubling aspects to the image of writer-as-mother, the envisaging of the labor of writing a book as birth and childrearing has proved helpful to Roberts. Towards the end of *The Book of Mrs Noah*, a painting of the annunciation of the Virgin Mary is used to symbolize a woman's act of creation in a way that collapses distinctions between the generativity of nature and the creative will of the Word. In the painting, Mary reads the story of Noah, while the angel speaks to her: "[m]editating on words, her half-shut eyes cast down, seeing nothing but the black marks on the white page, she conceives other words; new words. She creates the Word inside herself, by herself, using her own power ... She is the Ark, the maker of the Word. She is the author. Meditating on the Old Testament, then discarding it, she will write a new text, with herself as the subject that speaks."[160] In Roberts's annunciation, in which words are made flesh and the flesh makes new words, the woman writer conceives herself, in giving herself subjectivity and speech. This image of writing oneself as a giving birth to oneself reminds me of a phrase of Hélène Cixous: "[w]riting, dreaming, delivering; being my own daughter of each day."[161]

Maitland also writes of the annunciation, imagining Mary's "assent" as "the moment of conception,"[162] "an assent to the totality of herself, to a womanhood so vital and empowered that it could break free of biology and submission, any dependence on or need for masculine sexuality."[163] Her 1999 novel *Brittle Joys* portrays the annunciation as the invention of the craft of glass-blowing: "[l]ying on the leather that covers her hand is a sphere, her glowing blue, light-refracting, light-distorting bubble, free of the rod, free and filled with inspiration. It has a navel, a small round scar, that joins it to her and to history, but she has set it free ... She is pregnant,

159. *BMN*, 56.
160. Ibid., 214–15.
161. Cixous, *Coming to Writing*, 6.
162. *DJ*, 28.
163. Ibid., 30.

breathed into, inspired by the spirit. This is the annunciation."[164] This, as in Roberts's image, presents a woman's inspiration in artistic creativity as part of her bodily capacity to nurture new life.

Writing-as-mothering, as "annunciation," is particularly appropriate as an image of the fiction of autobiography, while maintaining a sense of the very close connection between the writer and the subject of the autobiography. The self that writes a life is not the same person who lived the events being remembered and narrated; the person disclosed on the page is in many ways an entirely separate creation, a daughter, almost. As Roberts reflects in *Paper Houses*, "[w]ho was that 'I,' that young woman of twenty-one? I reconstruct her. I invent a new 'me' composed of the girl I was, according to my diaries, my memories (and the gaps between them), and the self remembering her. She stands in between the two. A third term. She's a character in my story and she tells it too. She's like a daughter. Looking back at her, thinking about her, I mother myself."[165]

I find the image of annunciation helpful both in terms of the presentation of my own stories—the insertion of an autobiographical self who is in some sense my own creation—and in terms of my understanding of the authors Michèle Roberts and Sara Maitland's incarnation in their writing. In the following chapter I stay with the symbolism of the Virgin Mary, by considering "reading these stories beside my own"[166] in terms of encounter, that of visitation.

164. *BJ*, 227.
165. *PH*, 14.
166. Sands, *Escape from Paradise*, 167.

2

Visitation

Reading and Writing Encounters

As discussed in chapter 1, in this book I envisage both my own self-narration and that of the writers I engage with as 'annunciation,' inspired by Michèle Roberts and Sara Maitland's reimagining of this New Testament story. In their presentations of the annunciation, Mary's act of creativity is self-contained, independent, solitary. Thus, as a feminist theological way of thinking about literature, it is incomplete. What is needed is a sense of the communality of women's writing; that stories are generated by and through relationships; that we make stories for other people as well as ourselves.

For this I turn to the following episode in Luke's account of Mary the mother of Jesus: her visit to her cousin Elizabeth, also miraculously pregnant, her story also not listened to or believed by those around her. Encountering Mary, Elizabeth feels the child in her womb leaping for joy; she declares Mary "blessed among women" (Luke 1:41–4). Encountering Elizabeth, Mary utters the words of the Magnificat (Luke 1:46–55), after two thousand years still recited daily in evening prayer: "my soul magnifies the Lord, and my spirit rejoices in God my Saviour . . . He has brought down the powerful from their thrones, and lifted up the lowly."

In this chapter, I take the image of the visitation as representative of the creative power of encounter with other women, reading their stories beside one's own. My theological reading of Roberts and Maitland's writing is a visitation; in turn their writing is generated from multiple and interrelated visitations. I consider this in terms of the communal context of feminist writing practice, feminist revisioning of women encountered in myth and history, and the very real relationships that readers have with books.

Visitation

WOMEN'S FRIENDSHIP AND STORYTELLING

As with the annunciation, my notion of the visitation is structured by its retelling in the work of Roberts and Maitland. Michèle Roberts uses the first chapter of Luke to explore female friendship in a poem entitled "Magnificat," which describes the friend coming over to comfort the heartbroken narrator as "fierce as a small archangel"; her sage words of comfort "an annunciation," the declaration of "the birth of a new life / . . . you commanded me to sing of my redemption." At the end of the poem she reflects on their friendship, "it was a holy communion / between women, a Visitation."[1] This presentation of women's friendship in terms of religious imagery is paralleled in Roberts's novel entitled *The Visitation*, with the protagonist's spiritual quest punctuated by visits from Beth, her best friend from university. While their friendship has many points of tension and conflict, it is Beth who is the bearer of Helen's moments of redemption: when she is struggling to write, Beth tells her that she admires her for continuing to try: "Beth's words of recognition . . . a loving witnessing of how she feels . . . Suddenly she's meeting her there, and in that barren place is a most warm consolation. Blessed are they that mourn, and show their trouble to friends, for that shall comfort them."[2] At the end of the novel, in conversation with a pregnant Beth, Helen comes to a cathartic understanding of her mental anguish, and this redemptive moment is described using imagery based on Luke 1:39-56: "saying, I am listening to you, saying, I am here . . . This is their loving labour, performed with one another, and it brings forth children, a mutual pregnancy, as they embrace and listen to each other, and the words inside them leap for joy . . . [Beth] commands her to sing of her redemption, her life, to speak, to write."[3]

A recasting of the visitation in terms of female friendship is more firmly placed in the context of the women's movement in Maitland's 1978 novel, *Daughter of Jerusalem*. Mary's visit to Elizabeth is retold as a moment of feminist solidarity: "there in one another's arms, and only there, they are affirmed, encouraged, borne up, freed . . . And in the arms of her friend, her sister, within the strength of another woman Mary conceives again: the flowering of the great song of praise and power and triumph, the love song

---

1. *ASW*, 9.
2. *TV*, 82.
3. *TV*, 173.

that unites her not just to Elizabeth but to all the other difficult women everywhere and everywhen."[4]

Daughter of Jerusalem juxtaposes the stories of biblical women with the story of the present-day feminist Liz and her ambivalence towards her struggle to conceive a child. The retelling of the visitation occurs after a description of Liz's consciousness-raising group, implicitly linking Elizabeth and Mary's support of each other with the relationships between women that were central to the second-wave liberation movement.

Consciousness-Raising

The practice of feminist 'consciousness-raising' has its origins in the group New York Radical Women, of which early members included key feminist writers such as Shulamith Firestone, Robin Morgan and Kate Millett. Anne Forer recalls the invention of the term consciousness-raising in 1967: "[i]n the Old Left, they used to say that the workers don't know they're oppressed, so we have to raise their consciousness. One night at a meeting I said, 'Would everybody please give me an example from their own life on how they experienced oppression as a woman? I need to hear it to raise my own consciousness.' Kathie [Sarachild] was sitting behind me and the words rang in her mind. From then on she sort of made it an institution and called it consciousness-raising."[5]

In the following few years, this practice of women meeting regularly in groups to talk about their experiences would spread throughout the US and across the Atlantic. The organization of political activism was not separated from this primary activity of identifying the ways patriarchal oppression functions in all aspects of women's lives, in ways not fully recognized until they were narrated and discussed. As Adrienne Rich asserts, "[t]he naming as political of women's personal experiences, to be explored and compared in consciousness-raising [CR] sessions, was a keystone of radical feminist theory." Rich draws attention to the practice of the consciousness-raising session itself, which would focus on "each woman's individual testimony."[6] Carol Christ has emphasized the spiritual implications of this practice, referring to the CR group session as "a ritualized setting in which women

---

4. *DJ*, 52.
5. Brownmiller, *In Our Time*, 21.
6. Rich, *Blood, Bread and Poetry*, viii.

gather together to share their stories."⁷ In feminist theology, the importance of women's sharing their stories with one another was encapsulated by Nelle Morton's phrase "hearing into speech," inspired by an incident at a week-long workshop she ran, in which a woman told the group her painful personal history, and the rest of the group sat and listened to her "in powerful silence."⁸ The woman then said to the group, "you heard me to my own story. You heard me to my own speech."⁹

Morton's account of "hearing into speech" echoes the transformative encounters of Roberts and Maitland's reimagining of the visitation. They demonstrate the generative power of what Carol Christ expresses as women's "creat[ing] new being" in telling each other "stories which have never been told before, stories utterly unlike the stories we have all learned from the culture."¹⁰ However, there is in Roberts and Maitland's writing an honest realism about the difficulties of feminist friendship and the consciousness-raising paradigm.

Maitland's retelling of the visitation has Mary's famous liberation song created out of the love between her and Elizabeth, but the protagonist of *Daughter of Jerusalem* has a more ambivalent attitude towards her feminist friends. Undergoing fertility treatment, with a doctor who thinks that her inability to conceive is psychosomatic, Liz is jealous of her best friend Nancy, who has children, and of Alice, who announces her unplanned pregnancy at a CR group meeting. Liz is resentful of the group's expectation that she takes part in a pro-choice demonstration, putting "moral pressure" on her to "be a good feminist, be a good sister."¹¹ In the doctor's waiting room, Liz thinks of her women's group as a "small minority of articulate women, educated, practised in tearing up your personal lives for the edification of your friends," which would be no use for "most of the women here . . . too embarrassed, too private, to gain anything from such a conversation."¹² A significant moment of the novel is a conversation between Liz and her friend Nancy; together they discuss the complexities of their relationships; their inability to live up to the feminist ideal. Their openness and solidarity is a redemptive moment; it is counterbalanced by the less wholesome—but

---

7. Christ, *Diving Deep and Surfacing*, 7.
8. Morton, *Journey is Home*, 205.
9. Ibid., 206.
10. Christ, "Why Women Need the Goddess," 229.
11. *DJ*, 45.
12. Ibid., 33.

powerful—image of Deborah and Jael (Judg 5). The encounter between Deborah and Jael, the peasant-woman who killed Israel's enemy Sisera while he slept in her tent, is, in Maitland's version, the dark face of women's liberation; Deborah's song a bloody and violent Magnificat: "Deborah and Jael look at each other, they smile at each other—they are friends . . . They know their husbands will never want to touch them again. They know who the enemy is . . . the whole victorious, manic, excited exultant army is silent with fear . . . What is the source of the joy that lights up these women? What are the words of the song they will sing together? What power drove the hand that drove the nail?"[13]

From the outset Roberts also presents the ambivalence of women's storytelling as liberative. Julie, the protagonist of *A Piece of the Night*, awakens her feminist consciousness through spending time with the women's group of her old school friend, Jenny: "[i]n this atmosphere of female warmth and support there is nothing to stop her cracking up completely, letting go once and for all."[14] The closing passage of the novel iterates the hope of shared storytelling: "[t]ell me about your past, Julie begins to urge other women, and they to urge her. The women sit in circles talking. They are passing telegrams along battle-lines, telling each other stories that will not put them to sleep, recognising allies under the disguise of femininity."[15]

This passage also features in a short story published in the Woman Writers Collective's *Tales I Tell My Mother*, "Martha and Mary Raise Consciousness from the Dead." Mary and Martha are associated with the "resurrection" of CR not only because of the story of their brother Lazarus in John 11, but also because tradition has divided them into domestic and contemplative, pitting sisters against each other (Luke 10:38–42), and one of the functions of the CR movement is to bring women together, when patriarchy has divided them. It tells of a burgeoning lesbian romance: sexual female friendship, also imaged by visitation, is portrayed in Roberts and Maitland's fiction.

In "Martha and Mary" and *A Piece of the Night* lesbian relationships seem to be a salvific alternative to the love of men; although Julie suffers when her girlfriend Jenny becomes the lover of another member of their shared household. In Maitland's *Virgin Territory*, the nun Anna comes to the realization of the damage patriarchal religion has done to her partly

---

13. *DJ*, 168.
14. *PN*, 100.
15. Ibid., 180.

through her friendship with Karen, a lesbian feminist. The exploration of archetypes is a central theme of the novel; Anna buys Karen a print of Käthe Kollwitz's lithograph of the visitation: "[i]t brought their two worlds together, close like the women in the lithograph. Karen smiled and hugged her and said, 'Of course, you do realise that the Visitation is the ultimate Dyke moment, don't you; when two women get together and in love proclaim their freedom, they sing that the personal is political and from their love will come freedom for all the world.'"[16] Yet lesbian love is no more ideologically pure than any other sexual desire, any other friendship, and Karen's love for Anna is not untainted by possessiveness.

Similarly, although optimistic, Roberts's "Martha and Mary" is not a wholly positive account of consciousness-raising: "I told the [women's] group a story, to keep them entertained, to laugh and preferably not to weep, hiding reality from them and myself with metaphor and rhythm."[17] This reminder of the artifice of any kind of storytelling—including the frank self-narration of a women's group—is echoed in Roberts's recollection of her own involvement in CR groups: "my articulateness sometimes felt like glibness to me: opinions rather than true explorations. I could tell my truth in poems, through metaphor . . . But I couldn't speak in poems at meetings."[18] Later, Roberts would satirically examine such experiences in *The Book of Mrs Noah*: "[h]ere I am, returning to a nice warm womb full of the nourishment and sweetness of women, a fine safe place in which to grow and change, and what do I find? Not only disagreement and conflict (women's groups? give me a coffee morning any day) but also untruths. To speak is a lie. To oversimplify. I don't believe in that conversation we've just had. The taking up of positions as in a war, no ambiguity allowed."[19] Like some instances of feminist fiction, the CR paradigm invokes storytelling as "talking to sisters/friends/comrades, opening up in a trusting way, telling all, telling the truth, utilising only that most reliable of narrators: oneself, or a character based on oneself . . . a narrator whose impulses were essentially *good*."[20] Roberts's fiction explores how storytelling and sisterly relationships are not always innocent and certainly not always easy: sisterhood can be more like that of Rachel and Leah than Mary and Elizabeth; for example the

16. *VT*, 146.
17. *MMT*, 72.
18. *PH*, 49.
19. *BMN*, 57.
20. *FSG*, 9.

sisterly rivalries of *In the Red Kitchen*'s Flora and Rose, Thérèse and Léonie in *Daughters of the House* and Catherine and Vinny in *The Mistressclass*.

Roberts's writing does portray the richness of sisterly relationships, "passionate love between friends,"[21] and redemptive possibilities of women's storytelling encounters—but in a way that recognizes sisterhood's impurities and limitations. In *Fair Exchange*, the 18th-century unwed pregnant women Annette and Jemima become friends through telling each other their stories—"[t]rue friendship . . . meant telling each other things; sharing secrets when necessary; witnessing each other's lives. You held the memory of each other, the events and changes."[22] However, they lose touch with each other, a source of deep regret for Jemima once she learns of Annette's death. *The Mistressclass* tells of the failure of sisterly relationships, but also how it generates stories; the voice of Charlotte Bronte describes her relationship with Emily: "[s]he traced whole stories on my back; she spelled out poems, line by line, all down my spine. When she'd finished, she twisted around, and I began. It was my turn. . . My sister: my first reader; my first audience; as I hers. Both of us writers and both of us readers, connected by the need for storytelling not to end."[23]

Collective Writing

Feminism has always been "a peculiarly literary movement,"[24] with its ideas developed in and communicated through poetry, fiction and theatre, collapsing the boundaries between political activism and artistic creation. Much of feminism's ideas and imagery were generated communally, flourishing in the network of activist relationships. The writing of the women's liberation movement was often produced collectively, with groups of women writing and/or publishing their work together. This was both ideological and practical—the writing would often emerge from CR and campaigning groups; the values of feminism are fundamentally communal; and it is easier to self-publish if one is part of a group. One particularly notable UK feminist writing collective was one in which both Michèle Roberts and Sara Maitland took part in, and was remarkable in the sense that most of its members went on to have successful careers publishing as individuals.

21. *BMN*, 104.
22. *FE*, 185.
23. *MC*, 95.
24. Walton, *Literature, Theology and Feminism*, 10.

The group, also including Zoë Fairbairns, Valerie Miner and Michelene Wandor, came together to produce a book of short stories, *Tales I Tell My Mother*. Roberts writes in the epilogue, "we are not unique; we represent only a fraction of the woman all over the country who are coming together in groups to leap forward from the isolation and social silence of the diary and the shopping list and the backs of envelopes in order to communicate to others via the alchemy of fiction the concerns of their lives as women and as feminists."[25]

In the introduction, Fairbairns explains their method: they met every two or three weeks in each others' homes, discussing the members' stories that had been circulated in the time since the last meeting: "[c]hanges were usually made in the light of the discussions, and no story has been included that does not have the unanimous agreement of the group that it should be included."[26] In her memoir, *Paper Houses*, Roberts recalls how they "criticised each other's work, gave each other ideas, discussed everything minutely and exhaustively."[27] *Tales I Tell My Mother* does not romanticize this process: Fairbairns writes, "we believe that collectivity has its limits, and each story is ultimately the work of its individual author, and is signed as such. Collectivity is a word that is bandied about a lot in the women's movement. Sometimes 'collective' is just a trendy euphemism for the same old committee. Sometimes it's an excuse for not doing anything. At its best though—and it has been good for us—it really can mean a group of equals, united by a genuine determination to get on with the job."[28] Roberts's epilogue also emphasizes that the success of the group was due to discipline and commitment, and before joining the group each member was already established in some way as a writer.[29] As well as a practical attitude to the work involved in the project, Fairbairns's introduction and Roberts's epilogue are honest—in their different ways—about the relational difficulties of working in such a way. Fairbairns lists the differences amongst the members, then asks "What can they find to agree on?," answered with

> Everyone else in the group is in a league to put her down.
> This is the finest and best group of women anyone had the privilege of being supported by.

25. *ET*, 160.
26. Fairbairns, "Introduction," 3.
27. *PH*, 130.
28. Fairbairns, "Introduction," 3.
29. *ET*, 160.

> She is the best writer in the group, if not the world.
> (Or the worst.)
> She is unfeminist, unsisterly, unworthy of the others.
> Nobody understands what she is on about, which is her failure.
> Nobody understands what she is on about, which is their loss.[30]

This admittance of their doubts and resistance to taking themselves too seriously would have enabled them to withstand the personal and creative difficulties of scrutinizing each other's work. This honest and humorous approach is characteristic of the British feminist writing of the time.

Aside from the Women Writers Collective, which also published *More Tales I Tell My Mother* in 1987, Maitland and Roberts would both contribute to a number of other collective projects. An essay of Roberts's was included in a collection of reflections on spirituality, *Walking on Water*, which Maitland edited along with Jo Garcia. Both Roberts and Maitland contributed to *Fathers: Reflections by Daughters* edited by Ursula Owen; *The Seven Deadly Sins* and *The Seven Cardinal Virtues*, both edited by Alison Fell. They were part of a feminist milieu, with its shared interests, ideals and images; they were also friends. Roberts writes how Maitland would drive her home from group meetings, "even when we had arrived at my house we would sit on in the car for another half-hour, furiously swapping perceptions and ideas."[31] When I first embarked on this project, I had known that the two writers would almost certainly be aware of each other's work, but I had not realized that they knew each other personally, until the jolt of reading in Roberts's piece in *Walking on Water* that it was her friendship with "you, Sara" that had kept alive her interest in spirituality after renouncing Catholicism.[32]

Michèle Roberts also worked with groups who published poetry collectively.[33] One group also met regularly to discuss one another's work; a practice of which Alison Fell wrote "has both broken the double isolation of being women and being writers, and also given us the courage to face the necessity of writing alone."[34]

Roberts's work inscribes the conflict between the feminist emphasis on working collectively and the artistic need to work alone. In *Paper Houses*,

---

30. Fairbairns, "Introduction," 2.

31. *PH*, 130.

32. *WWH*, 63.

33. See Blaug et al., *Cutlasses and Earrings*; Fell, *Smile*; Fell, *Licking the Bed Clean*; Kazantzis, Roberts, and Wandor, *Touch Papers*.

34. Fell, *Smile*, iv.

she remembers writing her first novel at night, a secret from her communal household, feeling guilty for working on "a private, individual project . . . I salved my conscience by going to lots of meetings."³⁵ *The Book of Mrs Noah* explores at length the tensions and possibilities of women's writing communities, affectionately and angrily parodying the feminist literary scene. As well as being a library of women's writing, the Ark is a home for women writers: "[w]omen come here to develop their craft, to discuss work in progress, to give and take criticism and advice on redrafting, to share fears, failures, ideas. Women who hate the very idea of writers workshops come here to get away from other women, to live in cells of silence and isolation, to be as selfish and unsisterly as they like."³⁶

Mrs Noah gets together with the "Sibyls"—five women writers suffering from writer's block—to discuss having a writing group; they each rehearse the typical debates of women's writing: one raises the objection that feminists are not inclusive of heterosexual women; another that what matters is writing well, rather than being female. The avowed feminist wants to reinvent language—"[i]ncoherence and irrationality and syntactical violence and multiple word-orgasms, that's what we need"—another asks for them to speak with "ordinary language"; one wants to "theorize" the link between gender and creativity.³⁷ Later on, one of the Sibyls is visited by her "seven deadly sins," number five being "unsisterly behaviour": "[y]ou don't work collectively any more. You want to be a star. You've stopped caring about your struggling sisters. Women all over the world are trying to fight their oppression and you sit at home cosily writing novels. You'd never have become a writer if it wasn't for the women's movement, yet where's your gratitude?"³⁸

In *Paper Houses*, Roberts writes that after the success of *The Wild Girl*, three of her feminist friends criticized her for becoming part of "the literary establishment"; this passage in *The Book of Mrs Noah* seem reflective of that. She believes that this "moralism" was caused by envy, and the inability to openly admit this envy.³⁹ One of the Sibyls admits how furiously jealous she sometimes is of her feminist writing colleagues, with publishers and critics pitting feminist writers against one another. She is her jealous of her

35. *PH*, 126.
36. *BMN*, 21.
37. Ibid., 49.
38. Ibid., 177.
39. *PH*, 255–56.

friend selected for top-twenty promotions, of one who has a cult following, of another who is "flavour of the month" at the moment: "I don't admit this; haven't men always said women are bitchy, envious and competitive? I punish myself instead. I stay away from you."[40] Another of the Sibyls says she is now fed up with the popular images and themes of feminist literature: "I'd rather not read about menstruation, says the Deftly Sibyl: I quite see that it was a revolutionary topic when first introduced into women's writing, but now it's become de rigueur I'm bored with it. I'm also bored by throbbing wombs, moons, grandmothers, lesbians, the lost mother, nuns, witches, food, and orgasms."[41] Written under the shadow of Thatcherism, *The Book of Mrs Noah* is a sometimes savage—but essentially loving—satirizing of the feminist movement. It is self-critical and self-mocking more than anything: after all, Michèle Roberts has never stopped writing about any of the things listed by the Deftly Sibyl.

Sara Maitland's affectionate send-up of feminism and collective writing also utilizes the image of Noah's Ark, and was also published in 1987: indeed, she comments within that "the story of the Ark seems to be a recurrent image for the frailty of our times."[42] Written with Michelene Wandor, *Arky Types*—"the most fun to write novel that I have ever been engaged in"[43]—consists of letters between a variety of characters, including Sara and Michelene, a literary agent, a publisher, Sister Mary Clare, Mrs Noah and Mrs Vicar. The Ark was also chosen for the comic potential of "mix[ing] sexual politics with zoomorphic metaphor":[44] the conflicts of the women's movement good-naturedly satirized in the characters of a worm and fugitive lesbian tortoises, who object to the Ark's heterosexist "couplism."

The book playfully discusses the process of collaborative writing: a publisher asks them to write a book after hearing "how you both spoke with such conviction about the ways in which writers could and did use each other's imaginations,"[45] before becoming evasive about the terms of their contract. The letters between Sara and Michelene discuss the possibilities of writing something together, including them getting irritated with each other: Sara writes, "I suppose I feel you're dictating to my imagination,

40. *BMN*, 190.
41. Ibid., 189.
42. *AT*, 33.
43. *RWB*.
44. *AT*, 121.
45. Ibid., 7.

and my imagination is digging in her heels."⁴⁶ Michelene responds to Sara's talking about them "finding" the book with "[w]riting isn't magic, it's fucking awful, hard work."⁴⁷ Sara, a committed Christian, enjoys the Jewish atheist Michelene's "knockabout comedy or religious debunking" but does not want it written "under my name."⁴⁸ Maitland and Wandor's writing encounter between non-religious Jew and Christian is also explored in the letters between Michelene and Sister Mary Clare, in which Michelene writes about Christian "co-opting" of the Hebrew Bible. These fictional difficulties are reflective of the questions Maitland and Wandor discussed in reality in writing *Arky Types*: Maitland says, "we went through a long period, some of which is incorporated into the book, . . . of working out how we might . . . find a way of writing which both reflected our very deep friendship and affection and didn't wipe out either voice, or try and create a liberal voice . . . apart from anything else it would be a very weird voice, a voice that was tidily, evenly shared between Michelene and I."⁴⁹

The writing of Sara Maitland and Michèle Roberts both testifies to the literary fruitfulness of the women's movement, of feminist friendship, consciousness-raising and collective writing. They also portray the flaws inherent in these writing encounters of flesh-and-blood women; visitations unique and precious in their imperfect reality.

Encounters Across Myth and History

Michèle Roberts and Sara Maitland's revisioning of Mary and Elizabeth is itself a kind of visitation: the rewriting of the story of these biblical women an encounter that reaches across what Maitland calls "the timeless space between the boundary of myth and history."⁵⁰ In this section I explore Roberts and Maitland's retellings of female characters from scripture, hagiography, fairytale, myth, and history as visitation, firstly in terms of a literary encounter between women, but also in terms of another meaning of visitation—a haunting.

---

46. Ibid., 33.
47. Ibid., 117.
48. Ibid., 33.
49. *RWB*.
50. *WFMW*, 82.

Sex, Sin, and Our Selves

Feminist Revisioning

Revisionist narratives and motifs are employed extensively throughout both Roberts and Maitland's work; much academic attention to Roberts's work is concerned with her revisioning;[51] retelling old tales is basic to Maitland's conception of herself as a writer, and is especially prevalent in her short stories. In "A Feminist Writer's Progress" she writes of herself in the third person: "[s]he knew... what her own quest really was: to retell the old stories again and fill in some bits that got left out. She knew what her own form was too—the intense and even constraining space of the short story, vibrating with the voices of tradition and memory."[52]

Roberts and Maitland's writing of mythical[53] figures is situated within the tradition of feminist revisioning, itself part of the wider literary tradition of appropriating and adapting[54] ancient stories and images, from epic poetry to Roland Barthes's assertion that "any text is an intertext."[55] Feminist adaption and appropriation was influentially referred to as "revisioning" in the sixth chapter of Alicia Ostriker's *Stealing the Language*. In identifying the particular purpose of contemporary women writers' retellings of traditional stories, Ostriker drew on Adrienne Rich's definition of revisioning as "the act of looking back" in order "not to pass on a tradition but to break its hold over us."[56] Myths are unmade and remade in feminist revisionary texts "not only to expose the patriarchal beliefs which underpin them, but to provide alternative myths which can offer women a more constructive view of their own gender."[57] In *Feminist Revision and the Bible* (1993), Ostriker says,

> As critic and poet, as Jew, woman and (dare I say) human being, I am involved in a collective enterprise which has as its ultimate goal the radical transformation of what used to be called 'the

---

51. See for example Falcus, *Michèle Roberts*; García Sánchez, "Michèle Roberts's Protagonists"; King, *Women and the Word*; Walton, *Imagining Theology*, 79–87; White, "Visions and Re-Visions."

52. *FWP*, 20.

53. Henceforth I will use 'myth' and 'traditional tales' as generic shorthand for scripture, hagiography, fairytale, folklore and classical myth and history, making distinctions where necessary.

54. See Sanders, *Adaption and Appropriation*.

55. Barthes, "Theory of the Text," 39.

56. Rich, "When We Dead Awaken," 91.

57. King, *Women and the Word*, 3.

Judeo-Christian tradition.' Yet my quest springs directly from the core of that tradition and is the inevitable consequence of it . . . I am engaged both theoretically and practically in the question of what will happen when the spiritual imagination of women, women who may call themselves Jews or Christians, pagans or atheists, witches or worshippers of the Great Goddess, is released into language and into history.[58]

While feminist revisioning has extended to all aspects of cultural discourse, it is arguable that "Bible, hagiography, myth, and fairy tale have been a major focus for reimagining because they represent and encode a culture's values in a more direct way than more complex and literary texts."[59] There is something particularly subversive about women's inscribing their own stories onto these ancient and renowned tales, because of their deeply personal significance, as well as their "archaic prestige."[60] Writers contemporary with Roberts and Maitland who have employed revisionary strategies include Angela Carter, A. S. Byatt, Liz Lochhead, Michelene Wandor, Jeanette Winterson, Anita Diamant, Carol Ann Duffy, Jenny Diski, Tanith Lee, and Margaret Atwood. Their literary revisioning takes various forms: for example as a prequel or sequel, employing first-person narration, or placing a minor character at center stage. The traditional stories may be given a contemporary setting, or have an alternative ending.[61]

Ostriker identifies four features of feminist revisioning: firstly, "the female poet gives voice to female silence";[62] secondly, attention is drawn to "the male gendered universal." Thirdly, the feminist revisionist writer "finds something in the myth which nobody noticed before, and which only a woman would be likely to notice . . . meanings already latent in a given story are recovered and foregrounded by a woman's perspective." Ostriker's final strategy, which she considers to be "the feature of female revisionism which scholars find most irritating and which I consider essential to the work of feminism" is the use of humor, the refiguring of "tragedy as farce": "[w]hat is supposed to be sacred becomes a joke. And I believe that

---

58. Ostriker, *Feminist Revision and the Bible*, 30.
59. Gilbert and Gubar, *Madwoman in the Attic*, 36.
60. Montefiore, *Feminism and Poetry*, 56.
61. See Harries, *Twice Upon a Time*, 99–102; Sellers, *Myth and Fairy Tale*, 13–14.
62. Ostriker, *Feminist Revision and the Bible*, 28.

whatever is sacred must become, somehow or other, a joke, if we want to free ourselves of mental tyranny."[63]

The way that feminist revisioning "defamiliarizes" well-known tales draws attention to the revisionist project: "it accentuates its argument to make clear that there is an argument, that an act of theft is occurring."[64] Yet the relationship of feminist revisioning with its source material is not simply one of "argument," in that, as stated by Donald Haase, retelling a traditional tale is to both accept *and* reject it.[65] Feminist revisioning has indeed sometimes been presented as "translating patriarchal texts back into the 'mother tongue.'"[66] However, this is more complex than an attempt at "correcting" ancient and timeless tales, as Jan Montefiore seems to assume when she argues that the force of the old tales is such that revisions "neither exorcise nor assume the power of their originals."[67]

Feminist retellings need not aim either to supersede the original or to uncover meanings regarded as authentic to a monolithic conception of women's experience. This would be the assertion of "a new tyranny," rather than a disruption of the hierarchical dualism of patriarchal discourse.[68] Instead, through their "mirroring" of the traditional tales,[69] feminist retellings emphasize that there is no "natural or unmediated" reflection of the stories.[70] Most feminist revisionists do not portray their telling of the story as "one 'true' version for all time," rather they stress that their revisioned tale "is only one version of the many possible versions. They encourage the reader to see the new telling "as one, but not the only, way to tell the tale."[71] Moreover, when dealing with fairytale and classical myth there is no "original" tale; rather they evolved from complex oral traditions, and have long been subject to continuous alteration. The written versions we know best— by Charles Perrault, the Grimm brothers, and Hans Christian Andersen, or Homer, Sophocles and Ovid—were shaped by their historical context and the ideological concerns of their authors. Historical-critical biblical

63. Ibid., 29.
64. Ostriker, *Stealing the Language*, 236.
65. Haase, "Feminist Fairy-Tale Scholarship," 30.
66. King, *Women and the Word*, 31.
67. Montefiore, *Feminism and Poetry*, 55.
68. Sellers, *Myth and Fairy Tale*, 137.
69. Bacchilega, "Cracking the Mirror," 10.
70. Haase, "Feminist Fairy-Tale Scholarship," 24.
71. Harries, *Twice Upon a Time*, 102.

scholarship has shown that the Bible's narratives were woven together from various written and oral sources by artful redactors; within scripture there are many different versions of the same story: the four Gospels, for example. In this sense, reimagining the stories in the light of feminist concerns is a seamless continuation of the tradition of myth, Bible, and fairy tale. As Sara Maitland writes, "the old stories" are "always and necessarily" told in the author's "own words and to [their] own ends."[72]

What I do find helpful about Ostriker's depiction of revisioning as "argument" with the source stories is that it is a relational image, ascribing personhood to both the reteller and the tale itself. Imaging retelling in terms of encounter between persons—be it violent, loving, erotic—articulates the depth and intensity of women's relationship with traditional tales and images, and the act of reinterpreting and rewriting them. As pieces of our cultural background, they are deeply familiar—belonging to "high culture" while being "quintessentially intimate"[73]—evoking affection, resentment, passion, and rage. Feminist revisioning is, in this sense, argument, but also conversation, wrestling, making love, encountering a friend.

There is not the space here to discuss in depth the multiple and significant differences between myth, fairytale, hagiography, scripture and history. In the latter three—and history most straightforwardly and significantly—the amount of 'reality' held by the stories and figures that are being reworked leads to problematic questions about stealing the lives and stories of others. Classical myth raises particular issues because of its privileged place in culture and literary tradition; also its role in psychoanalytic thought. Fairy tale is associated with childhood and thus with one's perceptions and expectations growing into adulthood, particularly for girls. With stories of saints—and more so with the Bible—notions of religious inspiration and the authority of the source text have tremendous bearing on the way it is retold: feminist revisioning of sacred stories will be especially passionate and conflicted, as we see in the revisioning of Roberts and Maitland.

Rather than attempting a critical survey of all of Roberts and Maitland's revisionist practice, in what follows I consider selected examples according to three (interrelated but distinct) modes of revisioning: archetypes, appropriation and encounter.

---

72. *ABS*, 124.
73. Ostriker, *Stealing the Language*, 213.

Archetypes

There is a feminist literary tradition of revisioning not only myth, but also the uses myth has been put to by the fathers of psychoanalysis: Sigmund Freud and Carl Jung. Feminist refiguring of Jung's thought on archetypes is significant in the use of female figures from myth in both Roberts and Maitland's work of the late 1970s and early 1980s, and is also apparent in the writing of their contemporaries. In Jung's thought, myth arises from the "collective unconscious," which manifests as specific ideas and images, termed "archetypes." These archetypal images "generate and shape all our most powerful thinking."[74] In the feminist project of uncovering and reworking the symbols and stories of patriarchal tradition, Roberts and Maitland have explored the way female archetypes have been harmful to women, and tried to recreate them in ways that would aid personal healing and the wider feminist movement.

Michèle Roberts's first three novels, and especially *The Wild Girl*, are deeply influenced by Jungian thought.[75] Amidst *The Wild Girl*'s reworking of early Christian texts, both gnostic and canonical, is a Jungian feminist critique of the Christian tradition's archetypal presentation of women as either virgin or whore—the dualism condemned throughout feminist discourse. Yet the novel also reflects Roberts's conviction at the time that the traditional female archetypes found in myth can be helpful for women. In "The Woman Who Wanted to Be a Hero," she wrote that the virgin can be seen as "the lesbian/independent woman"; "the mother as the woman who listens and receives and so conceives not just physical pregnancies but also spiritual ones." The whore becomes "the companion to men as the vibrantly sexual woman whose business is not necessarily to do with marriage and the bearing and raising of children" and "the sibyl as the woman who periodically needs to withdraw into what can be seen as depression or even madness but is in touch with ancient memories, inspiration . . . an artist."[76] All of these types are featured individually in *The Wild Girl*, and are combined in the character of the narrator, Mary Magdalene.

Although Maitland's 1984 novel *Virgin Territory* is set in the present day, it too is heavily concerned with mythical and religious archetypes—although in not such a directly Jungian way as Roberts's early work. The

---

74. Sellers, *Myth and Fairytale*, 4.
75. See *WWH* and Rowland, "Michèle Roberts' Virgins."
76. *WWH*, 62.

nun Anna sees her virginity as an alliance with "the Fathers," like the goddess Athena who had no mother and was responsible for extinguishing the monstrous female power of the Furies.[77] Anna's friend Karen suggests to her that the lesbian, as a woman who is not defined by her relationship to men, can be seen as "the positive image of the negative virgin."[78] Anna comes to think that "the bright virgin warrior, the beloved daughter" of the Fathers[79] can perhaps be transformed: "[C]ome into the woman-place with me. Give your virginity to me and I shall return it to you, all new and polished and as bright as the sun. I will enthrone us with the goddesses and we will be the true virgins forever; women who hold themselves, and hold themselves free."[80] Artemis, the virgin huntress who eschews the company of men and is also the goddess of childbirth, and the Amazons, warrior women who live without dependence on men, are held up throughout the novel as alternative female archetypes. Stories of fiercely strong and independent female figures from myth feature heavily in Maitland's first collection of short stories, *Telling Tales*, for example "Lilith," "Hyppolita," "Andromeda," and "The Lady Artemis."

Archetypes feature in Maitland's first novel, *Daughter of Jerusalem*, in the sense that the novel suggests that contemporary women's experience can be understood through traditional narratives; in Ostriker's words, "the faces in mythology may be our own faces which we must explore to gain knowledge of myth's inner meanings and our own."[81] In *Daughter of Jerusalem* each chapter ends with a retelling of the story of a biblical woman, with parallels between that tale and the previous episode of Liz's story—for example Liz's relationship with her women's group is placed in parallel with Mary and Elizabeth's visitation; the friendship of Deborah and Jael with that of Liz and Nancy. The story of Rachael attempting to overcome her "barrenness" with mandrake root echoes Liz's seeking the "magic" of the women in the maternity ward.[82] Maitland has explained that she added biblical characters to the social realist plot of *Daughter of Jerusalem* in order to demonstrate the connections between feminist interests and "that very

---

77. Keller, *Broken Web*, 52.
78. *VT*, 114.
79. Ibid., 127.
80. Ibid., 126.
81. Ostriker, *Stealing the Language*, 215.
82. *DJ*, 217.

legendary and all-so-long-ago experience of barrenness and of women's friendships."[83]

Maitland's religious faith has a bearing on the way that she revisions biblical archetypes of women, as compared to those of myth or fairytale, in that "Mary Magdalene is, for me, not a myth but a sister";[84] for Maitland "there is an underlying reality" to these narratives and metaphors.[85] Thus there are valid comparisons between her reimagining of biblical women as archetypes that apply to the present day, and the ancient Jewish practice of midrash—rabbis retelling biblical stories, drawing out further meaning from scripture's gaps and small details. Ostriker describes midrash as "composed not for a narrow audience of scholars, but for an entire community. It is this tradition to which I hope to belong. In midrash, ancient tales yield new meanings to new generations. Not surprisingly, many midrashists today are women; we should expect many more in future."[86] The biblical scholar Athalya Brenner terms as "neo-midrash" the recent Jewish feminist appropriation of "this ancient Jewish literary form," with its "hallmarks" being the reclaiming of biblical women "as exemplary life-models" and a "confessional approach."[87] Maitland's work could thus be categorized as such, in that she is a confessing religious believer, and some of her stories have been disseminated in a way that is at least partly directed towards the faith community (for example *Angel and Me: Short Stories for Holy Week* and *Stations of the Cross*). However, midrash is very much a Jewish tradition, and thus it is perhaps inappropriate to apply the term to Maitland's Christian retellings.

Appropriation

The second mode of revisioning of women from traditional stories that I read in Roberts and Maitland is 'appropriation': when the mythical woman is speaking for the writer, who uses one story to tell another or to make a point; expressing something that comes from outside the source tale. Of course, this applies in some sense to all retelling, and perhaps all reading—as Mieke Bal writes, "projection," or "reading into," is always "part of any

83. King, *Women and the Word*, 83.
84. *AT*, 72.
85. Alexander, *Contemporary Women Novelists*, 82.
86. Ostriker, *Nakedness of the Fathers*, xii–xiii.
87. Brenner, *I Am*, xvii–xviii.

form of processing signs in reading, looking, listening and talking alike."[88] Bal posits the "productive potential of 'pre-posterous'" reading—the "thoughtful deployment of anachronism in the interpretation of historical artifacts"—and argues that "[a]ny exegesis is pre-posterous by definition and no appeal to the 'original text' can change that."[89] Yet it seems to me that a "projection" of the author's self or concerns comes across more intensely in some stories than in others.

A number of Maitland's retellings convey a clear feminist message, for example Delilah in *Daughter of Jerusalem* reflects on why she cut Sampson's hair, realizing that she hurt him and ultimately herself due to her assent to misogynist attitudes: "[s]he had been brought up among real men, who killed in the army and came home at night to kill again on the bodies of their women, who had been hard brutal men without softness. That was how a man should be, not amenable to the wishes of a woman, not lured by beauty, not kind and compassionate with her weakness."[90] However, Maitland's appropriation of traditional tales is not usually didactic in the manner of the Delilah story; rather she takes an element of the source tale and expands on it in order to explore issues which are important to her. In *Women Fly When Men Aren't Watching*, the story of Cassandra—who was cursed by Apollo to always tell the truth but never be believed—becomes a story about the former surgical practice of severing the connection between the brain hemispheres of epilepsy sufferers. It is also a story about the distance between experience and language: "[t]here is a gap and she knows there is a gap between what she sees and what she says."[91] "Rapunzel Revisited" perhaps reflects Maitland's living on her own for the first time after the end of her marriage, enjoying this new found silence and solitude. The elderly Rapunzel retreats to her tower again, where

> [t]here is no plot, no narrative. Nothing happens. But still the wind swings in from the sea and the birds sing before the day's dawn; and still she listens to the sounds of silence which she had missed, despite the delights of the Court. Still she finds witches and whimbrels to enchant her days and still she looks through the refracting lens of all the stories to try and find her own truth, her own story. The story of a woman who has been child and beloved

---

88. Bal, *Loving Yusef*, 77.
89. Ibid., 13.
90. *DJ*, 110.
91. *WFMW*, 54.

and queen and has finished with all those tasks and must now try to learn to be herself.[92]

On Becoming a Fairy Godmother uses traditional tales to tell stories about menopause; foregrounding narrative elements that were already in the tales, for example Jocasta and Helen's being middle-aged at the point in their lives for which they are famous. Maitland imagines endings to well-known stories that reflect women's experience of aging: Eve, the first woman to grow old, finds that once she reaches the menopause she is able to return to Eden, yet chooses not to because she does not want to go back to a state of innocence; she wants to know "what happens next."[93] Similarly, a number of the stories in *Far North and Other Dark Tales* demonstrate Maitland's preoccupation with silence—such as the silent princess attempting to break her brothers' enchantment in "The Swans," or Philomel who has her tongue cut out in "The Swallow and the Nightingale."

Michèle Roberts happily describes as a "plundering" the historical inspiration for her novels *Fair Exchange* and *The Looking Glass*—William Wordsworth's lover Annette Fallon and Mary Wollstonecraft in the former, and Stéphane Mallarmé in the latter—in the foreword to both novels. The word "plundering" expresses Roberts's irreverent and instrumental use of historical figures. Writing *The Wild Girl* in the first person, Roberts felt she was "holding up a mask and speaking through it."[94] Roberts's Magdalene tells the author's stories and speaks with her voice in describing her spiritual experience: compare "[t]he universe breathed in and out and I dissolved in it, no longer I . . . This world shimmered and danced and changed constantly, and I, the not-I, was part of it, and understood it, and was it"[95] with the autobiographical description of "complete loss of ego, complete merging with the natural world around me . . . I saw how we were all the same, how the dance of atoms was in all of us, connected to one another in the shimmy of continual change."[96] Roberts's version of Noah's wife, a woman nameless and silent in the biblical text, is similarly representative of feminist spirituality and Roberts's own beliefs: "Jack's God sends us diseases and plagues and famines to show us his power. I can't understand why that's necessary when the terrible beauty of God shimmers as close to us as the

92. *WFMW*, 191.
93. *BFG*, 160.
94. *PH*, 248.
95. *WG*, 29.
96. *WWH*, 53.

raindrop on the end of a twig ... Jack's God is up, and mine is down. That seems to be one of the differences between the two. I wonder whether there are in fact two Gods, and whether they know each other. I wonder whether without knowing it Jack and I worship the same God."[97]

Roberts's Mrs Noah—like the wives of the patriarchs in Diamant's *The Red Tent*, Jenny Diski's *After These Things*, Ostriker's *The Nakedness of the Fathers*, and Maitland's earliest version of Sarah (in *Daughter of Jerusalem*)—does not share her husband's belief in Yahweh, but has a spirituality of her own. Over time, these retellings of the matriarchs have formed for me into an intertextual tissue, in which I cannot read one without the other; nor can I read the Genesis texts without their feminist reinventions that seek to recover contemporary women's lost heritage, to remember—"or failing that, invent"[98]—the link the between them and their foremothers: "now you come to me—women with hands and feet as soft as a queen's, with more cooking pots than you need, so safe in childbed and free with your tongues. You come hungry for the story that was lost. You crave words to fill the great silence that swallowed me, and my mothers, and my grandmothers before them."[99]

This brings us to the third mode of revisioning that I read in Roberts and Maitland: the writing of mythical women as an attempt to encounter an other, with a self-consciousness about the difficulties of doing so.

Encounter and Ghostly Visitation

Diamant's opening words of *The Red Tent* express the ghostly character of her revisioning of the story of Dinah: "[w]e have been lost to each other for so long. My name means nothing to you. My memory is dust. That is not your fault, or mine. The chain connecting mother to daughter was broken and the word passed to the keeping of men, who had no way of knowing. That is why I became a footnote, my story a brief detour between the well-known history of my father, Jacob, and the celebrated chronicle of Joseph, my brother."[100] This example of the revisionist imagination that focuses on "on gaps and gap filling" and "excavates what is not in a text,"[101] is similar to

97. BMN, 72–73.
98. Wittig, *Les Guerilleres*, 89.
99. Diamant, *The Red Tent*, 4.
100. Ibid., 1.
101. Brenner, *I Am*, x.

Michèle Roberts's approach in *The Wild Girl*, *The Book of Mrs Noah* and *Impossible Saints*. However, Roberts foregrounds the *inaccessibility* of women's literary and spiritual heritage.

While feminist literary revisioning maybe seen as "invention" as a valid response to the failure to "remember, remember, make an effort to remember" of Monique Wittig's famous phrase,[102] the same cannot be said for the historical-critical strand of feminist biblical scholarship. However, there are parallels, at least in terms of a *re-membering*. Elisabeth Schüssler Fiorenza's paradigm-shifting work *In Memory of Her* was a call to use historical tools in the attempt to reconstruct, to piece together from the fragments that have been preserved or found anew, the history of women's role in the origins of Christianity; to make reparation for the systemic failure of a true preaching of the gospel in which the anointing woman's story is told "in memory of her" (Mark 14:9).[103] More recently, Jane Schaberg has taken a feminist historical approach to reconstructing the biblical figure of Mary Magdalene, whose colorful afterlife as the penitent whore obscures her more shadowy historical presence, perhaps intimated at by her central role in a number of apocryphal/gnostic texts. Schaberg remembers John Dominic Crossan's paternalistic comment to her in a debate on the historicity of the Gospels' empty tomb narratives—"Jane, if I could give you the empty tomb, I would"[104]—and her decision that she would take it for herself, that she did not need to be given it; she would use all the "master's tools" at her disposal to build (like all historical interpretations, but here acknowledged) an account of her own making and with her own agenda. *The Resurrection of Mary Magdalene* conjures a figure viewed in insubstantial glimpses, but nevertheless a visionary whose spiritual leadership is related to that of Jesus, but not dependent on him.

There are a number of similarities between Schaberg's ghostly Mary Magdalene and Michèle Roberts's fully-fleshed one, also incarnated on the basis of texts such as the *Gospel of Philip* and the *Gospel of Mary*. Roberts reports in her Preface to the 2007 edition of *The Wild Girl* that she received visitations from her Mary Magdalene, who appeared to her in dreams and spoke to her; in the Author's Note she conceptualized this revisioning in the following terms: "I wanted to dissect a myth; I found myself at the same

102. Wittig, *Les Guerilleres*, 89.
103. Schüssler Fiorenza, *In Memory of Her*.
104. Schaberg, *Resurrection of Mary Magdalene*, 252.

time recreating one."[105] This "recreation" involved extensive research of biblical scholarship and the texts of Nag Hammadi and other apocrypha: "[i]t wasn't just a kind of possession or an inspiration, it was very researched." The research and the writing were inspired by Mary Magdalene's presence in dreams, but also by her absence, and the absence of women in general, from the canon of western culture: "I wanted to take on the sacred books of our culture because they left us out."[106] In both Roberts and Schaberg's imagination, the resurrection of Jesus that Mary Magdalene is witness to is not a physical one. Both Roberts and Schaberg recreate from fragments their own vision of a Mary, and the sadness of this reconstructive work, marred by loss and brokenness, is in both imaged in terms of burial—in *The Wild Girl* Mary buries her book, her Gospel; for Schaberg the absence of the historical Mary Magdalene is symbolized by the abandoned excavation of her city of Migdal.[107]

Roberts's Mary Magdalene's words are not lost, however, because her daughter uncovers them and passes them down the generations. Less optimistically, the autobiography of the protagonist of *Impossible Saints*, Josephine, is concealed in tiny scrolls inside the beads of her rosary. When her niece, Isabel, discovers it, "[r]olls of paper spilled across the floor, and Isabel realized that she no longer had any idea of what order they'd been arranged in."[108] This passage may be read as representative of the revisionist project of the whole novel. Roberts's creation of Josephine was inspired by the historical figure St. Teresa of Avila, who, like many women mystics, was able to achieve speech amidst a silencing culture by working with the grain of the religious authorities of the time. Like Teresa, Josephine writes a version of her *Life* that coheres with approved dogma in order to escape the suspicion of the Inquisition; she survives "[b]y speaking the language they understood. Being careful to use the words they used, the concepts they were familiar with, that they had designed."[109] In interviews Roberts has presented this as a celebration of the cunning strategies that have enabled women to transgress patriarchy[110], but in the novel this is more ambivalent. Josephine comes to be ashamed of herself, for "bowing and scraping and

---

105. *WG*, 7.
106. *GCG*, 18.
107. Schaberg, *Resurrection of Mary Magdalene*, 47–64.
108. *IS*, 238.
109. Ibid., 33.
110. *IGS*, 140.

currying favour," for "permission to carry on writing sweet little books they [the church authorities] heartily despised."[111] She is called to write her real *Life*, her true life's work, which expresses her beliefs in the divinity of the material world and the interconnection of all things.

Yet, after her death, this treasure is lost, and her writing becomes jumbled up in the hands of her female heir. Isabel realizes, as she attempts to reconstruct her aunt's life, that she is "making it all up . . . relying on hearsay, the stories she herself told me, the bits I put together for myself."[112] Feminist readers and revisionists today, like Isobel, or Michèle Roberts, are left an "impossible" task of reconstruction, our only clues being fragments, or that which is missing, the "crack in the grammar," the "something left out, shouting from the margins, in the gaps in between,"[113] from "official" works written to appease those in charge. In the words of Heather Walton, "[t]he story of Josephine is a story of women and writing. She is forbidden to read, her books are burned, her words are lost; really lost. It is also a narrative of revisioning; of the impossibility of restoring the past and the limits of remembering."[114]

Josephine's incorrupt body becomes a commodity amidst church intrigue and the business of relics; her body is dismembered and lost amongst the other bones of the eleven thousand virgins. The feminist theological historian, Virginia Burrus, comments that "we cannot expect to recover the 'fleshly' experience of ancient women or even to discover more than meager fragments of the 'words' with which they represented their own bodies."[115] But in Roberts's work we see the attempt to make something from these fragments, as imaged by the golden bone collage at the opening of the novel. *Impossible Saints* does not create a shining and whole "alternative hagiography,"[116] but it does use the shattered pieces of tradition in productive ways. The bizarre, macabre, unsettling and deeply funny magical realist retelling of stories of the women saints of Voragine's *The Golden Legend*, scattered amongst the main narrative of Josephine, employ Bakhtin's "carnivalesque" strategy of disrupting the dominant cultural discourse.[117] The

111. *IS*, 130.
112. Ibid., 261–62.
113. Ibid., 34.
114. Walton, *Imagining Theology*, 87.
115. Burrus, "Word and Flesh," 31.
116. See Sellers, *Myth and Fairytale*.
117. See García Sánchez, "Michèle Roberts's Protagonists," 240.

relationship of fathers and daughters, women and patriarchy, is explored through the horrific and the comic. *Impossible Saints* itself is like the mosaics of the golden chamber—"[t]he patterns were severe and mysterious. No one could say what they meant."[118]

Sara Maitland's engagement with women saints also suggests that the discerning of "tenuous patterns of meaning" is the only way that contemporary women can relate to those "lives which no longer have a social context fully comprehensible to us."[119] For Maitland the difficulty of revisioning is not how historical or mythical women are fragmented or buried in patriarchal culture, but the intractable otherness of the women she meets in the revisionist encounter. This first comes across in "A Feminist Writer's Progress," in which Maitland explains how she came to the realization that she could not remold mythical women according to feminist idealism. The sense of the writer's distinctness from—and lack of control over—the tale she is telling features in the story "The Swallow and the Nightingale." It concerns the sisters Philomel and Procne, who take revenge on Procne's husband, Tereus, for cutting out Philomel's tongue in his rage and shame at having had sex with her. The sisters' revenge is to cook his and Procne's son in a stew and serve it him, so that Tereus unknowingly eats his own child, until Philomel enters carrying the boy's skull. Maitland then inserts the voice of the author, telling of how ancient Greek poets end this story "awkwardly," by sending the gods to intervene and turn the three characters into birds—echoed in her own awkward and abrupt ending, depending on the divine intervention of the author. She asks if this "terrible story" is about "men's shame and women's shamelessness? A rare dangerous story about a woman who loves something more than her own child? Is it a story about cultural difference, about Greek and barbarian, about male and female, about speech and silence, about tongues and penises?"[120]

This strategy, of breaking the fourth wall and including the revisionist struggle with a story as part of the story itself, is a feature of "Triptych," from *A Book of Spells*. A story told in three sections (hence the title), the first is a straightforward narrative of Hagar in the desert. The Sarah section opens with the words, "[i]n the tent it is cool. The tent is cool but she is sweating" before the voice of the writer interrupts: "[f]or years I have heard Sarah's voice; for years I have strained my ears to hear it, identified with it. Not

118. *IS*, 3.
119. *RL*, 63.
120. *FN*, 263.

just I think the sharing of names, though that should not be discounted. It is easy for a woman like me to hear the voice of a woman like her; two women, of different time, place, space, race, but two women of privilege, articulate, sophisticated, adept, self-controlled. Women, even, of power, by class, education, marriage, status. I hear her voice too easily, Hagar's too furtively." Maitland starts again to tell Sarah's story, and once again her own voice intrudes: "no matter how I context it, Sarah's laugh in the tent, by the oaks of Mamre, rings uncomfortably in the ear. . . . Why is she laughing? . . . She is laughing because it is too late."[121] The story continues (and is much the same as the 1978 version in *Daughter of Jerusalem*), concluding that Sarah was laughing at herself, for thinking that she had outwitted Abraham and his God by contriving to have a child through her own will, through Hagar: "[i]t is best to laugh at foolish women who think they can get their own way in a world where even God is a man and on the other side."[122]

The shift away from narrative, commenced with the retelling of Sarah's point of view, is fulfilled in the "Abraham" section. Maitland writes that she had intended "to write it here, like the others, trying to recreate it, enter in to it, understand it; tell it," but will not, because she "can't be bothered" and "almost everyone knows it already."[123] After some "edgy, cranky, cynical" Bible commentary, she writes that "those priestly, juridical editors" of the Bible, "fail to write out, or suppress, the abiding emotional reality of Sarah and Hagar. At their every appearance the text vibrates, leaping, shining, buoyant, alive. It is there, it is undeniably there—Hagar praising in the wilderness, Sarah laughing in her tent. Their vitality searing the pages across the long silences." For Maitland, to read of Sarah and Hagar, to enter into imagination and write from their perspective, is an encounter with an other. She encounters Sarah more easily than Hagar, because of the similarities between them, but in "Triptych" it is the difficulties of encounter with Sarah—"[w]hy is she laughing?"—that are put in print. Maitland resists entering into such an encounter with Abraham, however—to "bring that hyped-up prose, that imaginative understanding, that poetic psychoanalysis, to bear on that poor crazed old man"—because "it is too soon and too late. To understand all is to forgive all. And I do not want to forgive."[124]

121. *BSP*, 113.
122. Ibid., 116.
123. Ibid., 117.
124. Ibid., 119.

The difficulties of the revisionist encounter are also discussed in the 1993 short story "Requiem," about the second-century Roman martyrs Felicity and Perpetua. They are known through Augustine of Hippo's sermons on them and Perpetua's own written testimony. The sections of "Requiem" are titled after those of the funeral Mass. It is another story of visitation: both women are mothers—noblewoman Perpetua having recently given birth, and the slave Felicity going into premature labor in prison. During the three weeks of their imprisonment they did not speak to one another—"Perpetua dreams her dreams and declares her visions . . . Felicity walks her own silent road . . . She clings to her silence in the dark and neither will comfort the other."[125] This changes during the night before the execution: "[i]t is their secret: who made the first move, who made the even harder gesture of accepting, affirming, responding to that move, I do not know. But in the morning they go out, shining bright and holding hands. They are singing, they are singing and their songs are an offence to the ogling crowd. They are women together and their hands are clasped round each other's in victory . . . they march as free women, and their fingers are entwined."[126]

The author has told her readers that this is "a story about four people," "Felicity, Perpetua, Augustine and Sara,"[127] and her consideration of her treatment of these ancient figures is included within the story: she wants to share in Felicity and Perpetua's "sweet knowledge of death."[128] Although Maitland tries to understand Augustine (unlike Abraham), and his valorization of women's death, she refuses to forgive him (as with Abraham), "[b]ecause he does not know how much he needs our forgiveness . . . he has hurt us; we live, past and future, recast in his model." It is Augustine's appropriation of Felicity and Perpetua that is his sin: "[e]ach time he names them, he names his own desires, . . . that they should not be how they are. They must diminish themselves for him: that cannot be easily forgiven."[129] Maitland moves on to "Sara's story," which "ought to be the easiest to tell, because I do not have to listen to other voices, do not have to deal justly with the other voices, with their time, their space, their social constraints," but is not, because "[m]y entry into this story is through their text and my

125. *WFMW*, 78.
126. Ibid., 79.
127. Ibid., 76–77.
128. Ibid., 79.
129. Ibid., 81.

context." She tells of her "obsession" with Felicity and Perpetua—like Jacob and the angel, she has "wrestled" with them, and they "do not let me go." In writing about them in the revisionist encounter, "I want to use them for my own morally uplifting purposes. They resist me. Their voices are clear and individual."[130] There is a shift to a more jovial tone in a dialogue between Sara the author and Perpetua:

> SARA: I want to make a story about your life, about your courage and your death, your dreams, your madness and your love.
>
> PERPETUA: I have already made that story. My life is my own.
>
> SARA: But it's history. Women need to know it better.[131]

Sara asks why Perpetua had to become a man in her visionary dream in which she wrestles in the arena; the martyr tells her feminist hagiographer, "I'm not fixing up my dreams to match your theory of feminism. I am who I am."[132] The "Second Lesson" of "Requiem" is a reflection on quantum physics and the theory of relativity, that space and time are not the certainties we once thought; throughout the story this comes across in reference to communicating with the women martyrs "across time and space." Their dialogue "wavers and breaks up . . . impossible to sustain. Our voices die away, battered by the differences of vision, of understanding."[133]

Maitland's struggle with the historical Perpetua speaks of the discomforting nature of what A. S. Byatt refers to as "relations between living and dead minds."[134] This reminds us of another meaning of visitation, one that encapsulates the complicated and difficult aspects of women's relationships—whether literal or literary—which cannot be adequately contained by the overwhelmingly positive image of Mary and Elizabeth. 'Visitation' may also mean 'haunting,' an encounter with ghostly presences that intrude on the interests and desires of the contemporary writer. This is suggested in Roberts's description of Josephine's official *Life*, like other mystical writing produced to appease the church authorities: "all the time she's there, breathing quietly under the surface of the prose, poking her finger through from

---

130. Ibid., 82.
131. Ibid., 83.
132. Ibid., 83–84.
133. Ibid., 85.
134. Byatt, "Choices," 17.

time to time, like a ghost longing to be let in."[135] Vinny in *The Mistressclass* writes the names, dates or quotations of famous writers on the pavements outside places where they lived, but only of dead writers: "Vinny doesn't inscribe the kerbs outside the houses of living writers. Phantoms they may be for readers who've never met them, but nonetheless it's mainly the unseen presences of the dead that fascinate. Written language, stored in books, let you travel backwards, through and beyond death. It let you stand in the presence of the person who made it."[136]

The ghostly reading encounter is not always positive, however, and re-visioning is not straightforward, not always freely chosen. As Léonie finds in Roberts's *Daughters of the House*, "[t]he grave in the cemetery had been forced open, made to give up its dead. At the same moment mouths had opened to shout words that Leonie tried not to hear . . . But history was voices that came alive and shouted."[137] When making golden bone collages, we may not find the materials of history always as compliant as we would wish.

Yet for Maitland, thinking in terms of the incarnation, these dry bones live. In 1998 she wrote a book with the poet Wendy Mulford, entitled *Virtuous Magic*, in which their poems and stories seek to engage with certain women saints, making "the imaginative effort to find a link across the centuries."[138] They note that the nature of sainthood is such that the "lives of the saints" only come into being after death.[139] As such, and in the stories of their lives, saints are "boundary transgressors";[140] "[t]he saint both inhabits her mortality and presses against its limits, so that her life is always crossing through the boundaries both of this world and another . . . the stuff of myth and fairy-tale."[141] Similarly, the theologian Elizabeth Stuart discusses in her *Spitting at Dragons: Towards a Feminist Theology of Sainthood* how saints "rupture in their own persons the fault line between heaven and earth, divinity and humanity"[142]—which Maitland and Mulford call "the

135. *IS*, 34.
136. *MC*, 107.
137. *DH*, 170–71.
138. *VM*, 4.
139. Ibid., 71.
140. Ibid., 370.
141. Ibid., 366.
142. Stuart, *Spitting at Dragons*, 68.

logically-fixed boundary between time and eternity," first transgressed by the Incarnation, and now "relived, represented" in the saints.[143]

In terms of genre, hagiography crosses boundaries of history, myth, folk tale and didactic text. Maitland and Mulford (and, in a different sort of way, Michèle Roberts's *Impossible Saints*) explore how the traditional hagiographical tales of women saints are disruptive of culture's dominant values, "turning upside-down everyday logic, common sense and decency and flying in the face of accepted codes of good behaviour."[144] Many of the stories of women saints describe their attempts to escape from marriages forced on them by their family—an inverse of the fairy tales in which marrying a prince is the desired end. This aspect of the lives of women saints is one that feminist revisioning must reclaim from the patriarchal presentation of women saints as submissive and self-effacing exemplars of womanhood. Stuart argues that the concept of sainthood may also be reconceived in a way that does not reinforce hierarchal thinking, and suggests that contemporary believers' "friendship" with saints, across the boundaries of life and death, time and space, is "subversive of hetero-reality."[145]

For Maitland and Mulford, this friendship encounter involves retelling the saints in creative writing, yet they find themselves unable to make the saints into whom they want them to be, to "insert them into our prefabricated theoretical and feminist theological frameworks. They defy inclusion. They remain Other."[146] Encountering women such as Joan of Arc, Margaret of Antioch and Teresa of Avila, Maitland and Mulford are confronted by the intractable otherness of women across time, space and reality. However, in revisioning the saints, they discovered that the shapes and patterns of their own life stories did seem to intersect with those of the saints. They suggest that this "struggle" to "articulate their meanings for us as individuals" may, "in light of the Incarnation," possibly be "in itself a theological conclusion."[147] As Maitland writes at the end of the Felicity and Perpetua story, "[w]e may not take each other's lives, each across time and space . . . We may say, here are good things, here are limitations, but there are more things in heaven and earth than we dreamed of; and we explore

---

143. *VM*, 370.
144. Ibid., 369.
145. Stuart, *Spitting at Dragons*, 83.
146. *VM*, 374.
147. Ibid.

the past, as we explore the future, for visions of possibility, for the expansion of consciousness, for the channels of hope."[148]

There is a parallel here between Maitland's encounter with the stories of the saints, and how I encounter hers and Roberts's writing in this book—reading their stories beside my own. Hence I now turn to the visitation encounter between writers and their readers.

Encounters of Flesh and Words

While Maitland's writing emphasizes the relationship of the contemporary writer with women of myth and history, in Roberts's work the most significant reading/writing encounter is with other writers. In *The Book of Mrs Noah*, the writers on board the women's library of the Ark creatively encounter not only each other, but the women writers from the past: "[e]very woman who has ever lived has deposited here her book . . . all the stories, from past present and future, are here, rubbing shoulders in the dark."[149] Roberts has described how, as an undergraduate, studying the writings of medieval mystics she encountered "a tradition of women writers which would nourish my own struggles to write," albeit unconsciously at the time.[150] A sense of communion with other writers, and the intense spiritual significance of books, echo throughout her work, but come most to the fore in Roberts's more recent fiction. She says, "I'm drawn back and back to women, religion and female religious figures getting replaced by writers. I am fascinated by Charlotte Brontë, George Sand and Elizabeth Gaskell. They're my saints now I think."[151] The notion of writers as the new saints is explored in *The Mistressclass*: Vinny reflects that,

> Reading is a form of resurrection . . . Language goes on, despite death, the skein that binds the generations, making itself new between the life and death of every poet. Language is as certain as death but triumphs over it. So you didn't need religion. What you needed was poetry . . .
>
> the language of criticism depended on theories that wore out as they become unfashionable and were replaced. Whereas the language of poetry and novels was hammered out of something else; metaphor; purer and sparer. Like bones and blood. Clothes

148. *WFMW*, 85.
149. *BMN*, 20.
150. *PH*, 11.
151. *GCG*, 25.

changed from generation to generation, but flesh was flesh. And poems were like bodies.[152]

For Roberts, it is poets who enact the incarnational "boundary crossing" that Maitland perceives in the saints.

Roberts's writing on the flesh of beloved words reminds me of the words of Hélène Cixous, that in literary criticism, "[e]verything begins with love. If we work on a text we don't love, we are automatically at the wrong distance."[153] She goes on to speak of this in terms of "touch": "I choose to work on texts that 'touch' me. I use the word deliberately because I believe there is a bodily relationship between reader and text."[154] This intimacy between reader and text is expressed in the title of the volume of autobiographical literary criticism, *The Intimate Critique*,[155] which is pervaded by a sense of the reader relating to books in much the same way as they relate to persons. Lynne Pearce interprets the interaction a reader has with certain texts as a "relationship with a textual other," in which the implied personhood of that "other," and the affective nature of the reading process, make it very much "a relationship."[156] Wayne Booth claims that a metaphor of "friendship" with books enables the conceptualization of the ethical expectations we have of the books we read—"the company we keep"[157]—in that "[t]he fullest friendship arises whenever two people not only offer each other pleasure or utilities but believe that they are equals in all their aspirations and thus are good for and with each other."[158] When we relate to texts with love and friendship, we ascribe to them a subjecthood that will involve ethical considerations as well as affection.

I now turn to a particular relationship between reader and text—that between myself and the work of Michèle Roberts and Sara Maitland.

---

152. *MC*, 108–9.

153. In Sellers, *Writing Differences*, 147.

154. Ibid., 148.

155. Freedman, Frey, and Zauhar, *Intimate Critique*.

156. Pearce, *Feminism*, 17. See Llewellyn, *Women's Spiritual Reading*, 192–234, for an insightful qualitative study of the communal nature of women's relationships with beloved texts.

157. Booth, *Company We Keep*.

158. Booth, "Way I Loved George Eliot," 7.

Their Stories Beside My Own

In August 2010 I went for a day trip to Edinburgh. As I lived in Glasgow, this should be unremarkable—however, since moving to Glasgow I had not actually been to Edinburgh, other than passing through on the way to elsewhere. It was a slightly perverse, tongue-in-cheek sign of devotion to my adopted city, that after nearly two years I had not thought its arch-rival worth visiting. Hence an odd feeling of disloyalty, at how jaw-dropping I found Edinburgh's vistas, how magical its steep, windy and quaintly-named streets. I was going to a concert in the evening, and thought I would go early to take a look at what was happening at the festivals. I went alone, which was not insignificant. While I actually prefer to be on my own when shopping, discovering new places, visiting museums, and so on, it does make me slightly uncomfortable: a bit anxious, a bit of a pariah. Yet, since the end of a significant relationship a couple of months earlier, I had decided to ignore these twinges of social awkwardness, and make the most of my time in Scotland, make the effort to do things I wanted to do, with or without company. I was also thinking a lot about the next day, when I was to meet someone who I had encountered several weeks previously, and until a few days before not known whether I would (or should) see again, but very much wanted to. Visiting Edinburgh during festival time would take my mind off what tomorrow may, or may not, bring.

On leaving the train station, I picked up several programs and brochures for the various festivals. Once I got up to the High Street and found myself somewhere to sit and flick through them, it was ten minutes after 2 p.m. I turned first to the Book Festival program, and on the page titled "Tuesday 17th August": "Michèle Roberts, 14.30." I looked at the map and worked out that I might just about make it to the festival venue in time; so I dashed through the crowds along Princes Street, amazed by the serendipity of it all. I only just made it to the box office before the close of the lecture theatre doors ("Please! I'm writing my PhD on her!").

I was glad to have made the session, in which she read from and talked about her latest book, *Mud*, a collection of short stories. Struggling to get my breath back and cool down, it felt strange to be sitting amongst an audience looking at this woman, who did not know me, but that I had spent so much time with and knew so well. Loved, in fact. Of course, I was aware that the person I know and, yes, love, as "Michèle Roberts" is an imaginary figure, a creation of her writing and my reading, not the flesh and blood person reading on stage, who I do not know at all. But it took the embodied presence of the person behind the idea, to make me realize that my relationship to that imagined person was one of love. I decided to go to the book signing afterwards, and to mention my PhD to her. She reacted with a frightened noise—only half-joking, I think—and after signing my copy of the new book she wished me luck with the PhD. But I did not leave contact details or try to ask any serious questions. There are plenty of academic interviews with her already. There is enough material out there to get a very good sense of the 'fictional' person. I was not going to press my company onto the real one.

Any long piece of literary research will create a certain level of intimacy between the researcher and her subject; but it is a complicated relationship: just as Maitland worries about appropriating Perpetua, I feel guilty about taking pieces of hers and Roberts's work and rearranging them according to my own design. I think of all the things that I do not write about, because I do not like or understand them, or they simply do not fit. Like Maitland and her women of myth and history, I am often confronted with the otherness of these authors I work on, troubled by things I object to on ideological or aesthetic grounds, but also know that this other is the creation of my own reading. But sometimes it is difficult to maintain the position that my relationship as a reader is with a fiction—the authorial self disclosed in writing and interviews—when the flesh-and-blood author is still living. I met Michèle Roberts very briefly, but I have spent an amount of time with Sara Maitland, and thus have a real life relationship with a real person that is distinct from, but not unrelated to, the reading relationship I have with the fictive author.

What I find curious about my story about meeting Michèle Roberts in Edinburgh is not only that I was narrating it to myself self-consciously as it unfolded (the novelistic nature of the providential timings was not lost on me, and as I ran along Princes Street I was already thinking how I would tell this story to others), but that it is a very Michèle Roberts-esque episode. My plan to wander the streets of a strange city, a lone *flâneur*, nursing a heart simultaneously bruised and hopeful, by chance encountering a writer whose work I knew so intimately. It is the bare bones of the sort of tale that might appear (albeit far more beautifully written) in one of her episodic novels or collections of short stories. My relationship with her writing, with the fictional person of the writer Michèle Roberts, is such that it structures my interpretation of my own experience. It is not just that in Roberts and Maitland I read parallels with my own stories; my stories are sometimes generated by the visitation encounter between their writing and my reading. They "open up for me a path which is already mine, yet not altogether mine."[159]

Maitland and Mulford write that the "idiosyncrasies of our own histories" make them "pervious" to the lives of certain saints.[160] In my interaction with the narrative selves of Michèle Roberts and Sara Maitland, certain similarities have led me to identify with them to some extent—like both of them, my childhood was bookish, imaginative and amongst a large family; I had nervous breakdowns in my teens and early twenties; my religious beliefs and upbringing have had a profound effect on who I am. I share with Roberts and Maitland a feminism that, although it may be held up to scrutiny, criticized and made fun of, is essential to who I am. Like Roberts, I have found spiritual satisfaction in making things with my hands (and reading her work has helped me to understand this better); like her I often say too much, and love too much and too easily. Like Maitland, I present myself to the world with something of a cultivated eccentricity, and another point of commonality is that I feel most fulfilled and joyful when alone in the midst of nature and wildness.

Both Roberts and Maitland wrote and published a lot around the time I was born, and the photographs in *Paper Houses* of Michèle Roberts with her friends wearing plaid shirts and holding huge mugs of tea, remind me of my parents' photo albums of their student days. Roberts and Maitland were born within a year of each other, a decade before my mother's birth; they were friends with each other in a world really very different from mine, and it is the differences between the two of them and between myself and them, as well as the similarities, that have made working on them so fruitful. So much of their work has emerged from their engagement with the stories of other women that to work on them is to encounter a literary and spiritual tradition, a women's community. I do not feel like they are versions of me, or mothers, or sisters, or friends—although possibly they are a mixture of all those things—and perhaps if I had grown up Roman Catholic and had a more of an innate sense of what sainthood means, I would say yes, they are my saints. It is this visitation encounter that has brought into being—albeit fragmented, "fragile and finite"[161]—the stories and theological reflection that I present in the following chapters of this book.

159. Cixous in Sellers, *Writing Differences*, 148.
160. *VM*, 374.
161. Sands, *Escape from Paradise*, 167.

3

Selves

FIVE DECADES AGO, VALERIE Saiving opened an article in *The Journal of Religion* with the following words: "I am a student of theology; I am also a woman. Perhaps it strikes you as curious that I put these two assertions beside each other, as if to imply that one's sexual identity has some bearing on his theological views."[1] This is widely regarded as the opening trumpet-blast of feminist theological method, and the use throughout the article of the now anachronistic masculine pronoun emphasizes just how much of a departure Saiving's ideas were from the prevailing culture of the time. Saiving's argument was that contemporary theologians' thought on "the human situation" and the doctrine of sin reflects male experience, and not women's experience; more specifically, that the "feminine temptations" for contemporary women are not pride or desire for power, but "underdevelopment or negation of the self."[2]

The themes raised in Saiving's article recur throughout the remainder of this book. Her words created a platform for women theologians to rethink the most basic workings of their discipline. The idea of self-negation as "the female sin" became standard in feminist theology, and its implications extended to other areas of Christian doctrine, especially soteriology and Christology. Yet it was soon critiqued for its universalizing of "women's experience," for applying to all women something which is perhaps specific to a particular demographic elite.

However, in the painful recognition of its own white, western, middle-class bias, feminist theological discourse has sometimes overlooked the continuing relevance of the issues raised by Saiving. She asks questions

---

1. Saiving, "Human Situation," 100.
2. Ibid., 108.

about how we conceive of our selves and our relationships with others—how to love and yet maintain one's own integrity—and these are not questions that are readily answered. In the following theological reflection on these issues, I draw on the 'annunciation' of personal narrative, the 'visitation' of my reading encounter with Michèle Roberts and Sara Maitland, and a wide range of theological resources, in order to reflect on these questions. I am not seeking systematized solutions, but a gathering together of fragments, "no answers to be believed in, but challenge and insight, delight and strength, that are fragile and finite but real."[3]

SELFHOOD, CONNECTION AND FEMINIST THEOLOGY

The Human Situation

In her discussion of "women's sin," Saiving takes as her starting point the theology of modern 20th century theologians such as Anders Nygren and Reinhold Niebuhr, whose analysis of the human condition is that our natural state is one of pride and arrogant individualism, resisting dependence on the loving creator God. This "root sin" stems from existential anxiety:

> While man is a creature, subject to the limitations of all finite existence, he is different from other creatures because he is free ... This freedom of man, which is the source of his historical and cultural creativity, is also the source of his temptation to sin. For man's freedom, which from another point of view can be called his individuality and his essential loneliness, brings with it a pervasive fear for the survival of the self and its values. Sin is the self's attempt to overcome that anxiety by magnifying its own power, righteousness, or knowledge.[4]

The opposite of this self-aggrandizement is self-giving love, "the true norm of human existence and the one real solution to the fundamental predicament in which man stands."[5]

Although Saiving does not quote directly from Anders Nygren, she refers to a notion of love that, "taking no thought for its own interests but seeking only the good of the other,"[6] applies to his theology of agape.

3. Sands, *Escape from Paradise*, 167.
4. Saiving, "Human Situation," 100.
5. Ibid., 101.
6. Ibid.

Nygren's *Agape and Eros* asserts selfless, unconditional agape as the only true Christian love. Since Nygren, the theology of love has been dominated by the ideal of human passivity in the receiving of God's generous love, while extending that unconditional love to other human beings.[7] Love that is particular or self-generated has no relation whatsoever to the agapic ideal: "[t]here cannot actually be any doubt that Eros and Agape belong originally to two entirely separate worlds, between which no direct communication is possible."[8] Furthest of all from Christian agape is self-love, which, according to Nygren, is "man's natural condition, and also the reason for the perversity of his will":[9] "[a]gape recognizes no kind of self-love as legitimate."[10] Thus "[c]oncerns for the human sělf, for subjectivity and for their development are thus eclipsed from any legitimate theological focus."[11] Although Nygren's devaluing of "the love of an aspiring soul, a love that climbs towards heaven,"[12] and of any "notion of reciprocity, let alone mutuality,"[13] has been widely criticized, reworked and rejected in contemporary theology, Saiving's focus is the assumption of "the human situation" as prideful self-love. Her contention is that "[c]ontemporary theological doctrines of love have . . . been constructed primarily upon the basis of masculine experience"; that a focus on women's experience demonstrates "certain aspects of the human situation which are present but less obvious in the experience of men," and thus that "these doctrines do not provide an adequate interpretation of the situation of women—nor, for that matter, of men."[14]

Saiving elucidates these significant differences in male and female experience, drawing on cultural history and contemporary psychological and anthropological accounts of human development and gender. She argues that, for social reasons rooted in biology, "man's sense of his own masculinity . . . is . . . characterized by uncertainty, challenge, and the feeling that he must again and again prove himself a man. It also calls for a kind of objective achievement and a greater degree of self-differentiation

---

7. See Jeanrond, *Theology of Love*.
8. Nygren, *Agape and Eros*, 31.
9. Ibid., 101.
10. Ibid., 217.
11. Jeanrond, *Theology of Love*, 116.
12. Renshaw, *Subject of Love*, 43.
13. Ibid., 47.
14. Saiving, "Human Situation," 101.

and self-development than are required of the woman as woman. In a sense, masculinity is an endless process of *becoming*, while in femininity the emphasis is on *being*."[15] Thus contemporary theology's preoccupation with "anxiety, estrangement, and the conflict between necessity and freedom; its identification of sin with pride, will to-power, exploitation, self-assertiveness,"[16] and account of redemption in self-renouncing relationship with God, speaks to the situation of men rather than that of women.

In contrast, the situation of women is such that "the feminine temptations" may be characterized as: "triviality, distractibility, and diffuseness; lack of an organizing center or focus; dependence on others for one's own self-definition; tolerance at the expense of standards of excellence; inability to respect the boundaries of privacy; sentimentality, gossipy sociability, and mistrust of reason—in short, underdevelopment or negation of the self."[17] Saiving's explanation of this is that women's maternal capacity for "surrendering her individual concerns in order to serve the immediate needs of others" may lead to "diffuseness of purpose"; dependence on other people, and lack of respect for personal boundaries: the negative side of woman's "receptivity to the moods and feelings of others and her tendency to merge her selfhood in the joys, sorrows, hopes, and problems of those around her."[18]

Feminism and Autonomy

In the 1970s, Judith Plaskow's doctoral dissertation (later published as *Sex, Sin and Grace*) took up Saiving's argument, but developed it further using the ideas of the contemporary women's movement. In her critique of the doctrine of sin in the theology of Reinhold Niebuhr and Paul Tillich, Plaskow employs a concept of women's experience as "the interrelation between cultural expectations and their internalization,"[19] applying the feminist analysis that women's situation as passive and self-negating is a result of socialization: "steered toward certain functions from the time they are born and taught to see these functions as expressing their true female nature."[20]

15. Ibid., 105, emphasis in original.
16. Ibid., 107.
17. Ibid., 107–8.
18. Ibid., 109.
19. Plaskow, *Sex, Sin and Grace*, 2–3.
20. Ibid., 64.

She proposes that "the particular sin of women [is] the adoption of society's view of themselves to the detriment of their freedom."[21]

Plaskow summarizes Simone de Beauvoir's account of women's lives as "the story of conflict between efforts toward autonomous existence and the necessity of being-the-other, between vocations as human beings and obligations as women."[22] This is the story of Michèle Roberts's first novel, *A Piece of the Night*, in which Julie struggles to gain a sense of herself apart from the expectations of her family and desire of her husband. She lives her life "two inches behind the front of her skin, that part of her created willfully by herself, when she puts on her make-up, and by Ben, when he makes love to her."[23] The possibility of authentic existence is found in grief while visiting her dying mother: "Julie wrapped in her bedspread breaks all the rules of years ago, sits on the stairs and cries softly outside her mother's room. The nice girl, the mad bad girl cries all through the night, she cries herself awake."[24] This "awakening" is echoed in Sara Maitland's novel *Virgin Territory*, which ends with Anna confessing "to the sins of cowardice, lack of self-knowledge and authenticity,"[25] "stepping outside her own conditioning, out of her carefully constructed sin . . . an enormous effort laying claim to new possibility."[26]

While feminist theology of sin is not limited to a notion of "women's sin" being the failure to "awake" to feminist consciousness, Plaskow's writing contributed to feminist emphasis on the virtues of autonomy and rejection of malestream theology's idealization of service and self-sacrifice. In the theology as exemplified by Niebhur, "[t]he language of self-sacrifice conflicts with personhood and becomes destructive" in its suggestion that "the struggle to become a centered self, to achieve full independent selfhood, is sinful." This "serves to reinforce women's servitude," becoming "another voice in the chorus of external expectation defining and confining the way women live"; for a woman to believe in the primacy of sacrificial love is to "stifle in herself the desire to be a separate person some part of whose mind, time, and feelings are inviolable."[27] Barbara Andolsen argues

21. Ibid., 64.
22. Ibid., 31–32.
23. *PN*, 67.
24. Ibid., 109.
25. *VT*, 204.
26. Ibid., 209.
27. Plaskow, *Sex, Sin and Grace*, 87.

that the "receptivity" idealized by Christian theologians "has been distorted into demeaning passivity, submissiveness, and self-surrender," when it would be better for women to assume activity.[28] The British feminist theologian Daphne Hampson's renowned *Theology and Feminism* claims that the theme of God in Christ's self-emptying, or kenosis, "is far from helpful as a paradigm";[29] for her, "[a]utonomy is what feminism is about."[30] Christian feminists have struggled with how to reconcile the conflict between feminist insistence on the need for women to assert themselves as active and autonomous, with Christianity's fundamental principles of service and self-sacrifice. Others have concluded that, for women, these theological tropes can only ever be harmful: what is needed is a whole-scale reworking of our envisioning of how we relate to ourselves, each other, and to the divine.

Feminism, Connection, and Creation

Feminist theology has not sought to replace a paradigm of women's self-surrender with one of self-serving individualism, to reinscribe the distortions of "hypermasculine" culture by extending its ideals to women. Rather "[t]he concept of mutuality is understood to redress the repudiation of self . . . by displacing the binary discourse of self-interest versus other-regard with a discourse on shared power."[31] The feminist theological response to the arguments of Saiving and Plaskow has been to assert "not less but more (and different) relation; not disconnection, but connection that counts."[32]

Both Catherine Keller and Mary Grey write that, despite the damaging aspects of being acculturated to identify with others rather than develop an independent sense of self, it may be for women a "paradoxical" blessing, in that it provides a greater sense of the connection and relationality that is at the heart of things. According to Keller, "awareness of the fluent sociality of our own selves is more likely to have been incorporated into the very structure of our personality, reinforcing rather than repressing connective sensibilities."[33] For Grey, "by witnessing to a profounder ethic for relating,

28. Andolsen, "Agape," 77.
29. Hampson, *Theology and Feminism*, 155.
30. Ibid., 1.
31. Renshaw, *Subject of Love*, 15.
32. Keller, *Broken Web*, 3.
33. Ibid., 202.

women are actually revealing a world that is relational at its very core . . . not because of any myth of the feminine, or because of physiological makeup, but being largely left out of the competitive/aggressive/dominance ethic which controls the public arena, these relational strengths—vital for all humanity—have been preserved."[34]

Within a cultural symbolic in which "woman is to nature as man is to culture"[35] the association of the natural world with the female also means that women are identified with eros rather than agape; with sensual, physical, instinctual passion, rather than a transcendent, unconditional love bestowed by an agent who is free and independent. Feminists have sought to reclaim eros from patriarchy, celebrating love that is earthy, engaged, and embodied. This subverts the binary that privileges (masculine) agape over (feminine) eros. It also displaces the emphasis on nonreciprocal love that is thought to be to women's detriment, with eros a love that is willed and mutual, a dynamic energy flowing between persons. Following Carter Heyward's *The Redemption of God*, much feminist theology has adopted Heyward's refiguring of eros as "sacred yearning for mutuality, justice, and equality in relations,"[36] from the personal relationships of family, friends and lovers, to the relational structures of power that we call politics.

The feminist theological concern with relationality extends far beyond relationships between persons: our world and everything in it is imaged as one interconnected whole, in which all is held together by a web of relations. Women are thought to have something of a privileged access to this intrinsic relatedness because they are less inclined to the separative egoism that asserts human subjectivity as transcendent from nature, and because of women's symbolic association with the natural world. Women's identification with nature—its fertility and decay as well as its rhythms and cycles—"has been the very fact which doomed [them] to carry the burden of degraded sexuality throughout history to this day,"[37] and has been a barrier to women's full participation in culture and deprived them of full humanity. Yet feminists have taken this ancient association and reworked it: firstly by drawing a parallel between patriarchy's subjugation of women and humankind's "dominion" over the natural world (Gen 1:28); secondly

---

34. Grey, *Redeeming the Dream*, 31.
35. Ortner, "Is Female to Male as Nature Is to Culture?".
36. Renshaw, *Subject of Love*, 82.
37. Grey, *Redeeming the Dream*, 49.

because it is claimed that a sense of connection to nature is a spiritual blessing and profound truth.

The writing of Michèle Roberts also attests to the blessing and truth of our intrinsic relatedness with the whole of creation. In *A Piece of the Night*, the flipside of Julie's diffusive sense of self is her intuition of cosmic relatedness: "[t]he lines of definition others drew for her and taught her to draw were false, she was certain of that; she as she was then could see in her body all creation pulsating, the flow of energies into tides, migrations, seasons, separated from the natural world only by the gate of skin, a fragile barrier, easily ignored."[38] Josephine, the protagonist of *Impossible Saints*, has mystical experiences of the essential connectedness of the universe, imaged as a "body":

> The earth was a great body and she belonged with it and was part of it . . . she could see that the earth was alive, teeming with life, holding everything in a continuous dance, it was a vast memory swarming with past, present and future life, this was what God was, this profound understanding, in this untranslatable speech, that we were all made the same, part of each other, rocks and stones and trees and people all whirling about together living and dying and being transformed into each other.[39]

In a non-fiction essay, Roberts writes of her interest in the "old tradition" of mystical thought which presented the divine as "incarnate in all creation, no longer transcendent but immanent," with mystics having "spoken for centuries of personal experience of fusion with the divine as a physical reality."[40] She speaks of the participation of "each of us" in creation in terms of "the dance and flow of atoms,"[41] with "God" as "shorthand for the astonishing and complex processes of the world of which we are a part—not observing it but belonging in it,"[42] and also in terms of human creativity. From her earliest novels, Roberts's writing conjures a vivid sense of sight, sound, scent, taste and touch. The sense of the material evoked by her prose is a reclaiming of body and of nature from religious and patriarchal dualism, but it is also a celebration of our creative activity. Human beings partake in the divine not just through orgasmic moments in which ego

38. *PN*, 19.
39. *IS*, 189–90.
40. *FSG*, 43.
41. Ibid.
42. Ibid., 44.

dissolves and returns to unity with the cosmos, but through preparing and eating a good meal; thus Roberts's foregrounding of the sensual, tactile and everyday is profoundly theological.[43] One example is the character Hattie of *In the Red Kitchen*. She expresses the sacramental significance for her of cooking and creating:

> It was through learning to cook that I finally broke into the world, joined it and was joined by it. At first food was just a drug to dull memory and pain. Then I discovered that flour and butter working between my fingers, carrots falling apart under my quick knife, egg whites rising in the bowl as I beat them, all began to give me a sense of my adequate power, my reality. Inventing then writing down recipes I unmade and remade the world . . . Through cooking I learned how much I was part of the world around me.[44]

Roberts writes in a poetic ecofeminist tradition exemplified by Susan Griffin's influential *Woman and Nature: The Roaring Inside Her*, an exploration of patriarchy's subjugation of women and natural world. This is linked with separation: man views himself as distinct from and superior to the rest of the world, in a way that woman is not: "[h]e says that woman speaks with nature. That she hears voices from under the earth. That wind blows in her ears and trees whisper to her . . . But for him this dialogue is over. He says he is not part of this world, that he was set on this world as a stranger. He sets himself apart from woman and nature."[45] Separation is also the means by which man possesses and controls the world: by dividing up time and space,[46] by naming,[47] and in the mores and laws of religion: "[s]eparation. The clean from the unclean. The decaying, the putrid, the polluted, the fetid, the eroded, waste, defecation, from the unchanging. The changing from the sacred."[48] Griffin portrays the symbolic association of woman and nature, and the denigration of both, in terms of fertility and agriculture: "[b]y the sweat of his brow, he makes her yield. She opens her broad lap to him. . . . Silently she works miracles for him. Yet, just as silently, she withholds from him. Without reason, she refuses to yield. . . . He is determined

---

43. See Fisk, "To Make and Make Again."
44. *RK*, 87.
45. Griffin, *Woman and Nature*, 2.
46. Ibid., 107–11.
47. Ibid., 190.
48. Ibid., 95.

he will master her. He will make her produce at will. He will devise ways to plant what he wants in her, to make her yield more to him."[49]

Woman and Nature is presented as two voices speaking, and the suppressed voice of woman, written in italics, cries out amidst the discourse of science, whose discoveries have come to undermine the ideals of rational humanity's transcendent and unique place in the cosmos. Amidst woman's configuration in patriarchal culture, and her own sense of herself and her history, a different way of thinking emerges: "*[t]he shape of the cave. Space divided and not divided. Space mutable, we say, separation becoming union. . . . The rectangular shape of his book of knowledge, bending. The shape of our silence, the shape of the roofs of our mouths.*"[50] In this vision of unity, "*there is no end to any act. . . . in every particle every act lives, and the stars do not frighten us, we say, starlight is familiar to us.*"[51] Griffin writes, "*[w]e know ourselves to be made from this earth. We know this earth is made from our bodies. For we see ourselves. And we are nature.*"[52]

The current environmental crisis gives particular weight and urgency to ecofeminist claims that western civilization's objectified and instrumental view of the natural world has led to widespread destruction and endangering of life on this planet. Griffin's interrelation of feminism, poetics and ecology is given theological treatment in influential works such as Catherine Keller's *From a Broken Web*,[53] Mary Grey's *Redeeming the Dream*, Rosemary Radford Ruether's *Gaia and God: An Ecofeminist Theology of Earth Healing*, Sallie McFague's *The Body of God: An Ecological Theology* and in the writings of Goddess thealogians such as Carol Christ and Starhawk.[54] Whether invested in the symbolism of the Hebrew Bible, Christian tradition or Goddess worship, they all stress the interdependency of all living things, the value of communion, and the need for an end to dualistic conceptions of humanity over and above the rest of nature, all of which are related to issues of economic and social justice, as well as ecology.

49. Ibid., 52–53.
50. Ibid., 161, emphasis in original.
51. Ibid., 172, emphasis in original.
52. Ibid., 226, emphasis in original.
53. It is Keller's work that I find to be the most theoretically sophisticated and rhetorically convincing—as well as pleasurable to read—and I am indebted to her work throughout this chapter.
54. See Christ, *Rebirth of the Goddess*; *She Who Changes*; "Ecofeminism and Process Philosophy"; and "Embodied Embedded Mysticism"; and Starhawk, *Spiral Dance*; *Webs of Power*; and *Earthpath*.

Using various approaches, these feminist theologies argue that a profound reworking of metaphysical ideas about God is also necessary; theist doctrines about God's transcendence, immutability and sovereignty—described by Catherine Keller as "separation deified"[55]—have been extremely harmful. Feminist theologians have drawn on systems theory, James Lovelock's Gaia hypothesis, and the process thought of A. N. Whitehead and Charles Hartshorne to present a God immanent in the world, intimately connected rather than separate from it, changing along with the world while engaging with it.[56] Mary Grey summarizes Carter Heyward's theology as the subverting of "the God who stands over-against humanity: by contrast, God is interpreted as source of relational power," and redemption is "voluntary participation in making right relation here and now among ourselves."[57]

I discuss the implications of these relational, ecological theologies in chapters 4 and 6, particularly as regards issues of sin and evil. In the present chapter my focus is the tension between empowered, autonomous selfhood and the call to right relation, defined as loving identification with the joys and sufferings of other people and the natural world within the web of life. This is a tension which feminist theologians are well aware of. Catherine Keller calls "[w]omen's self-definition in terms of relationship" a "psychosocial bondage," but does not think that women "seeking an empowering center in themselves," apart from "selfhood drained away in futile assymmetries," are involved in the repudiation of connection. Rather, "[l]iberated from relational bondage, we range through an unlimited array of relations."[58]

Recognizing that women must move away from "living a 'mediated' existence" in which they define themselves according to their relationships with others, for Mary Grey the situating of "the complex web of interrelating on a much wider plane, including nature and the cosmos itself"[59] may be a corrective to women's dissolving into their relationships with other people in that it displaces culture's idealization of romantic and familial relationships. She writes that our "personal relationships can seldom bear the immense weight invested in them," and for her the way to avoid mak-

---

55. Keller, *Broken Web*, 39.
56. See Grey, *Redeeming the Dream*, 32–35.
57. Ibid., 89.
58. Keller, *Broken Web*, 3.
59. Grey, *Redeeming the Dream*, 39.

ing "unrealistic demands" on "our interpersonal relating" is to "develop our personal strengths and face our 'aloneness' in the world," as well as to radically rethink the nature of relation.[60] Carter Heyward's feminist reconfiguring of eros takes care not only to emphasize the political aspects of this life-giving force, striving for social justice; it also stresses that "right-relation" must be truly mutual, with equal relationships between whole and self-assured persons. She speaks of "breaking free" of the "the chilly delusion" of "self-possession" as "we come into our power to call forth the YES that connects us . . . our openness to sacred movement between and among ourselves";[61] yet she also acknowledges that "we can never live simply 'for ourselves.' Nor can we live simply 'for others.' Women in particular must not allow our integrities to be formed by the spurious lesson we have been taught that we should be more for others than for ourselves. To live with integrity, we live with others: we are 'for' ourselves and 'for' others."[62]

Heyward's conception of mutual relation, in which we live for ourselves while living for others is certainly an attractive one. But it seems to me to be an ideal that is not easily enacted in reality.

Our Boundaries, Our Selves

Initially, my attention was drawn to feminist theology's valorization of autonomy because of the interesting conflicts it produces, with both the fundamentals of Christian theology and religious feminisms's own emphasis on the essential relatedness of all creation and the divine. I was intrigued by Christian feminist theologians attempts to reconcile belief in the importance of self-development with the doctrine and symbolism of self-sacrifice (see chapter 4) and their own spiritual yearnings (see chapter 5); also by how religious feminist account of selves in relation—inextricably connected but empowered and self-determining—necessarily strikes a delicate balance. In short, my concerns were primarily theoretical. But in thinking about gender and self-negation, as well as how the self is constructed and disclosed in narrative (as discussed in chapter 1), I have come to believe that feminist theology has been too quick in passing over the ethical dimensions of Saiving's account of the "feminine temptations."

60. Ibid., 39.
61. Heyward, *Touching Our Strength*, 22.
62. Ibid., 26.

Sex, Sin, and Our Selves

Feminist theology of sin has focused on injustice, with "structural sin" the inevitable dark side of our essential connectedness, but has perhaps neglected the very profound issues of selfhood and boundaries in interpersonal relationships. Susan Thistlethwaite suggests that feminist emphasis on "relationality" is a result of "white women's sin" as laid down by Saiving—the temptation to smooth things over, to collapse everything into one and not respect the "boundaries" of difference[63]—but, on the whole, feminist theology since the 1980s has been wary of an analysis of women's psychology that seems to be universalizing and not accounting for ethnic and socioeconomic differences. Anglo-American feminism is also cautious of repeating ideas that seem to have an essentialist concept of male and female differences; perhaps understandably, considering the widely-held currency of claims of the intrinsic difference between men and women's perception and communication, especially in personal relationships.[64] Yet issues of integrity, authenticity and boundaries are hugely important in our lives; for men as well as women.

I have come to see that this is no more so than in my own life. Very often, my 'sins' are what Saiving calls "feminine" ones, and the realization of this has come as a surprise to me. I have always seen myself as rather independent, proud, assertive, and not at all lacking in "personality." But I also recognize that, for all my feminist principles, I tend to see myself through the eyes of others. I forget that other people are not me. I often want to smooth things over; I go along with things. I find myself saying too much, spilling out, not respecting other's boundaries or my own. I desperately want union with others and this often results in me losing my self. With family, friends, and lovers, I often struggle to distinguish their pain from my own; to separate my memories and narratives of the past from those of the people I love.

In romantic and sexual relationships in particular, I have a tendency to fragment; in the heady rush of new love I lose all sense of my own interests, plans, and desires. In the heartbreak of the end of a relationship I become unable to focus my attention or settle down to anything, and need to be constantly in the company of others. Eventually this passes, and once again independent solitude comes as a relief to me. But, as I enter my thirties, I still wonder if I will ever be able to love another person in that way

---

63. Thistlethwaite, *Sex, Race and God*, 86.

64. See Fine, *Delusions of Gender*, for a robust critique of discourses of innate cognitive sexual differences.

and not let myself dissolve into them. Whether I can ever share my life without losing it.

And I cannot go into more specific detail here about my past and present familial and romantic entanglements. I cannot tell them here as stories, because stories create an identity, and these are stories about identity being absorbed or fragmented. Stories incline to closure, and these are stories without an ending, only a pause. And while none of my stories belong to me alone, these most of all are those of my family, friends, and lovers, and I have decided not to dissolve the boundaries of privacy any more than I already have.

From this perspective, feminist theology of selves in relation seems all rather inadequate. Contextualizing interpersonal relationships amidst the cosmic relational web may provide a joy and sense of perspective that is a comfort. Yet it is also a form of resigned Stoicism, one that on its own does not meet the ethical demands of feminism; hence feminist theology introduces a redemptive element that is more about an ideal than what actually happens. Carter Heyward's idea of divine eros "subordinates experience to the ethical principal of right-relation, thus leaving us with a moral imperative rather than a phenomenal experience of just love."[65] Although Grey admits, in a more grimly realistic vein than Heyward, that "'mutuality in relation' implies a reciprocity in relating which may be the ideal but, sadly, is beyond the grasp of most people,"[66] her work still hinges on the hope of redemption.

Feminist theological ideas about relationality are idealized: "anti-tragic," to use the terminology of Kathleen Sands.[67] For both Heyward and Grey, the hope of relational redemption is eschatological in character, concerned with what is to come. For me the problem is not so much the belief in the possibility of a better world to come, but the denial of the unique, particular, irrevocable tragedy of so much of this world, including our selves and our relationships, subsumed into a hopeful redemptive narrative. I might, on my better days, have a feminist panentheist faith in ultimate redemption. But that cannot, and does not, detract from the small and particular tragedies of relationships between selves and others. Yet I want to turn now to another kind of universal narrative, one that may offer some solace in providing ways of understanding the tension between the

---

65. Renshaw, *Subject of Love*, 83.
66. Grey, *Redeeming the Dream*, 87.
67. See Sands, *Escape from Paradise*.

desire for union and the need for separation. I do not read it as the one true explanation, but as a story: an origin myth, as well as a tragedy.

Feminism and Psychoanalytic Accounts of Selfhood

In what follows, I discuss how the psychoanalytic story of the making of the human self may illuminate understanding of selfhood, separation and gender. The link between feminist theological questions and psychoanalytical accounts of selfhood is made in the work of Catherine Keller,[68] the writing of Michèle Roberts, and (to a lesser extent) Sara Maitland. As will become obvious, I am not attempting to give a thorough account of psychoanalytic philosophy—and still less its practice—rather, I am selectively looking at ways that feminism has reworked psychoanalytic accounts of selfhood to understand the gendered ways we relate to ourselves and to each other.

Freudian

Sigmund Freud famously attributed himself, along with Copernicus and Darwin, the third person in the trinity of thinkers who dismantled humankind's belief in its privileged place in creation.[69] Copernicus showed that the earth is not at the center of the universe; Darwin that—as the product of an evolution that is randomly selected rather than designed—humanity is no different from the rest of the biosphere. Freud's contribution, as he saw it, was to demonstrate that the human person is not the master of itself, that we have drives and desires over which we have little knowledge and no control. While Freud's ideas undermined the logic of the patriarchy of Enlightenment modernity, with 'man' the rational master of his own destiny, from a feminist perspective they have been deeply ambivalent in their account of 'woman.' Feminist thinkers have denounced Freud's misogynist errors in his theory and treatment of his female patients;[70] others have defended his theory as "not a recommendation *for* a patriarchal society, but an analysis *of* one."[71] Many feminist thinkers take a more nuanced approach, not accept-

---

68. Keller, *Broken Web*, 94–153.
69. See Brunner, *Freud*, 32.
70. See for example Friedan, *Feminine Mystique*, and Figes, *Patriarchal Attitudes*.
71. Mitchell, *Psychoanalysis and Feminism*, xv, emphasis in original.

ing everything Freud wrote, but finding the fundamentals of his thought to have proved persuasive, especially in providing an account of femininity defined by non-differentiation and passivity, and masculinity defined by separation and autonomy.

First published in 1978, Nancy Chodorow's *The Reproduction of Mothering*, a "revised standard version of psychoanalysis," explores "the preoedipal phase so hastily passed over by Freudian theory"[72] in asking why, despite huge shifts in socioeconomic circumstances, in childrearing it is nearly always women who take on the nurturing role of primary caregiver. Drawing on the object-relations theory of the British school of psychoanalysis, which attends to the interpersonal relations of early childhood, Chodorow argues that, "[w]omen mother" because they were mothered by women: "[w]omen's mothering . . . produces asymmetries in the relational experiences of boys and girls as they grow up."[73] Because "[m]others tend to experience their daughters as more like, and continuous with, themselves," girls remain longer than boys as "part of the dyadic primary mother-child relationship."[74] Mothers perceive the boy child as "a male opposite" and thus they are more quickly "pushed out of the preoedipal relationship, and have had to curtail their primary love and sense of empathetic tie with their mother." Thus boys tend to have "a more emphatic individuation and a more defensive firming of experienced ego boundaries."[75] The girl child grows up with "empathy"—"experiencing another's needs or feelings as one's own"—"built into" her "primary definition of self."[76]

Chodorow sees this pattern as 'social' rather than 'natural,' the result of the nuclear family structure that has come to predominate in the western world; as such she, in Keller's words, "mobilizes the revolutionary potential of psychoanalytic theory for social critique."[77] In Keller's analysis, the problems of "insufficient differentiation from the mother," "female self-devaluation" and "the subsequent affective and cultural deprivation that reproduces the entire cycle again" comes down not to connection itself, but patriarchal structures. The "empathic continuum initially common to both sexes" becomes distorted, is denied to the male and overwhelms the

---

72. Keller, *Broken Web*, 124.
73. Chodorow, *Reproduction of Mothering*, 169.
74. Ibid., 166.
75. Ibid., 166–67.
76. Ibid., 167.
77. Keller, *Broken Web*, 131.

female.[78] Yet this is something that we—as societies and individuals—may possibly be able to change, so that both male and female children grow into adults who value connection with others, without becoming lost in that connection.

Kristevan

In Freudian accounts of human development, the child emerges as a person—a subject—through differentiation from the mother. This is an important aspect of the psychoanalytic theory of Julia Kristeva. Her work follows on—with crucial departures—from Jacques Lacan and his concept of the 'mirror stage,' in which the child's recognition of itself in a mirror heralds its sense of itself as a unified subject, which is also associated with the acquisition of language. Freud's 'Law of the Father' becomes bound up with the very basis of sociality—language itself—and this domain is labeled by Lacanians 'the Symbolic.' To become a subject, the child must leave the realm of non-differentiated identification with the mother, and acquire the demarcated words and laws of the Symbolic. Where Kristeva departs from Lacan is her theory that another kind of language, another mode of life, "the Semiotic,"[79] continues to exist as a substrata of the Symbolic. The child begins its life in the "choral" realm of "continuous relation to the mother" and becomes a subject through breaking with the Semiotic and acquiring the Symbolic, which "constitutes itself at the cost of repressing instinctual drive."[80] Yet Semiotic language—the non-referential noises of the child learning to speak—remains with us, and is detectable in the sounds we make when words fail us, and—crucially, for Kristeva—in poetic language.

Literature that shatters our sense of self, that restores us briefly to the pre-Symbolic sense of continuity, is "revolutionary," in that it "underscore[s] the limits of socially useful discourse and attest[s] to what it represses."[81] For Julia Kristeva, reading modernist and avant-garde literature—for example the work of James Joyce, Samuel Beckett, Phillippe Sollers, and Vladimir Mayakovsky—leads to a self-shattering jouissance in its accessing of the instinctual drives that came before—and continue to lie beneath—the

78. Keller, *Broken Web*, 136.
79. I capitalize 'Symbolic' and 'Semiotic' to distinguish them from other meanings of 'symbolic' and Ferdinand de Saussure's 'semiotics.'
80. Kristeva, *Desire in Language*, 136.
81. Kristeva, *Revolution in Poetic Language*, 16.

Selves

imposition of demarcated subjectivity through the acquisition of symbolic language: "the symbolic covering (constituted by acquired knowledge, the discourse of others, and communal shelter) cracks, and something that I call instinctual drive . . . rides up to destroy any guarantees, any beliefs, any protection, including those comprised by father or professor."[82] In Kristeva's schema, liberation is not through the privileging of the experience of women as autonomous and discrete subjects; rather it is through the undermining of subjectivity and thus the social order.

However, for Kristeva neither the Semiotic or Symbolic are the enemy, instead they are both necessary, inextricable; they both bring us pleasure, they both bring us pain. We need the Symbolic to be, to function, and amidst its security we both delight and suffer "at finding oneself different, irreducible, for one is born by a simply singular speech, not merging with the others."[83] Wanting to escape the "overly constraining and reductive meaning of a language made up of universals," we have "black thrusts of desire" towards the Semiotic, but fear the "void" and "the unnameable."[84] The Symbolic represses the Semiotic but it also depends upon it as its basis: "[o]ur discourse—all discourse—moves with and against the chora in the sense that it simultaneously depends upon and refuses it."[85] While the child achieves subjectivity through "abjecting" itself from the body of the mother,[86] the chora and the body of the mother are not one and the same. Rather, amidst the chaos of the drives of non-subjectivity, the child is grounded by the mother's body, which becomes a locus of the mediation of the Symbolic.[87]

Kristeva's experience as a mother comes to play in her psychoanalytic theory. She writes of how women may perceive from both angles—as the child and as the mother—the sense of original continuity with an other, and the tension between "I"/ "Not-I." "Stabat Mater," her famous piece first published in 1976, is a consideration of motherhood, religion and the Virgin Mary, written in two columns: one a scholarly discussion, the other a poetic meditation (although—as Grace Jantzen has observed—the two forms bleed into one another).[88] Being pregnant and giving birth "extracts

82. Kristeva, *Desire in Language*, 162.
83. Ibid., x.
84. Ibid.
85. Kristeva, *Revolution in Poetic Language*, 26.
86. See Kristeva, *Powers of Horror*.
87. Kristeva, *Revolution in Poetic Language*, 27–28.
88. Jantzen, *Becoming Divine*, 202.

woman out of her oneness,"[89] but also makes her all the more aware of persons' separateness from each other. Kristeva writes of her son, "[m]y body is no longer mine"[90] and "[t]here is him . . . his own flesh, which was mine yesterday."[91] She describes the strangeness of the "abyss that opens up between the body and what had been its inside," the child who, "once the umbilical cord has been severed, is an inaccessible other."[92] At the same time, through the sense of continuity with her child, the "spatial memory"[93] of infant intimacy with her own mother is restored to her: "[r]ecovered childhood, dreamed peace restored . . . smiles in the blackness of dreams, at night, opaque joy that roots me in her bed, my mother's, and projects him, a son, a butterfly soaking up dew from her hand, there, nearby, in the night. Alone: she, I, and he."[94]

At the beginning of the piece, Kristeva mentions how the "maternal" has been presented as "an identity catastrophe that causes the Name to topple over into the unnameable that one imagines as femininity, nonlanguage, or body."[95] This masculine poststructuralist construction, of which she herself has had a role in sustaining, takes on a rather different tone when considered from the perspective of a mother. As well as desiring and fearing primal non-differentiation, and harboring the "fantasy" of the "lost territory" of her own idealized mother-child relationship,[96] the woman who is a mother, as "the threshold of culture and nature," also experiences her own body as the curious site of connection and separation, sameness and otherness.[97]

Anglo-American feminism can be notoriously squeamish about French feminist 'biological essentialism,' and anything suggestive of

89. Kristeva, *Tales of Love*, 259.
90. Ibid., 241.
91. Ibid., 243.
92. Ibid., 254.
93. Ibid., 256.
94. Ibid., 247.
95. Ibid., 235.
96. Ibid., 234.

97. Ibid., 259. Of course, not all women are mothers, or have the potential to be mothers, and having not had a child I do not think that I have any more access to this experience of the contingency of connection and otherness than do men. However, as a cisgendered woman I might be able to have a child; there is for me the possibility of motherhood that men do not have, and it would be wrong to insist that this can have no bearing whatsoever on my conception of subjectivity compared to that of a man.

Freudian 'anatomy as destiny,' and I share these worries if psychoanalytic theory is taken literally, rather than poetically. I tend to think that the origin myths of psychoanalysis only really work as "a metaphor for the psychic structure of the bourgeois nuclear family,"[98] but nevertheless I find them compelling, and, although far from universal, the bourgeois nuclear family has great social importance. Children are raised in a wide variety of circumstances, with multiple divergences from the 'holy family' of mother-father-child; nevertheless it remains true that we are all born of a woman; we all have made our dwelling in a woman's womb. And, like Grace Jantzen, I see great symbolic significance in this, although not in same way as her positive ideal of "natality" (drawing on Hannah Arendt);[99] rather, that we all began as connected, as part of another, and then become separated. The tragedy of the necessary severing of that original communion is partly biological, cultural, psychological and mythic. I must stress that I do not write of it as a 'fact,' but it does for me provide a powerful account of the human experience of the simultaneous yearning for connection and need for independence: fear of loneliness and horror of loss of self. I also find interesting the psychoanalytic account of the role of language in the construction of selfhood. The new-born infant's separateness is confirmed by socialization through language; ironically, the tool that enables us to communicate with others is that which creates our ultimate differentiation. However, the imaginative use of language awakens the Semiotic, undermining the individuated ego and restoring the bliss and terror of primal connectedness.

I now turn to the ways in which the narrative and images of this psychoanalytic account of selfhood are employed in the work of Sara Maitland and Michèle Roberts.

Sara Maitland

Like its U.S. counterpart, the British feminist movement of the 1970s and 1980s was profoundly interested in psychoanalysis, although its explicit connection to socialism meant that UK feminism was also concerned with placing the ideas of Marx and Freud in conversation with one another. The work of Sara Maitland and Michèle Roberts, coming from that particular place and time, reflects this discussion. Debates about psychoanalysis and feminism feature in their fictional depiction of the feminist movement,

---

98. Mitchell, *Psychoanalysis and Feminism*, xxi.
99. Jantzen, *Becoming Divine*.

for example in Maitland's *Daughter of Jerusalem* and *Virgin Territory*, and Roberts's *A Piece of the Night*, *The Visitation*, and *The Book of Mrs Noah*, and throughout Roberts's memoir of the period, *Paper Houses*. Exploration of the psychoanalytic account of selfhood is a significant theme in the novels of both authors.

As well as in psychoanalytic theory, the relationship between mother and daughter became an important object of analysis in second wave feminist discourse, with women exploring how female internalization and perpetuation of patriarchy played out in their experience of their own mothers. First published in 1977, Nancy Friday's *My Mother My Self*, which attested that "[a]ny effort to change and shape our lives must begin with the first woman in whose image we live,"[100] was a bestseller, and complex and difficult mother-daughter relationships abound throughout second wave feminist literature. Maitland's characters Elizabeth in *Daughter of Jerusalem*, Anna in *Virgin Territory*, and Phoebe in *Three Times Table*, are all 'daddy's girls' who identify with their father, and struggle to live up to his expectations. The resolution of Elizabeth's conflict with her mother is a turning point of *Daughter of Jerusalem*; *Three Times Table* tells of the isolated anguish of Phoebe, her mother, and her daughter, but in the end they find solace in connecting with each other. In *Virgin Territory*, however, Anna does not remember her mother, who left her and her father when she was a baby; a plot point used within the novel's complex system of metaphors to explore issues of religion, language, gender, and human development.

While Maitland is far from being a follower of Kristevan thought, her novel can be read within the structure of Kristeva's theory of the Symbolic and Semiotic, with the voice of the Fathers representing order and paternal law, and the voice of the brain-damaged infant, Caro, speaking for the Semiotic, the chaotic maternal realm. Kristeva's "brinks"[101] set themselves up against each other "on the battleground of Anna's flesh."[102] She meets Caro when she volunteers to assist her parents in a program of exercises attempting to normalize her—"trying to pattern her, Anna felt, as she had been patterned into a good nun." In her identification with Caro, Anna starts to hear her voice, enticing her to "[c]ome down here into the dark . . . Forget your rules, your order, your commitment to the light."[103] "Down here" is the

100. Friday, *My Mother My Self*, 2.
101. Kristeva, *Desire in Language*, x.
102. *VT*, 132.
103. Ibid., 53.

chora, a place of chaos, anterior to the order of the Fathers, and associated with the primal chaos that precedes God's creation in the Genesis narrative. The Fathers say to Anna, "remember, in the beginning there was not; and we were there when there was not. Our goodwill created all things, and we hold it in being. If we are angry it will all go, fall, explode, implode, there will be no more light, no more matter, no more anything, nothing real, no ground, no time."[104]

Anna fears that if she leaves the tyranny of Fathers, the realm of the Symbolic, there will be disintegration and she will cease to be a human subject; something confirmed by Caro's words, which also emphasize how the Semiotic always remains beneath the Symbolic:

> Damaged. Damaged. Damaged. Inside all of you is me. The screaming. The no words. Incontinence. I made different choices, not towards the light and bright. Gold flames and singing. I carry your darkness too. I am the dark hole under your careful houses . . . I am where you might be and I cannot be moved. You left me behind. You make me carry the darkness of not-made. I am creation's joke. What is human? you ask and you answer it is words you say and reason. It is conscience and thinking about others. It is speech and responsiveness and social. So I am not human I am animal. I am freak. I am in you.[105]

Yet Caro's way is not just an unnerving darkness, but also play and freedom: "I can play and play eternally. My play is delightful anarchy. Not for learning, for taming, for training, for ordering, not for decorum and deportment. But for joy and kaleidoscopic light shattering and reforming in the depths of the unmade stars."[106]

The Semiotic does not conform to the logic and rules of language, thus Caro's voice is "a black quiet muttering,"[107] "the voice of the voiceless moments."[108] Sometimes in depicting the voice of Caro, Maitland departs from the rules of grammar, stretching out the words on the printed page, representing the stutters, moans and other sounds of Semiotic language. For example,

---

104. Ibid., 56.
105. Ibid., 72.
106. Ibid., 132.
107. Ibid., 53.
108. Ibid., 54.

Sex, Sin, and Our Selves

> Go down into that silence, even quieter. Consent. Consent to me.
> Come down deeper below
> the words. Let it break down all the way.
> E ven to the bot tom of the se nse. and
>   be   low.
> da   na   ga   el.
> And when there is silence and the blood red moon setting. the stars dying when we stride without fear on the vast vacuity of chaos. then there can be birth and creation. then there will be calm.[109]

Anna fails in her attempts to argue with the Fathers, for "words were the possession of the Fathers, and in using them she was dragged back into their power."[110] Yet she knows that "[t]here was a great power in naming, calling things by name was the act of creation,"[111] and when she finally defeats the Fathers it is through words as well as screams, and she resolves to use their ways against them.

In a non-fiction essay, Maitland writes in a Freudian vein when she asserts that, "[f]atherhood is, partly and importantly, that which frees one from childhood and the private, and unites one with the social and the historical. We all have to forge our identities over against the mother and her loving, the good father is one who enables this process."[112] In *Virgin Territory* this process has gone wrong: rather than abject the mother in identifying with the father, the child has too soon been abandoned by the mother. This is particular, pertaining to the physical circumstances of Caro's birth, leaving her brain-damaged, and Anna's abandonment by her mother, but it also has a universal element, a representation of mothering within the distortions of patriarchy:

> The child knows that the mother, the body of the mother, is a treacherous rat. She gnaws through the umbilical cord too soon. Wait, the child screams, wait. The cord is thick and strong and pulsing. It joins the baby to the placenta, to the source of nourishment and peace, to the primordial paradise. . . There should be time but they snap the baby off and there is a dreadful gap between blood-breathing and air breathing . . . swung against the nothingness of air where there should be the weight of water. . . The baby

---

109. Ibid., 133.
110. Ibid., 166.
111. Ibid., 94.
112. *WR*, 155.

> is snatched up to heaven to the bright courts of the fathers. The mother, defeated, rushes off to hide in the desert. The mother sells the child to the Fathers, over and over again.[113]

It seems that the root of Anna's problems is her lack of a mother: she identifies with her father to the extent that she remembers nothing about her mother. Anna has strove to be "brave and clever and virtuous and good, her father's daughter. The Fathers' daughter, sprung to live on the emanation of the Father's Word, armed against darkness and chaos"; like Athene, choosing the Fathers over the mothers; "[t]he bright virgin warrior, the beloved daughter." Having repressed the need for a mother, as Anna's mental state worsens she finds herself longing to be held, to be "wrapped in a soft blue blanket with a satin edging, wrapped warm and held close. She wanted a mother."[114]

Once she has chosen to leave the tyranny of the Fathers, Anna does not opt for the extremes of Caro's choral existence, but a middle way: "[t]hose painful exercises in normality are appropriate for me. I want to be a grown-up, you see, that is what I have chosen. You have given me a love gift, a new part of myself, a new way, but I don't have to come all the way down with you."[115] For Anna, learning how to be a grown-up means that she must go in search of mothers, to find new ways of imaging the divine, to perhaps seek out her literal mother. She decides first to return to South America and the Amazon: "she would have to go travelling unprotected, commit herself to the great river and float down into the dark interior; she had to go and seek the country of the Mothers."[116]

Although Maitland has said to me in conversation that she does not fully subscribe to the "ontology" of the psychoanalytic account of selfhood, and uses these ideas as a literary device rather than holding them to be philosophical truths,[117] it continues to be a theme of her later work. The short story "Sybil" in *On Becoming a Fairy Godmother* uses the oracle at Delphi as an image of the "brink" between order and chaos: the priestess squats over "the deep crack, the fissure in the solid ground . . . and from its depths the voice of the god speaks to men through a woman."[118] Like

113. *VT*, 43–44.
114. Ibid., 127.
115. Ibid., 199.
116. Ibid., 203.
117. Maitland, conversation with the author, June 2011.
118. *BFG*, 199–200.

Anna in *Virgin Territory*, the sybil experiences the void and devastation of ceasing to be protected by "the almighty father-lover," for "the good will of the father creates and sustains the daughter, the words of the father created and sustained the universe," thus "if the father is angry it will all go, fall, implode."[119] She says that the mothers have abandoned the daughters, and here this abandonment is associated not only with birth but also with menopause, no longer having any link to the womb:[120] "the moon waxes, wanes . . . But not me i've snapped the cord, cut the bond, the cord that bound me . . . cored me to mother . . . i've been a woman—kore, parthenos, gune, meter—bound to the rhythm, to the beat, to the drum. not now, i'm free—free to, free from, free for, free fall."[121]

Michèle Roberts

Psychoanalytic themes are more prevalent in Michèle Roberts's work than in Maitland's, and she gives more credence to its theoretical claims; however, she is often at pains to insist that her writing is not the handmaid of critical theory.[122] In the 1980s Roberts's writing was heavily saturated with Jungian thought, and *A Piece of the Night*, *The Visitation* and *The Wild Girl* echo her attempts in undergoing psychotherapy to "integrate the split-off archetypes within me"[123] and an androgynous ideal which combined the masculine animus—"dividing, ordering, separating, naming"—and feminine anima—"receiving, opening, waxing and waning, relating, uniting."[124] By the late 1980s, Jungian ideas had largely disappeared from her work, and began to reflect the continental philosophical tradition that followed Lacan's development of Freud. In *Paper Houses*, Roberts relates how she would telephone her friend Mandy for the "low-down on Foucault, or Lacan, or Cixous," because she did not have time to read them closely herself.[125] Psychoanalytic poststructuralist theory is most utilized in Roberts's

---

119. Ibid., 212.

120. Maitland explains that the sybils at Delphi were women of post-menopausal age, dressed as pre-pubescent kore to preserve ritual purity without the risks associated with using young girls (*BFG*, 219).

121. *BFG*, 202.

122. *IBR*, 96.

123. *WWH*, 60.

124. Ibid., 65.

125. *PH*, 185.

writing in terms of women's relationship to language and the unconscious. She tells María Soraya García Sánchez, "women have been so repressed into the unconscious of the culture . . . that (a) it's where we've belonged but (b) it's where we can begin to invent ourselves . . . I have been encouraged by those French philosophers like Kristeva and Cixous and Irigaray who . . . suggested to me . . . that because so many meanings of woman were repressed, it was very liberating for a writer to dive down, and see what she can find, and bring it back up to the surface."[126] For Roberts, accessing the unconsciousness through writing is associated with the body of the mother. As well as writing realist portrayals of difficult mother-daughter relations (for example in *A Piece of the Night* and *Daughters of the House*), the psychoanalytic image of the lost mother abounds throughout her fiction.

Flesh and Blood—perhaps Robert's most experimental novel—consists of multiple stories of fantastic and horrible times and places, which spiral inwards in a strange labyrinth. At the center is the narrative of the angel Cherubina. She describes the dreamlike country of Paradise: "[p]ut together the desire and the maps, the broken pots and the mysterious words, a phrase of guttural music—but you have not found it. You are not there yet. You need to trip, to wobble off-balance. You arrive unexpectedly. At this particular moment it's the last thing on your mind, coming here. You find it by accident. You fall into this place."[127] Paradise takes the form of a Middle East landscape, thus alluding to the biblical worlds but also to the tale-telling of Scheherazade, mentioned in the opening story. The reader follows the narrative to the Turkish baths: "[o]n your blissful skin the hands of the masseuse play a writing game. They spell out, in fingertalk, words and phrases, they trace love messages for your shut eyes to read."[128] This leads to the next section, "Anon." All the other chapters are titled after their narrator, thus the "anonymity" of the piece at the heart of the novel alludes to the state of existence that is prior to naming:

> mamabébé love you are here with you together us now over and over so non-stop mamabébé so wanting you born this love us so close skinskin talking heartbeat belonging with you allowed love home flesh my mamabébé our body singing to you so beautiful love listen mamabébé listen:

126. *IGS*, 140.
127. *FB*, 104–5.
128. Ibid., 108.

> swimming in our waters we listen
> to ourheartbeat
> we is one whole undivided
> you/me broken now mended
> you/me restored mamabébé
> our body of love pickedup putbacktogether
> repaired
> made whole again[129]

This writing of union with the mother's body—of merged subjectivity and the representation of Semiotic language—works well within the context of the novel, a moment of beatific calm amidst the disturbing narrative whirlwind. The reader comes out from there, back into the previous stories, one by one, returning at the end to the opening narrative of Freddie/Frederica, who tells us at the beginning that she has murdered her mother. Frederica feels that she has killed her mother by entering the world of adulthood and becoming pregnant, reminding her of the primal loss of becoming a separate subject. The resolution at the end is informed by the experience of the center:

> this is an elegy for the mother I remember . . . She talked to me in a secret language of mamabébé. She was my place once and I was hers. I didn't give her up without a struggle . . . a love song for my daughter not yet born, who swims inside me dreaming unborn dreams, my flesh and blood, made of love in the land of milk and honey, the land of spices and stories.[130]

Flesh and Blood may be an exquisitely-written literary exploration of psychoanalytic imagery, but Roberts's main source of inspiration is her imagination and attempts to work out the struggles and anguishes of her own life. In a 2003 interview with Jenny Newman, she says, "I felt very separate from my mother . . . she was the paradise from which I had been 'expelled untimely.' The image of the maternal body as paradise became very important to me. Obviously it's there in psychoanalytical literature, but it was my journey to discover it. . . a religious or mystical feeling or quest: to get back to some pre-linguistic state of bliss, which is about unity, non-separation."[131] For Roberts, writing is the "quest" to return, momentarily, to the lost paradise; an attempt to recreate "she who is paradise itself

---

129. Ibid., 109.
130. Ibid., 173–74.
131. *IJN*.

for the baby, the growing child: the mother."[132] *The Book of Mrs Noah* uses the image of the Ark as a womb and women's library to explore ideas about motherhood and writing; like *Flesh and Blood*, the narrative shifts and fragments, winding along the canals of Venice. On the final page, Mrs Noah reaches the end of her journey:

> Creation starts here, in the Ark. Love actively shapes the work. My mother nourishes me with words, words of such power and richness that I grow, dance, leap. But the purpose of the Ark is that I leave it . . . Cutting the cord, she gives me speech. Words of longing for that world I've lost, words of desire to explore this absence of her. I must go further into absence, and find more words . . . Writer. Mother. Two words I have linked through this voyage on the Ark, this arc of stories, a distance of so many nights, such longing. This long twist of words spun out of loss."[133]

Influenced by object-relations theory on artistic practice as the attempt to make reparation for the loss of connection with the mother, Roberts writes that "[i]n the art we make, we make that lost body, we make it up, we re-make it, we remember it, we re-member it."[134] The creative impulse rises up out of "this overwhelming sadness at absence," through which "we learn to create something beautiful: our words, later on our gifts, later still our works of art. We re-create the mother inside ourselves, over and over again."[135]

For Roberts, as for Kristeva, the pre-Symbolic union with the mother is associated not with absence of words, but a different, non-denotive type of language. In *Daughters of the House* Léonie has visions of a "golden woman in red," a symbol of the divine feminine, remembered in the folk-religion of the countryside, but suppressed by the parish priest.[136] In the presence of this figure, Léonie finds that "[s]omething was restored to her which she had lost and believed she would never find again . . . A language she once knew but had forgotten about, forgotten ever hearing, forgotten she could speak. Deeper than English or French; not foreign; her own. She had heard it spoken long ago . . . The secret language, the underground

132. *FSG*, 20.
133. *BMN*, 274–75.
134. *FSG*, 20.
135. Ibid., 21.
136. *DH*, 87.

stream ... that joined her back to what she had lost, to something she had once intimately known"[137]

Linking with Kristeva's thought on poetic language, in Roberts's work it is through writing poetic language that one accesses a mystical state of continuity, a loss of distinction between self and world that reminds us of the primary connection with the body of the mother. In *Impossible Saints*, Josephine finds in writing that "currents of language poured through her, molten gold, when that feeling she called God burned and shivered and danced up and down her spine ... Her lap was filled with treasure and pearls. Words fell on her and fed her like manna ... Inside the golden cocoon of writing she died. She died to her self, her old life, her former way of stringing sentences together. She dwindled down into darkness, knew nothing, was extinguished."[138]

Yet the relationship between language, mystical connection and infant paradise regained is an ambivalent one: through language it is reaccessed, but also lost. This is not only in the process of becoming a separate subject through acquiring speech, but also in the experience of communication that expresses and makes real, but also divides and negates. In *The Looking Glass*, Genevieve reflects on storytelling:

> you might lose something precious by making and telling a story, because then all its parts stretched out, beads strung one by one onto a string in time ... whereas while the unspoken words remained inside you all of them connected one to the other in a mad circling dance which was indescribably beautiful, wholly present in just one second, an eternal now. When you smoothed and flattened and straightened the story out, made it exist word by word in speech, you lost that heavenly possession of everything at once ... Speaking and telling, you threw joy away and had to mourn the loss of paradise, the shimmering eternal moment which was outside time ... Perhaps Eve's punishment, thrust forth from paradise, was to become a storyteller. Not in order to defend herself but simply to have to speak.[139]

Storytelling and writing is that through which we regain the lost paradise, but is also entwined with that through which we were expelled from paradise in the first place.

137. Ibid., 86.
138. *IS*, 35.
139. *LG*, 274–75.

The narratives and metaphors of psychoanalysis, particularly in Roberts and Maitland's writing about the loss of the maternal body, provide a tragic origin myth for the tension between our desire for connection and need for separation. This account gives an explanation for the differences between men and women's connective sensibilities as the socially contingent products of a patriarchal culture. As such, it offers hope that the blessing of women's relational capacities—particularly as regards the rest of the cosmos—can be extended to men; that the curse of women's diffusiveness at the expense of autonomous selfhood can be overcome. Yet the root of the painful ambivalence towards individuality and non-differentiation is not only socially constructed; it is something basic to being human, something tragic and universal. This tragic origin myth can help us in trying to understand the difficulties in our unique and particular relations with others, without prescribing ideal solutions. Roberts's work in particular points towards glimpses of comfort in moments of connection—in poetic language, sex, making things, communion with nature—without an "anti-tragic" belief in ultimate restoration.

4

Suffering, Sacrifice, and Sin

KATHLEEN SANDS HAS CRITICIZED feminist theology for its dependence on "another, higher world in which 'what is' and 'what ought to be' are eternally the same."[1] In this chapter's consideration of feminist reworking of Christian thought on self-sacrifice, suffering and sin, my overarching argument is that, however necessary the feminist deconstruction of the soteriological aspects of Christian theology, feminist treatment of these issues tends towards purity and simplicity. This is to the detriment of a real engagement with the complex and painful realities of the world, and it is my contention that theology would do better to attend to how things are, rather than how we want them to be.

SERVICE, SACRIFICE, AND THE SUFFERING BODY

When, following on from Valerie Saiving, feminist theologians such as Judith Plaskow and Barbara Andolsen claimed that Christian[2] valorization of self-abnegation is harmful to women, it soon became clear that this is a critique that goes to the very heart of the Christian religion.[3] The ideals of service and self-sacrifice are not incidental to Christianity. Rather, they are its very basis: the Son of God becoming human and submitting to a painful and humiliating death, in order to save humankind from sin. In a highly influential essay, Joanne Carlson Brown and Rebecca Parker argue that Christianity's glorification of suffering in the symbol of the cross is "an

---

1. Sands, *Escape from Paradise*, 59.

2. Although Plaskow is a Jewish theologian, the Christian theology of Reinhold Niebuhr and Paul Tillich was the focus of her doctoral dissertation.

3. Plaskow, *Sex, Sin and Grace*; Andolsen, "Agape."

abusive theology."[4] For women in particular, "[i]f the best person who ever lived gave his life for others, then, to be of value we should likewise sacrifice ourselves. Any sense that we have a right to care for our own needs is in conflict with being a faithful follower of Jesus. Our suffering for others will save the world . . . Those whose lives have been deeply shaped by the Christian tradition feel that self-sacrifice and obedience are not only virtues but the definition of a faithful identity."[5] They claim that "suffering is never redemptive, and suffering can never be redeemed."[6] This became what Susan Frank Parsons would call a "feminist orthodoxy"[7] to the extent that Lisa Isherwood, in her *Introducing Feminist Christologies*, begins the chapter on "Suffering Christ" with the sentence, "[i]t may not surprise readers that this chapter is shorter than the rest."[8] In feminist theology, it is best to only glance at the image of the suffering Christ, not to gaze for too long. Yet the crucifixion has cast a long shadow on western Christianity, and perhaps feminist theology has looked away too quickly, has set its face towards the bright dawn of Easter Sunday in a denial of the darkness of Good Friday.

Redemptive Suffering

Feminist condemnation tends to focus on the specific notion of redemptive suffering that is arguably the most blunt-edged version of Christian atonement theology: the penal substitution doctrine of atonement: "[a]t the center of western Christianity is the story of the cross, which claims God the Father required the death of his Son to save the world. We believe this theological claim sanctifies violence."[9] The formulation of penal substitution, in which Jesus' death on the cross enacts vicariously the punishment for sin that God's justice demands of humanity, may be the least subtle of substitutionary doctrines of atonement. It also has a cast-iron logic and violent poeticism that have strengthened its influence. Of all the models of the atonement, this is the one with the best hymns. I absorbed it as a child: the

---

4. Brown and Parker, "God So Loved the World," 26.
5. Ibid., 2.
6. Ibid., 27.
7. Parsons, *Challenging Women's Orthodoxies*.
8. Isherwood, *Introducing Feminist Christologies*, 87.
9. Brock and Parker, *Proverbs of Ashes*, 8.

"deeper magic" of C. S. Lewis's *Chronicles of Narnia*, in which Aslan dies in the stead of the treacherous boy Edmund.[10]

These days the doctrine of penal substitution seems to me to be a theology so unjust, so nasty, so limited in its imagination about the divine, that I cannot fathom how I could have once believed in it. The feminist argument that this specific Christian "glorification of suffering" is an "abusive theology"[11] now seems obvious. Yet I do remember the moment when, after a few years of studying theology, I finally realized how truly horrible the penal substitutionary model is: reading the preface to *Christianity, Patriarchy and Abuse*, in which Elizabeth Bettenhausen describes a collective of feminist theologians rewriting some of the gospel episodes according to the imaginative premise of Christ's coming in the form of a woman. One of the stories rewritten was Christ's flogging by Roman soldiers, in which "She" was blindfolded and raped by them. Bettenhausen then wonders what if this, rather than the cross, had been the atoning paradigm for Christianity: the penal substitution coming from gang rape rather than crucifixion. She asks, "[w]ould women ever imagine forming a religion around the rape of a woman?"[12] The question was like a punch in the stomach, and my answer—and Bettenhausen's—was of 'of course not: that would be horrendous,' and it led me to conclude that the torture and horrific murder of a male savior, in order to satisfy divine justice, is no less hideous.

Michèle Roberts has written on this topic in a similar vein to feminist theologians: that the notion of Christ's vicarious sacrifice is irredeemable, a doctrine "that damages and stunts children's moral, psychological and emotional growth."[13] The attitude of Roberts's character Josephine well expresses the experience of many people subject to substitutionary atonement theology, including my own: "[a] crucifix on the wall of every room reminded her of Christ's death on the cross. Her fault. Her sins nailed him up there . . . She hurt Christ twice: first by being born at all, being born in a state of original sin and so forcing him to come down to earth and die painfully on the cross in order to save her, and secondly, she hurt him afresh by not being grateful enough."[14] In *The Book of Mrs Noah* a medieval nun moves away from such an understanding of God: "I don't like the crucifix;

10. Lewis, *Lion, the Witch and the Wardrobe*, 176.
11. Brown and Parker, "God So Loved the World," 26.
12. Bettenhausen, Foreword to *Christianity, Patriarchy and Abuse*, xi.
13. *FSG*, 33.
14. *IS*, 46.

it dominates my cell, but I won't look at it. I won't be responsible any longer for his pain, my poor torn brother. Nor can I console him. I have abdicated my position at the foot of the cross. For me, now, Jesus is only one more wretch condemned to death by a cruel Father-God . . . I can't love a God who requires such suffering, who wills his son to be tortured to a slow death . . . I have given up that God."[15] My autobiographical reasons for feeling so strongly against this doctrine—every bit as strongly as Roberts—are the same reasons why I cannot join her, and feminist theologians such as Isherwood, in permanently shutting my eyes to the cross.

At the age of thirteen, I started cutting myself. I have never known precisely why, nor why I carried on doing so for ten years. I can ascribe many reasons to it: the most obvious being that it was the only way I knew to convey quite how bad I felt. It was always more about the blood and disfigurement than the pain: these red tears were a weeping I could control, and my mutilated flesh bore on the outside the wrongness I felt inside.

When at the age of fifteen I re-embraced the faith of my younger childhood, the motivation and manner of my self-harm changed. My charismatic evangelical faith had no place for the value of suffering or the practice of penitential discipline. Instead, we were encouraged to be joyful: being unhappy was "not good witnessing." I felt horribly guilty for being miserable, and for being unable or unwilling to hide it. Although we were not surrounded by visual images of the crucified Christ, the emphasis on the doctrine of penal substitution meant that the suffering and bleeding Jesus was ever present in words, if not in pictures, in the prayers, sermons, and songs we sang. Surrounded by all this bloody symbolism, I began to cut myself in order to punish myself, for specific sins such as rage and jealousy, and the more general sin of not loving God, who had died for me, as much as I ought to. The cutting did not lead to the relief of guilt, instead it led to more: I was damaging "the temple of the Holy Spirit" and "whoever sins against the body sins against God" (1 Cor 6:19–20). A particularly zealous friend said to me, "what does this show of your attitude to God, that you would mutilate his creation like that?" I would tell myself that I did not need to shed any more blood, that Jesus shed all the blood that is necessary to cover my sin. But the problem was that I still believed myself to be owned by a God who had demanded blood in the first place.

Along with any number of contemporary theologians—feminists not least among them—I believe that Christian theology must, like Jesus

15. *BMN*, 106.

Christ, be utterly incarnate, rooted in and growing from embodied human beings in a particular place and time. Theology is done by bodies and about bodies. Thus, when doing theology, I cannot but be aware of this particular body, my body, its surface delicately laced with pink and white lines, a network of scars mapping out over a decade of self-harm. Thinking about the wounds of Christ, I look at my own wounds; faded, now, but still very much there. Some of them were brought about by a mistaken notion of love for the crucified Christ, and as such they support what certain feminist theologians say about the cross and redemptive suffering. Others of my scars—wordless, enfleshed cries of dereliction—testify to a truth obvious to the point of banality: that suffering exists. People hurt, often overwhelmingly so, and in the enduring image of the human Jesus Christ on the cross, in the compelling narrative of his anguish, arrest, trial and crucifixion, Christianity affirms the reality of suffering, a reality that even God's Son was subject to.

Yet *any* valorization of Christ's suffering has been a subject of debate in feminist theology.[16] Notions of atonement that present Jesus' death not as a propitiatory sacrifice, but as God's identification with the weak and the powerless, a symbol of non-coercive authority that responds to evil with love, are also criticized by feminist theology. Such theologies of the cross (Jürgen Moltmann's *The Crucified God* perhaps being perhaps the most notable) are placed in the tradition of Abelard's 'exemplarism,' which "suggests that we come to know love most fully by being moved by torture and execution as an act of self-sacrificing love for us, which then becomes the model for our own lives."[17] Christ as 'suffering servant' is accused of reinforcing women's sense that to be righteous is to deny oneself and submit to any suffering; that true love is to lay down one's life for the other; this has contributed to a culture in which victims of domestic violence choose to remain in abusive relationships.[18] Mary Daly claims (with her typical rhetorical overstatement) that, in the church, the imitation of Christ is only ever "theoretical" for men; it is women who do it in practice.[19] Other feminist theologians interpret Christ's serving role, as demonstrated in the footwashing of John 13, as an example of service that displaces self-centeredness, one rooted in

---

16. See Ramsey, "Losing One's Life."
17. Brock, "Communities of the Cross," 121.
18. See Brown, Miller and Bohn, *Christianity, Patriarchy and Abuse*; Ruether, *Introducing Redemption*, 98–103.
19. Daly, *Beyond God the Father*, 100.

generous, mutual love rather than self-humiliation.[20] Yet it may be argued that the footwashing is as problematic as the cross: in an imperfect world rife with inequality and exploitation, the idealization of servitude tends to contribute to injustice. Even an emphasis on the footwashing as a loving action *between friends* (who thus relate to one another as equals) is still open to abuse. I have seen a number of people (men as well as women) worn away by years of loving service to their church, their friends, their family, but not themselves received even a tenth of the generosity that they have shown.

Some feminist theologians have followed liberation theology in emphasizing the political meaning of Christ's execution. They wish "to explore the implications of . . . God's own move into history at the side and on the side of those same persons on the margins," without forgetting that "[t]he process of kenosis or emptying is one that has reinforced the pain for persons already lacking power, especially when it is urged prescriptively."[21] These tend to stress that the cross is the inevitable but awful consequence of Jesus' struggle against oppression. For Beverley Harrison, "[i]t is one thing to live out a commitment to mutuality and reciprocity as the way to bear up God in the world and to be clear-eyed and realistic about what the consequences of that radical love may be. It is quite another to do what many Christians have done—that is, to rip the crucifixion of Jesus out of its lived-world context in his total life and historical project and turn sacrifice into an abstract norm for the Christian life."[22] Rosemary Radford Ruether claims that the cross represents "the risk that Jesus and all people take when they unmask the idols and announce the good news that God is on the side of the poor and those who struggle for justice."[23] The "good news" of the resurrection was not the result of the cross, instead it represents "a refusal to accept the message of the cross, an insistence that life will win over death in the end," and the only significance Ruether ascribes to Jesus' cross is as "a crime intended to silence him and to destroy his movement."[24] In Ruether's soteriology, "[t]he God of the resurrection did not cause the cross, but was momentarily crushed by the cross, only to rise again, overcoming it with a rebirth of protest and new hope. In the resurrection we say No to unjust

20. Schneiders, "The Footwashing."
21. Ringe, *Luke*, 158.
22. Harrison, *Making the Connections*, 19.
23. Ruether, *Introducing Redemption*, 103.
24. Ibid., 101.

death and Yes to life abundant for all of us together."[25] She argues that to regard the death of Jesus as having any intrinsically redemptive meaning is mistaken and harmful not only because it promotes suffering, but also because it is a barrier to true redemption: the active striving to change the world and ourselves.

Representation of the Suffering Body

Christian feminists have long challenged the patriarchal teachings that women cannot represent Christ's priestly role because Christ is male. They have pointed out that this begs the question, "can a male savior save women?"[26] If it is the Son's taking on of human nature that enables his salvific work, and if, according to the maxim of Gregory of Nazianzus, "the unassumed is the unhealed," can it really be said that he assumed the nature of women as well as men? As Elizabeth Johnson has argued, "God's saving solidarity with all humanity is what is crucial for the birth of the new creation. *Et homo factus est* . . . But if in fact what is meant is *et vir factus est* . . . then women are cut out of the loop of salvation, for female sexuality is not taken on by the Word made flesh."[27] Yet a number of feminist theologians have not wanted Christ on the cross to assume a female body: the degrading, exposed violence of crucifixion has been inflicted on the female body again and again; Tina Beattie claims that representations of a female crucified Christ, such as Edwina Sandys's 1974 sculpture "Christa," commissioned by the United Nations Decade for Women, serve only to "perpetuate the violence done to women."[28]

Depictions of a female crucified Christ raise the issue of sexual violence and gender, because the naked, tortured female body is immediately sexual in a way that the male body of Christ is not. Marcella Althaus-Reid asks why "is the tortured male body of Christ less offensive and infinitely more divine than a woman's tortured body? Why is it that, confronted by the naked body of a female Christ, the heterosexual gaze is still fixed on the shape of breasts, the youth of the body and its sexual desirability?"[29] The viewer's reaction to "Christa" images demonstrates that patriarchy has

25. Ibid., 107.
26. See Ruether, *To Change the World*, 45–56.
27. Johnson, *She Who Is*, 153.
28. Beattie, "Sexuality," 143.
29. Althaus-Reid, *Indecent Theology*, 111.

configured the female body not only as 'other' to normative humanity (and divinity), but also as sexual object. The Christa forces people to consider the maleness of God in a manner far more shocking—and thus perhaps more powerful—than other feminist subversions of the gender of God, such as Mother or Sophia (Wisdom). Thus I would suggest that its place in feminist reworking of Christian symbolism is as a shock tactic first and foremost, to be held alongside other models for the divine feminine, rather than the primary paradigm.

Of the works featured in Julie Clague's article discussing a number of representations of a female Christ on the cross, perhaps the most shocking example is James M. Murphy's "Christine on the Cross." On an inverted crucifix, with her hands bound above her head, a naked woman stands with her legs apart and feet nailed to the arms of the cross. It is a brutal image, one that uses religious symbolism to represent women's suffering as victims of sexual violence, and the imagery of pornography to provoke theological questions. The artist explains, "[e]very Easter for about five years I attempted to sculpt a crucifixion but did not complete it. Last Easter my sketch in soft clay took the shape of a woman. I realized thereby that the world's rejection and hatred of women culminates in crucifying the female Christ ... I thought that the crucifixion of a woman would be accurately expressed by spreading her legs, not her arms, on a lowered cross-bar. Such a posture symbolizes hostility toward woman, with implications of submission, sexual humiliation and rape."[30] In 1984 the pioneering feminist biblical scholar Phyllis Trible used "Christine on the Cross" as part of the meditations in Holy Week services, along with material from her renowned *Texts of Terror*. The thinking behind "Christine on the Cross" is similar to that of *Texts of Terror:* feminist biblical interpretation "in memoriam," attending to the terrible moments of literary violence in texts such as Judges 19, in which a woman is raped and killed, her body dismembered and sent to the twelve tribes of Israel.[31] The power of the Christa image lies in its role as a reminder of the violence that women are subjected to; that remembering this pain and defilement is a sacred task. In the image of a woman on the cross, the violent degradation of women's bodies is enacted on the body of God. Christa functions not only in memoriam, but, for survivors of sexual abuse and domestic violence, as a means for healing through identification. Susan Thistlethwaite, who initially felt that the Christa would be a

---

30. In Clague, "Christa," 93.
31. Trible, *Texts of Terror*, 3.

legitimization of women's "routine crucifixion" in patriarchal society, writes that "'Christa' is not experienced by many women as legitimating violence against them but as identifying with their pain and freeing them from the guilt that somehow . . . they deserved what they got."[32]

The female crucified Christ, as a "graphic portrayal of female suffering," has the role of exposing "the reality of the cross as a site of patriarchal violence."[33] However, some feminist theologians continue to claim that we would be better off without any representations of Christ on the cross, male or female. Rita Brock has claimed that the image of the crucifix emerged after the violence of medieval Christendom: "[i]t took Jesus a thousand years to die. The crucifixion is one of the most recognizable images in all of Western art. Once he dies, that is all he seems to do. His death becomes the screen onto which is projected every imaginable human suffering. Jesus' death has become so characteristic of Christian imagery and theology, it is nearly impossible to imagine a time when his crucifixion did not claim the center of Christian art and piety. But there was such a time."[34] Aside from having a somewhat reductive historiography in linking the emergence of veneration of the crucifix with the wars and conquests of the medieval age, Brock's work suffers from her dismissal of arguments that representations of Jesus' death have enabled Christians to "imagine God's compassion for human suffering," the image of the cross "a sign of divine solidarity with human pain."[35] Embodiment is central to her theology, yet she seems to deny that any good can come from representation of Christ's body in pain or as victim of patriarchal violence. This religious feminist affirmation of bodiliness, but not Christ's crucified body, forms part of its denial of the reality of suffering bodies.

Alyda Faber has critiqued another work of Brock's, written with Susan Thistlethwaite, for weakening their otherwise unflinching examination of the global sex industry, *Casting Stones: Prostitution and Liberation in Asia and the United States*, with a "theodicy of the body." Brock and Thistlethwaite write of the deeply horrific violation of women's bodies throughout the world, yet "their epistemology of eros as perdurable substratum of the body" entails that "[t]he broken body is a secondary imposition upon the body in its erotic fullness . . . Reclaiming the body for theology, they

32. Thistlethwaite, *Sex, Race and God*, 93.
33. Clague, "Christa," 83.
34. Brock, "Communities of the Cross," 110.
35. Ibid., 114.

Suffering, Sacrifice, and Sin

recover an ideal body, scraped and changed by suffering, yet essentially unalterable."[36] It seems that the broken body is not the true body. Belief in the essential reality of the good, whole body, charged with eros and undamaged by the disfiguring of patriarchal violence, creates an ontological dualism in which "[a]ttention to particular experiences of the maimed body . . . are made to fit into this dualist framework of good and evil." Faber argues that, rather than believing that the making of "unabashed assertions about violence as an evil distortion of a pre-existing and perdurable good" are sufficient resistance to violence, feminist theology would do better in "drawing political attention to violent destruction" by ceasing to "confine" violence to "speculative discussions about evil" in which "violence becomes unrepresentable in terms of damage done to bodies."[37]

It seems to me that there is a parallel here with feminist denial of the representation of Christ (or Christa) on the cross: just as the ontological reality of the suffering body is eschewed in favor of an idealized, erotic body, so is the possibility of representing human, embodied suffering as in any way divine. Yet, arguably, throughout the world and throughout history, pain and suffering is not a distortion of human bodily experience: it is *constitutive* of it. In the words of a liturgical prayer by Nicola Slee, "hurt is at the heart of things."[38] I have identified with the wounded body of Christ because my own body has been wounded. My wounds were not brought about through the direct action of patriarchal violence in the same way as his; it is more complicated than that. They are the product of human embodied existence that includes illness, grief, conflict, culpable fault, and the damaging symbolic of patriarchy. My scars are there, they are real, and they are mine: I do not want a theology that refuses the representation of the wounded, suffering body because it falls short of the feminist ideal of embodiment. It sometimes seems that feminist theology has such strong belief in how things *ought* to be, that it is unable to honor how things actually *are*. Its idealism and energy is concerned with defeating suffering rather than reflecting on it; with overcoming the damage of patriarchal violence rather than attending to its reality. Thus to represent the suffering Christ, to identify with him and to even consider ascribing any kind of redemptive value to the painful experiences that have made us who we are, is a kind of heresy in certain strands of feminist theology. In proclamations that suffering is

---

36. Faber, *Wounds*, 147.
37. Ibid., 209.
38. Slee, *Praying Like a Woman*, 10.

only ever bad, "can never be redemptive and can never be redeemed,"[39] I see the same totalizing dualism that caused me such anguish in its guise in Christian fundamentalism. I was taught that if something is even slightly tainted with sin then it is ruined utterly; that God demands perfection, or else punishment, and thus Christ bore the penalty required to save you in your total corruption. When feminist theology declares that the crucifix can play no part whatsoever in enabling us to attend to the reality of embodied suffering in the world, because it was an instrument of torture used to silence Christ in his struggle against injustice, and its representation has made victimization into a virtue, then it is using the same dualistic logic that demands purity at any cost. What I want are ways of identifying with the suffering body of Christ that acknowledge that suffering is how things are, rather than how they ought to be.

There are ways in which the body of Christ on the cross can be used to provide female imagery for the divine in a way that includes the suffering of embodied existence. Janet Soskice, drawing on the work of historians such as Caroline Walker Bynum, notes how "[a]ncient and venerable exegetical traditions have seen the blood and water flowing from Christ's pierced side as emblematic of birth";[40] the feeding of the Eucharistic body like that of a mother breastfeeding her child. While symbolism of birthing can be associated with Christ's tomb and baptism, it is in the veneration of the crucified Christ that Jesus as mother mysticism, such as that of Julian of Norwich, is the most concerned with the fleshly realities of female existence. Mary Grey considers how the cross as medium of atonement can be presented in terms of birthing, for birthing encompasses "dimensions of painful, suffering love," which include "conflict and even death," while at the same time being "an alternative to victory through violence."[41] Especially when considered from an historical and global context, in which women are very likely to die in childbirth, Christ's experience on the cross has significant parallels with the creative agony of giving birth: "[i]n the birthing experience we are given a 'letting go' of self—in pain and struggle—for the creation of new being. We are given the sense of our physical bodies falling or even being torn apart. We have lost our 'centered self.' Nobody can reach us in this struggle—neither husband, lover, nor parent."[42] The connection of

39. Brown and Parker, "God So Loved the World," 27.
40. Soskice, *Kindness of God*, 87.
41. Grey, *Redeeming the Dream*, 146–47.
42. Ibid., 148.

Christ's crucifixion with the lived experience of birthing is made explicit in the following passage by Sara Maitland: "God also brought new life, gospel life to birth, stretched out for hours on the cross, autonomy removed by aggressive experts, the eternal Word reduced to wordless cries, bleeding down into the dark, overwhelmed by the sense of desolation, the doubt as to how much more you can put up with. And afterwards the joy, the new life, the sense of mystery and distance."[43]

Maitland's thought on the representation of the cross from a Christian feminist perspective has been ambivalent. On one hand, in 1987 she wrote along the lines of feminist liberation theology of the cross, that "God did not enter into history and bodiliness in order to suffer but in order to redeem—the suffering is quite incidental (even if inevitable). If we want to 'identify' ourselves with Christ's primary act it must be through a passionate involvement in the process of history and its transformation. The consequence of God's suffering, like its purpose, is not that we should suffer more, but that we should suffer less."[44] In *Virgin Territory*, Anna considers getting a tattoo of a cross, but the "magical" tattoo artist tells her, "[y]ou don't want a crucifix, you want a Christ. But that one is too painful; too guilt-ridden," and suggests that instead she get a tattoo of a fish, representative of Jesus but also the grace of God.[45]

Perhaps it is that Maitland's thought on representation of Christ's suffering has changed over time, or simply that in some circumstances a cross is appropriate, that we do not have to choose between fishes and crucifixes. In 2009 she published a book of stories accompanying the artist Chris Gollon's paintings of the Stations of the Cross, commissioned by the church of St. John on Bethnal Green. The practice of the Stations of the Cross is exemplary of a medieval spirituality that emphasized identification with the suffering of Christ, and Maitland writes in the introduction that she is reluctant to dismiss this spirituality on the basis of modern tastes. She writes that the Stations emphasize the love "of a God who would undergo this painful, humiliating and drawn-out process."[46] Despite the problematic nature of this understanding of God's love, for Maitland this is a practice that is worth continuing, as a reminder of "the reality of political oppression,

43. WR, 154.
44. RL, 138.
45. VT, 176.
46. SC, 2.

physical pain and mental anguish, and Jesus' sharing in that."[47] She believes that Gollon's paintings are "a challenge to our current sensibility—which wants to be protected from too much darkness by 'quick fix' solutions."[48] Thus the paintings and stories use the traditional fourteen stations, ending with Jesus laid in his tomb, rather than including the resurrection, as in some contemporary practice; Maitland argues that an "immediate, unbroken move to a Station of the Resurrection calls into question the reality of Jesus' death. It gives, in an odd sense, credibility to the accusation that Christianity offers only an escape out of the pain of the world, rather than a profound engagement with it. Resurrection should not be easy consolation in the Church, but a longed-for renewal in the world."[49] When feminist theology wants to focus on the embodiment of the incarnation and resurrection, but not the suffering and death of the crucifixion, it makes the same mistake.

The stories (and paintings) of *Stations of the Cross* are not, however, a gratuitous and bloody celebration of pain and torture, such as Mel Gibson's 2004 *The Passion of the Christ* film, which takes high medieval iconography out of its historical context and presents it as a religious snuff movie. Rather, they relate the stuff of human experience—good, evil, complicated. In my visitation encounter with Maitland's retelling of the passion narrative, I am reminded that, whatever ill use it has been put to, the story of Christ's passion has a compelling plot and an incredibly rich array of symbols and cast of characters. The cross is much more than a vehicle of substitutionary sacrifice, or glorification of suffering: is a symbol and story through which we can explore that which is deepest and strongest; the most painful and the most wonderful.

The cross is the place from which to see the worst of humanity, the crimes we all take part in—not in the abstract theological sense in which the sins of all humanity nailed Christ to the cross, but in the real, political way that we are all complicit in injustice; the way that we can all be cowardly and sadistic. In Maitland's version, from the perspective of a Roman guard, we are told how he and others of his battalion—normal human beings—became grotesque when scourging an innocent man who would not be broken: "[i]njustice at the top leads to shame at the bottom and shame

---

47. Ibid., 3.
48. Ibid., 6.
49. Ibid., 4–5.

leads to cruelty. But we did it ourselves."⁵⁰ The Jews of Jerusalem, "forced to ask the occupying army, their conquerors, to do their dirty work for them" are ashamed and confused, "colonized and defeated" in the "dark moment, stirred up by the authorities and over-excited by Passover, they had called Caesar 'King.'"⁵¹ The daughters of Jerusalem (Luke 23:8) are not innocent mourners: they say, "[w]e are the crowd who bewailed and lamented him. Because, yes, there was madness and folly; but also there was a great sadness. He raised our hopes. . . . He made us remember and believe again, that things do not have to be like this; that God is faithful, even when we are faithless . . . There was something about him that called to us: our brother, our son, our friend and, in betraying him, we betrayed ourselves. So we wailed and lamented."⁵² After Jesus speaks to them, telling them to weep for themselves and for their children, they start to talk to one another and become friends; a feminist friendship rooted in "exploring, and arguing and talking . . . We know that sharp friendship keeps us safe from a kind of madness, and that fierce laughter gives women strength . . . We know that 'we' is a stronger word than 'I.'"⁵³

In Maitland's retelling of the sixth station, Veronica is the woman with the issue of blood from Mark 5:25–34, washing Jesus' face just as his healing enabled her to be washed at the mikvah for the first time in twelve years: "[h]e did not need to know why I had done it, he did not need to know who I was, or remember what he had done for me. It wasn't a payment of a debt, not in the last count. It was an exchange of gifts."⁵⁴ Mary forces herself to look away from her son carrying his cross, so as to not hold him back: "'[w]ho is my mother?' he had asked, and he had answered his own question, 'She who hears my words and keeps them.' It was the least I could do."⁵⁵

Being led to collect his cross, Jesus momentarily

> feels a kind of joy, and under his breath he repeats his own words, "For this I was born, for this I have come into the world." And "this" is not the pain and dark of the night; "this" is not the anguished prayers in the garden or the pointless betrayals of friends. "This" is the sunshine and the morning; the fire flash of sun on

---

50. Ibid., 17.
51. Ibid., 28.
52. Ibid., 68–69.
53. Ibid., 72.
54. Ibid., 56.
55. Ibid., 40.

polished bronze helmets, the restless pigeons rising against grey stone and blue sky . . . He cannot help smiling for the pure delight of it; for the sweetness of those years of laughter and freedom.[56]

Maitland's Christ is glad of the beauty of embodied life in the world even as he faces pain and death: the suffering is just as real, but so is the joy also. In the following section, I turn to the reality of sin and evil and its treatment in feminist theological tradition.

SIN AND EVIL

A friend of mine, a lapsed Catholic, once told me about his first confession. As a young boy, sitting in the confessional, he desperately racked his mind trying to come up with something he had done wrong, something to confess. Thinking back to a family picnic some days previously, he decided upon a behavior that could be construed as a sin: "Father, I ate too many strawberries; I had more than my fair share." At risk of reading too much into the improvised false piety of a seven-year-old child, for me that rather charming 'confession' represents the twin poles of the church's traditional teaching on sin. On one hand, "I ate too many strawberries": delighting in sensual pleasure, giving in to fleshly temptation, indulging the appetites of one's lower nature. On the other hand, "I had more than my fair share": hinting at Christianity's condemnation of injustice, of depriving others and taking what does not belong to you.

Throughout patriarchal religious discourse, women have been accused of being susceptible to the first, of being base creatures who habitually eat too many strawberries (or apples) and, what is worse, tempt righteous men to do the same. Feminist theology has squared up to the misogynist myth of women's sinfulness, exposing it for the lie that it is, while simultaneously reclaiming the sensual delights of forbidden fruit, be they apples or strawberries. Feminist revisioning of the doctrine of sin is inextricably connected to this struggle against "the very naming of women ourselves as those who bring sin and embody sin, daughters of Eve."[57] Some interpret this as feminism's replacing Eve's original sin with women's original innocence. Angela West's 1995 book, *Deadly Innocence: Feminism and the Mythology of Sin*, argues that feminist theology, in refuting age-old patriarchal

56. SC, 19.
57. McReynolds and Graff, "Sin," 169.

portrayals of women as "the devil's gateway,"[58] has presented women as blameless and ignored how women are just as capable of evil and wrongdoing as men. West draws on her experience of conflict amidst the Greenham Common peace camps, and white feminist discomfort with the challenge of women of color, to argue that "the roots of violence, anger, rage, rivalry, guilt manipulation and scapegoating—all are present in women as they are in men."[59]

West does not do justice to the complexity of feminist thought on sin, but it is a fair point that there is in feminist discourse a general tendency to present women as innocent victims. In the words of Angela Carter, "women writers are kind to women. Perhaps too kind . . . I cannot think of any woman in any work of fiction written by a woman who is taken to . . . final revelation of moral horror. We forgive; we don't judge."[60] This is an issue that Sara Maitland has contended with in her fiction; particularly in her short stories which revision mythical tales of "wicked women."

Sara Maitland's Wicked Women

Maitland's moral treatment of her source tales is intrinsic to her own understanding of her writing, and it sets her apart from other, more well-known, feminist revisionists, such as Carter: "[w]hen Angela Carter was still alive, I was complaining to her that a reviewer had compared my short stories to hers, and I said I was fed up with being sub-Angela Carter, and she laughed and said, 'You don't want to worry because we are fundamentally different. I am a 60s libertarian and you are a 70s moralist.' And I think that was a very accurate perception of hers."[61]

The moral force inherent in Maitland's writing does not result in a heavy-handed or simplistic didacticism. Rather, as Michelene Wandor writes, "it is the tension between [Maitland's] knowledge of . . . hell and the security of her cultural heritage that provides the tensions and excitement of her writing."[62] In "A Feminist Writer's Progress" Maitland explains how, writing revisionist stories according to feminist principles, she came to find that she could not remold myth and fairy tale according to idealistic beliefs

---

58. See Joseph, *Through the Devil's Gateway*.
59. West, *Deadly Innocence*, 60.
60. Carter, *Wayward Girls*, ix–x.
61. *IBB*, 105.
62. *AT*, 170.

about women. This was due to the sense that "killings and betrayals and cruelties were all there in the stories and could not be escaped." For her it was not just the challenge of the stories, but also the challenge of her own experience, that she could not rewrite these tales to become more palatable to feminist sensibilities: when writing "truly out of her own experience as a woman she had to recognize the conniving, treacherous, unloving, unlovely things that she did." It was a sense of faithfulness to the tales themselves as well to herself that resulted in Maitland's revisioning of wicked women in a way that faces up to women's capacity for evil: "[t]he Goddesses side with men and women betray their sisters and their mothers and their daughters . . . Women choose badness and madness daily and mythologically, and the Feminist Writer could not go on with her quest without telling these stories too."[63]

A number of Maitland's wicked women are motivated by revenge against men. Their reasons are just, but they go too far. One of the most memorable of these is the story of Jael from the book of Judges. Strictly speaking, Jael is not a mythical wicked woman, in that, however terrifying she may be to the male imagination, she was on the good side of the narrative, the side of God and the Israelites. Yet Maitland's explicit description of Jael's murder of Sisera does not depict her simply as an example of God exalting the lowly, or of women's cunning, as in much feminist biblical interpretation. Instead, when Jael bangs a tent peg into Sisera's skull it is a reversal of rape.[64] Maitland makes clear that not only can women be violent, they may also enjoy violence. Despite the "tenderness" she feels for him, and her admiration of his beauty, as Jael hammers the peg she takes pleasure in what she is doing: "the pointed stick no longer alien but part of her person . . . the point is finding its own pathway into the depths of the man. He groans once, unable to resist the strength behind her stroke and she has heard that groan before. She breaks through her own carefulness, becomes berserk, and long after it is necessary, bang, bang, bang, rhythmical and powerful."[65]

Jael acts out of revenge: she and Deborah "know who the enemy is" and delight in the knowledge that from now on their husbands fear them, as does "the whole victorious, manic, excited exultant army."[66] This is an

63. *FWP*, 21.
64. Duncker, *Sisters and Strangers*, 136.
65. *TT*, 2.
66. Ibid., 4.

ambiguous story, simultaneously celebrating women's solidarity against the common enemy, revealing both the power and the disturbing aspect of women's righteous anger.

Another story that explores female rage and vengefulness is "Siren Song," in which Maitland collapses two separate myths: one the Homeric description of sirens as creatures that tempt men to their deaths, the other Ovid's tale that the sirens were friends of Persephone's who became bird-like in order to look for her after she was taken by Hades.[67] Maitland's sirens speak as one, explaining how they had been entrusted with care of Persephone when Hades raped her. They became sirens in order to exact revenge on males: "we rend them with our long talons, sear them with our sharp beaks, destroy them with our bright eyes and devour them for our amusement and nourishment . . . we laugh; and for a few moments our pain is softened, our grief is comforted, our anger is slaked, our desire is fulfilled."[68] Their hands could not protect Persephone, "so we have grown talons"; they could not run fast enough, "so we have grown wings"; they learned to sing because "[t]he cold wind of his coming carried our little weak voices into nothing."[69] They argue that "we are justified when we seek vengeance; for our malice is not without cause; our cruelty is small payment for men's lust."[70] Maitland's revisioning of the sirens is similar to Ostriker's interpretation of Margaret Atwood's poem of the same name: "the female power to do evil is a direct function of her powerlessness to do anything else."[71] As such, Maitland's sirens are objects of sympathy, but they are not morally rehabilitated: they "break a man on the snares and delusions of his own heart . . . for no higher gain than the satisfaction of our own foul lusts and greeds."[72]

A particularly disturbing tale of women's revenge against men is that of Philomel and Procne, which Maitland revisions as "The Swallow and the Nightingale" in *Far North and Other Dark Tales*. It opens with these sisters giggling over a cooking pot, as they prepare the body of Procne's son to feed to her husband. Tereus cut out Philomel's tongue so she could not tell anyone that he had raped her; Procne decides that because he "had

---

67. Warner, *Beast to the Blonde*, 400-2.
68. *FN*, 148–49.
69. Ibid., 151.
70. Ibid., 155.
71. Ostriker, *Stealing the Language*, 222.
72. *FN*, 153.

cut out their words, they would make him eat his word—his dearest word, his statement to the future, his glory, his son."[73] After he has eaten his own child Procne tells him what she has done, and Philomel enters carrying the child's skull full of wine. What most characterizes Maitland's version is the callously joyous nature of the sisters, their love for each other and self-assuredness of their desires. They are neither evil witches nor passive victims, but they are not heroines either. However much feminism may approve of women loving each other more than their husbands, there are few things in western culture that make us shudder more than a mother killing her own child, let alone doing so light-heartedly.

Maitland's tendency to explore deeply rooted taboos is continued in her revisioning of Jocasta, the mother and wife of Oedipus. In myth, Jocasta is not a wicked woman but an unfortunate woman, who commits incest unknowingly and kills herself from the shame once the truth is uncovered. In Maitland's version, "Loving Oedipus," Jocasta is morally responsible; the story opens with "[o]f course I knew."[74] Yet she is not presented as an object of moral horror: her romantic love for Oedipus is tied up with maternal guilt at having abandoned him as a baby, emphasized by the repeated reference to his crippled feet: "[t]enderness was always at the root of my desire for him. Tenderness and guilt—a powerful aphrodisiac."[75] Maitland is adept at provoking the reader's empathy, and thus this story—which shows just how thin the barriers between different kinds of love can be—makes uncomfortable reading: incest is arguably just as strong a taboo today as it was in ancient Greece. As such, the reader identifies with Tiresias, who looks upon Jocasta with "love and condemnation." She agrees with him that "[i]t was wrong," but argues that "I wanted him. I needed him. Is it wrong to take what you need?" Tiresias answers, "Sometimes."[76]

Moral evil and guilt, as well as the fairy tale tradition and the taboo of child-abuse, are explored in "The Wicked Stepmother's Lament," which uses a modern voice and modern references in telling an old tale. Maitland emphasizes the role of Cinderella's dead mother in the tale, quoting the Grimm Brothers' version at the beginning of the story: "she called her only daughter to her bedside and said, 'dear child, remain pious and good, and then our dear God will always protect you, and I will look down on you from

73. Ibid., 235.
74. *BFG*, 163.
75. Ibid., 164.
76. Ibid., 172.

Suffering, Sacrifice, and Sin

heaven.'" The wicked stepmother, the narrator, is able to abuse Cinderella because she follows her mother's instructions, and the stepmother "could not believe the sweetness of that little girl and her wide-eyed belief that I would be happy and love her if she would just deny herself."[77] This story is a comment on fairy tales and female passivity: the child "invented castles in the air to which someone, though never herself, would come and take her one day."[78] Although the child, and her mother, commit the 'women's sin' of self-abnegation, and the feminist reader can identify with the narrator's desire to provoke Cinderella into fighting back and becoming powerful through anger, the stepmother is "not looking for self-justification."[79] While the origins of the abuse are explained in terms of the more severe aspects of feminist anger, in the end it is caused simply by "belly-deep madness": "I beat her ... systematically and severely ... I used her and I worked her and denied her pleasures and gave her pain."[80] This story also discusses male roles in fairy tales: the father does nothing, and "even the most silvery of princes soon goes out hunting and drinking and fighting and whoring."[81] Most of all this story is concerned with women and morality in myth: "it's more complicated, more complex than it's told, and the reasons why it's told the way it is are complex too." The narrator does not want to retell the tale so that she is not guilty: "I want to carry and cope with my own guilt, because I want to carry and cope with my own virtue and I really don't see that you can have one without the other ... I'm not willing to be a victim. I was not innocent, and I have grown out of innocence now and even of wanting to be thought innocent. Living is a harsh business ... and I feel the weight of that ancient harshness and I want to embrace it."[82]

Maitland has commented to me in conversation that there is a tendency in feminist fiction to present the female protagonist as not responsible for her shortcomings—the result of patriarchal socialization—but her overcoming of adversity is accorded to her as an achievement, a virtue. For Maitland, if women are to be regarded as full human beings, then they must own their moral failings as well as their strengths. As a writer, Maitland is comparable to her revision of Eve in the story "Choosing Paradise." Eve

77. *BSP*, 150.
78. Ibid., 151.
79. Ibid., 147.
80. Ibid., 151
81. Ibid., 150.
82. Ibid., 148.

finds that once she reaches the menopause she is able to return to Eden. Yet she chooses not to, because she does not want to go back to a state of innocence; she wants to know "what happens next." This is the same reason why she first disobeyed God years before: "she ate the apple because she was curious, because she wanted to know what would happen if she did, what would happen next. She ate the apple because the snake's slitty-eyed smile was not simple, not pure."[83] Most of Maitland's revisions of wicked women are—despite the strong sense of moral awareness—neither simple nor pure, and many are discomforting to read. Yet this is what, according to Hélène Cixous, we need our writers to do, to make us recognize that the "tales of crime" that we shiver to read are really about ourselves, "though under an assumed name, under a pseudonym . . . we are in all the Greek tragedies, which are our tragedies, except that we are not encouraged to make the connection."[84] In Maitland's writing the connection is made, the painful and necessary recognition that "the faces in mythology may be our own faces."[85]

The emphasis of feminist theology, however, has not been on the personal sin and tragedy of individuals, but our part in wider social networks of sin and injustice, and our complicity in them.

Feminist Theology of Sin

Despite the sense of 'innocence' that pervades much feminist discourse, there has in feminist theology been extensive rethinking of the doctrine of sin. For the majority of feminist theologians the emphasis is not on women's innocence, but on a different way of sinning from traditional Christian theological accounts. Angela West portrays the Saiving-Plaskow idea of "women's sin" as "a deep lack of self-worth" that amounts to innocence,[86] but this is a misrepresentation, as Rosemary Radford Ruether points out: "analysis of the difference of female sin from male sin does not mean that women are sinless, nor is it a question of essentialist natures of women and men. Rather it means taking seriously gender difference in relative power and powerlessness, and socialization into different models of identity, in

---

83. *BFG*, 160.
84. Cixous, *Three Steps*, 49.
85. Ostriker, *Stealing the Language*, 215.
86. West, *Deadly Innocence*, 82.

relation to the doing of evil. This means that women sin not only by failing to become a self, but also collaborate with male projects of evil, such as war."[87]

As the final sentence above demonstrates, the emphasis of feminist theology of sin is not self-abnegation as a personal failing, but as a political one. Feminist theology's enduring contribution to the theology of sin, influenced by Latin American liberation theology, is its analysis of sin as corporate and embedded in the structures of society, as exemplified in the concept of patriarchy. Ruether argues that sin is "never just 'individual;' there is no evil that is not relational," and that the "false individualizing" of the nature of sin, typical of "[w]hite male ethics," seeks to "evade the reality and responsibility" of social evil.[88] In the words of Marjorie Suchocki, "[s]in is not a contained act, but an extended event in an interdependent world";[89] structural sin is the result of "the unavoidably relational nature of human existence,"[90] because our world is one interconnected whole, in which all is held to together by a web of relations. The flipside of social evil is good relationality, with redemption defined as "mutuality," the restoration of "life-giving connections."[91] Ruether claims that there is "an ethics implicit in healthy biotic relationality . . . good and evil, and hence ethics, are rooted in relationality itself, life-sustaining and renewing relationality versus a distorted relationality that destroys both sides of the relationship."[92] Although I would hesitate at a definition of evil as breakdowns in mutuality (such a polite-sounding phrase seems incongruent with the appalling cruelty of acts of infanticide, gang-rape, genocide), it seems to me an obvious truth that sin is inherent in social structures; that the world's interconnection is characterized by injustice.

Feminist theology has struggled to provide an account of sin that defines where social evil ends and culpable fault begins. Mary Potter Engel distinguishes between structural evil and personal sin: evil is defined as "patterns larger than individuals . . . that tempt us toward injustice" whereas sin is "free, discrete acts of responsible individuals that create or reinforce

---

87. Ruether, Review of *Deadly Innocence*, 127.
88. Ruether, *Sexism and God-Talk*, 81.
89. Suchocki, *Fall to Violence*, 45.
90. Brock, *Journeys by Heart*, 7.
91. Grey, *Sacred Longings*, 146.
92. Ruether, "Dualism," 36.

these structures of oppression."[93] Ruether writes that sin is the sphere in which human beings make personal choices, either "enhancing life or stifling it," but she admits that "[i]t is not easy to demarcate exactly this region of culpable evil, for the boundaries of freedom and fate are fluid and have changed with the acquisition of new types of power."[94] Autonomous selfhood becomes particularly hazy when it comes to matters of social sin.

Personal responsibility is further negated by the element of bondage to sin. According to Ruether, "we are born into" the social "pattern of domination and subjugation . . . the collective, historical, inherited aspect of sin, which Christianity called 'original' sin, mistakenly seeing its inheritability as biological rather than social. It is also the aspect of sin which becomes unfreedom, a power that defines and controls us and which we feel powerless to change."[95] We might not blame Eve any more, but we are still born into sin, innately guilty. There may be "possibilities for resistance," but we are "caught and bound" within "the web of corruption."[96] Ruether admonishes us to "take up the task in each day, in each relationship, in each generation, to enhance loving, truthful and just relations, and curb and cure hate, fear and violence."[97] Yet she does not really explain just how we may go about this. Our personal choices are severely limited by our social circumstances: people living in unjust poverty are often too busy struggling to survive to take part in revolutionary activity. For the rich minority, far away from the wars, famines and droughts that the globalized capitalism from which we benefit contributes to, nearly all of our lifestyle choices will have some negative impact on the relational web, either economically, socially, or ecologically. Angela West describes minority-world women's participation in structural sin in starkly realist terms: "it is the poor who are paying for our pleasures, our needs, our sins . . . it is we who are incurring an impossible debt that we can never hope to repay."[98]

Most of my research into feminist theology of sin was undertaken during the weeks following the 2011 riots—a week in August which saw looting and violence throughout London and several other English cities. The nation was trying to understand why this happened, why so many

---

93. Engel, "Evil, Sin and Violation," 155.
94. Ruether, "Dualism," 36.
95. Ibid., 38.
96. Fulkerson, "Sexism as Original Sin," 673.
97. Ruether, "Dualism," 39.
98. West, *Deadly Innocence*, 174.

people—most of them very young—had taken to stealing, violence, and vandalizing their own communities. The response of politicians, the media and general chatter, was markedly divided between left and right. There was a public outcry for retributive justice, such as evicting perpetrators from council housing; the left argued that this would further the inequalities that contributed to the cause of the riots. Anger at wanton destruction led to racism and classism rising to the surface. The riots first broke out during a peaceful protest over the police shooting of a young black man in Tottenham. On *Newsnight*, popular historian David Starkey blamed the riots on "black" gang culture, claiming that "the problem is that the whites have become black."[99] Melanie Newton, a specialist in Caribbean history, comments that the riots are connected to the history of slavery and that Britain has failed "to acknowledge how profoundly racism and empire have poisoned the country's public life. Racist language, couched as state militarism and punishment, remains . . . available when British elites do not want to have a real discussion about their social problems. Few British elites, in our own age or in any other, want to admit that, historically, states do tend to get the forms of criminality that they deserve."[100] Listening to these debates, I felt increasingly enraged; I wanted to do something to stop my country turning on those that it has failed; I wanted to help these people who have not had my advantages in life, who have no way out of poverty and have grown up aspiring to expensive TVs and trainers but not much else. But I failed to see that there was much I could do, apart from go on protest marches, and write letters to the Prime Minister (neither of which I could muster the effort to actually do).

The August riots reminded me of my sense of powerlessness and guilt amidst social evil; they also demonstrated the complication of individual moral failings and communal and structural injustice. Social inequalities explain much of the motivation for rioting, but personal responsibility also lies with the rioters themselves. At the same time, it is difficult to situate individual responsibility amongst the actions of a mob. 'Riot', like 'violence', is an emotive word that appears simple, but bears any number of complexities. There is a huge difference between smashing in a shop window to steal a stereo, and using scaffold-poles to attack passers-by. This is something that the rioters themselves seemed to recognize: *The Guardian*'s Paul Lewis notes that, "[e]ven in the midst of the seeming immorality of rioting

99. *Newsnight*, BBC2, August 12, 2011.
100. Newton, "Accidental Rudeness."

without a cause, there were signs of a moral compass, with young men trying to rein back others they felt were going too far."[101]

As I walk to my local swimming pool, through the council estates and high-rises of Maryhill, I think of the explanations for why there were no riots in Glasgow: a difference in the gang culture; the layout of the city being such that the most deprived estates are a bus ride away from the shopping areas; the torrential rain over those few days. I rarely go through these estates—less than five minutes walk from my home—I pass through only to go swimming or pick up mail from the delivery office. Instead I spend my time in the West End—often described as 'leafy,' 'bohemian,' 'gentrified'—with its boutiques, delis and university—a university in which, as Heather Walton comments, "[y]ou can differentiate the academic staff and students from the porters and cleaners who work here, by height alone."[102] I live on the cusp of two completely different worlds. I see this in stark statistical form in the Scottish Index of Multiple Deprivation:[103] the precise area where I live is ranked low for overall deprivation, with only seven percent of the population on a low income, and only five percent unemployed. But if I walk 200 yards along the road, going north-west, I am in one of the top five percent most deprived areas in Scotland, with forty-eight percent income deprived and thirty-nine percent unemployed. If the people of Wyndford had decided to riot on Byres Road, could I have blamed them?

Living so close to such glaring inequalities serves to heighten the guilt I feel at my privilege and passive complicity in the world's evil. In the UK, universities and churches have investments in companies that sell weapons to unstable regions where children are forced to become soldiers. Our clothes are made by people working under appalling conditions for miniscule wages, prohibited from forming trade unions. We eat bananas and drink coffee grown on vast plantations in majority-world countries, using their resources for our luxuries, rather than their basic needs. The computer I type on could well have been made using minerals from mines run by armed forces that use rape as a means of control. As a product of capitalism, I tend to see myself as a consumer rather than a citizen; my part in the world is defined by what I buy. Despite my attempts to buy recycled

---

101. Lewis, "UK Riots."

102. Walton, *Imagining Theology*, 49.

103. This utilizes data on employment, income, crime, education, health and geographic mobility, using small areas (i.e. the median population is 767) to identify and relativize the "pockets of deprivation" throughout Scotland. http://www.scotland.gov.uk/Topics/Statistics/SIMD

or second-hand goods, fair trade or locally grown produce, I inevitably make purchases that contribute to corruption and violence. I am tainted. I want be forgiven, but I don't know how or by whom.

Guilt and Forgiveness

Feminist emphasis on structural sin rather than individual sin places limits on the possibility of forgiveness.[104] In the minority-world, repentance ('turning around') is nearly impossible as it is so difficult to untangle our personal responsibilities from the morass of amorphous crimes that go hand in hand with global capitalism. Yet feminist theologians tend not to pay much attention to the issue of forgiveness, blithely stating that we should forgive ourselves and others while continuing to battle against sinfully unjust social structures.[105]

Marjorie Suchocki defines forgiveness as "willing the well-being" of the violator "in the context of the fullest possible knowledge of the nature of the violation."[106] Yet, in her relational theology, the interdependency of all actions and persons means that "each is implicated in the actions of all, whether strongly or slightly."[107] This begs the question, within such a framework, who is able to forgive who? When crimes are not attributable to individual actions, nor committed against individual persons but whole societies, forgiveness cannot simply be sought from other people. Hannah Arendt claimed that it is impossible to forgive oneself, that forgiveness "depend[s] on plurality, on the presence and acting of others." Thus, trying to forgive oneself is "without reality and can signify no more than a role played before one's self."[108] We cannot own the experience of those who have been hurt by our sin, therefore trying to forgive oneself is meaningless.[109]

For some, the solution to this is to turn to God, a being higher than the sinful social structures we cannot climb out of; just as in traditional atonement theology it is God's saving work that enables forgiveness from original sin. Many feminists find the notion of a transcendent and omnipotent God irredeemable, arguing that it will necessarily "return women to dangerous

104. Carmichael, *Sin and Forgiveness*, 117.
105. For example, Ruether, "Women and Sin," 234.
106. Suchocki, *Fall to Violence*, 144.
107. Ibid., 113.
108. Arendt, *Human Condition*, 237.
109. Ibid., 243.

structures of divine domination and dependency."[110] Ruether argues that seeking forgiveness from above reduces us to "powerless sinners who can only passively receive our redemption," resulting in "a spirituality . . . of passive collaboration with the powers of violence and oppression."[111] We must rather be self-reliant in "a constant alertness to the ways in which sin is maintained in our lives."[112] Ruether's demanding approach has been criticized for failing to provide any comfort or respite. Iain Torrance responds, "I am not convinced that 'mature spirituality' will, or even should, free me from grief, hurt and anger and primordial evil."[113] Joy Ann McDougall believes that feminist theology has been premature in rejecting relationship with a transcendent personal God, arguing that "feminist theology has cut itself off from its ultimate source of hope to heal the brokenness of women's lives."[114]

For Angela West, the result of feminism's "unforgiving idealism" is a "terrible burden of self-judgment."[115] She argues that the solution is to return to traditional doctrines, to submit to God's judgment, thus enabling liberation from "the crushing burden of self-righteousness, from the burden of having to judge oneself by the ideals one has adopted."[116] The feminist liturgist Janet Morley uses the language of "burden" in one of her prayers of confession, a prayer which expresses minority world collusion in structural sin, without recourse to the language of absolution: "we lay before you / the sufferings we see on the news / the heavy loads that we impose / whether we know it or not . . . our desire to forget, our exhausting efforts to believe / that we are separate from this sin / these sufferings. / Remembering them is painful to us /The burden of them is intolerable."[117] Morley's prayer, with its talk of letting go of burdens, reminds me of Sharon Ringe's interpretation of Luke's account of Jesus' anointing by a woman, "a woman who was a sinner" (Luke 7: 36-50): "[h]er sins are already 'forgiven.' The word in Greek has the same root as the noun in 4:18, 'to proclaim release to captives.' It speaks not of a measured doling out of only the amount of pardon

110. McDougall, "Sin," 219.
111. Ruether, *Introducing Redemption*, 102.
112. Ruether, "Women and Sin," 234.
113. Torrance, "Response," 42.
114. McDougall, "Sin," 220.
115. West, *Deadly Innocence*, 135.
116. Ibid., 144.
117. Morley, *All Desires Known*, 134.

necessary to cover a specific quantity of sins, but rather of a letting go: her sins, whether many or few, have fallen away, as from open hands."[118] This model of forgiveness, as a releasing of the burden of sin, is one that enables the guilty person to own their sin, but also to let it go; to forgive themselves, amidst relating to others with love. I do not agree with Hannah Arendt, that one cannot forgive oneself; I believe that one must, to keep sane. This "letting go" does not mean passive collusion with sin; reading intertextually, I think of Mark's version of the anointing woman, of whom Jesus says, "she has done what she could" (Mark 14:8). It is important to do what we can; but as distinguished from 'doing one's best,' with its implications of a strident perfectionism that ends in failure and guilt.

Arriving here, I have had to let go of the model of forgiveness that I was raised with, and that permeates theological discourse on sin and forgiveness—the traditional forensic model, in which we are declared justified, pure, washed as white as snow. I have decided to cast away these visions of whiteness and purity. Susan Thistlethwaite's important work *Sex, Race and God* examines the challenge of black women's experience to white feminist theology. She concludes,

> I must acknowledge that women's nature is not inherently peaceful and benign but capable of tremendous violence, both overt and covert. I will not allow this insight to once again trigger white women's sense of guilt and spend the rest of my days wallowing. I must come to a forthright knowledge of good and evil, and live through the pain with both a hermeneutic of suspicion of racial privilege and a hermeneutic of the truth of white women's suffering as my tools. I don't know whether this is the best time for all white women to give up being perfect but I do know it's high time I did.[119]

Tragic Theopoetics

The work of Kathleen Sands suggests that it is through the medium of tragedy that religious feminists may learn how to be not-perfect. She argues that theology in the Christian tradition, including feminist theology, denies the reality of tragedy and persists in holding perfection to be possible. Her definition of tragedy speaks to the conflicts generated by feminist accounts

118. Ringe, *Luke*, 111.
119. Thistlethwaite; *Sex, Race and God*, 141.

of structural sin and the reality of human existence: tragedy is "irrecoverable loss and irresolvable contradiction";[120] "the moral paradox that beings who want goodness cannot remain uncontaminated by evil."[121] In Sands's thought, evil is held to have ontological existence: "[t]o pronounce something evil is to establish its existence, even while that existence is protested, resisted, refused, or terminated. Evil is not that which destroys itself but the decision to destroy; not that which is unintelligible but that which we may understand and yet refuse; not that which lacks being but the willful destruction or suppression of being."[122] She claims that, like Augustinian theodicy, feminist theology relies upon a privation theory of evil, as a distortion of what is true. For Sands, this amounts to pushing the tragic chorus off the stage of history, which does not put a stop to "irresolvable conflicts," but merely renders them invisible.[123] She believes that theology must "attend to the tragic," to "situate itself like a chorus on the heuristic edge of a community's narrative praxis."[124]

In an essay reflecting on her preaching practice, Heather Walton describes her difficulty in ending a sermon with advice on "application"—a necessary component of a good sermon, according to conventional wisdom. Influenced by feminist theology's call to do one's best for justice, in the past she would admonish her listeners "to join revolutionary social movements or, if infirmity and incapacity prevented this, to at least spend every spare moment sending letters to MPs, befriending refugees and opening their doors to the homeless." Looking back, she compares this approach to Solomon's judgment (1 Kings 3:16–27), instructing the two mothers to cut the surviving baby in half: "Solomon wants to do what many preachers want to do and that is to make a quick, clear judgment that resolves the situation and removes from himself all the guilt of association. He wishes to make a strong, clean cut rather than tend a weeping wound. When I picture the judgment scene it brings to my mind all the violent horror of innocent faith."[125]

For Walton and Sands, feminist theology should focus its energies on attending to real and present wounds, rather than trying to cut away our

120. Sands, *Escape from Paradise*, 2.
121. Ibid., 65.
122. Ibid., 8.
123. Ibid., 7.
124. Ibid., 13.
125. Walton, *Imagining Theology*, 72.

complicity in evil in the pursuit of perfection. The better part for theology is, like a tragic chorus, to give utterance to the pain of the world as it is; to relinquish the shining, white vision of purity, to "learn to think good and evil in the wild and colored world from which the possibility of tragedy can never be expelled."[126] Sands's writing hinges on the image of escape from paradise; Maitland's version of Eve chooses not to return, to stay in the outside world where things are "not simple, not pure."[127] This means "learn[ing] to do without the closure of absolutes" and thus "to weave more artfully the multicolored threads... Out here, beyond the walls of paradise" where the colors are harder to match, but also much more bright.[128]

126. Sands, *Escape from Paradise*, 38.
127. *BFG*, 160.
128. Sands, *Escape from Paradise*, 168.

5

Sex and the Sacred

When I was about eighteen, the PJ Harvey album *To Bring You My Love* spent much time on my Walkman during the bus journey to school. Even at the time, it struck me that the lyrics, with allusions of gothic romance and religious mysticism, seemed to describe the torments and joys of how I related to God in a way far more truthful and powerful than anything from the evangelical subculture that I was part of. I recognized, in the rattlesnake percussion and PJ Harvey's low growl that shifts in an instant to an angelic sigh, that dark, divine figure to whom I would cry out in rage and turmoil.

A couple of years previously, a friend of mine had become a Christian, and I started going to church with her occasionally. One morning the sermon was on Num 25:1–16. I was horrified not only by the story but by the enthusiasm with which the pastor rhythmically declared how God praised Phineas for his zeal in bringing down the spear through the Israelite man and Midianite woman "as they were having sex together," but was intrigued that my moral horror did not outweigh my increasing attraction to Christianity. And so that evening, smoking a cigarette under the cherry tree at the bottom of the garden, I asked God to come back to me.

In the few years following that moment, I channeled the passions and confusions inherent in being a teenager into religious devotion, which, as part of a charismatic church, took a form both expressly physical and romantic. We would pray for experiences such as being knocked bodily to the floor and shaken by the power of the Holy Spirit. We would sing worship songs that were essentially love songs directed to God. What compounded this way of relating to God was that those of us who were not married were not allowed any other outlets for erotic expression. We were supposed to be 'on fire' for God alone, not for anybody else. The problem was that God was not often immediately or obviously responsive, and I found many aspects of 'bible-believing' Christianity very distressing. I was deeply upset by the texts which told of a jealous God who demanded exclusive submission and devotion, and anything less was deserving of punishment; at the same time I was sustained by the unconditional love I read in texts such as Rom 5:8 or John 13–17. I now regard my desperate attempts to suppress or reconcile the conflicting elements within the Bible, and between scriptural texts and my own convictions, as a "doing violence" to myself.[1] As a sensitive teenage girl, I found myself caught in "this passion of the body wrenching itself,"[2] trying to reshape myself into the sort of person I believed that God demanded I be, for the sake of those moments of acceptance, of being held in God's love, feeling my self and all my torments evaporate. But the costs of these instances of grace far outweighed the benefits of that perpetual sense of unrequited love: by the age of eighteen, listening to PJ Harvey, I was starting to realize this.

These days it seems like a long time since I related to God in that way. But I maintain a certain nostalgia for that tormented desire, that yearning after the peace, the finality, of Polly Harvey's orgasmic roar. As a feminist, this is something of a guilty secret, something to confess to in hushed tones: that I sometimes miss the intensity of envisioning God as a lover, that I miss losing myself in the raptures of intense faith.

I have considered the tension between feminist calls to autonomous selfhood and relationality; I have also discussed how, when confronted by the suffering body, feminist faith in the body's sacredness seems to falter. Both these issues come into play—alongside the violence of Christian symbolism—with the central argument of this chapter: that, in its emphasis on the spiritual value of erotic experience, feminist theology has perhaps neglected the dangerous and frightening aspects of spirituality and sexuality, both aspects of human existence found in life's excesses and extremes.

Eros and Vulnerability in Feminist Theology

Power and Submission

A sense of feminist shame at one's prayerful urges may be read in some recent writings by feminist theologians. In 2008, the *Journal of Feminist*

---

1. Farley, "Feminist Consciousness," 43.
2. Kristeva, *Tales of Love*, 166.

Studies in Religion featured a roundtable discussion on "mysticism and feminist spirituality," in which Mary Potter Engel's contribution gives an example of religious feminists experiencing a conflict between their ideals and their spiritual desires. Engel's article explores her attempts to reconcile her feminist convictions with the mystical calling to be "no-self." A convert to Judaism, she was challenged by kabbalistic writings that propound a nullification of the self: "[t]his language, typical of mystics, was anathema to me—in spite of assurances that to be a 'vehicle of sanctity' is to know 'the joy of release from the self.' Alert to sexism's submersion of women's selves in the 'common' good and intent on becoming a free and empowered self, I found all talk of vehicles and nullification of self just one more turn of the patriarchal screw."[3] Engel's had been the typical feminist quest,[4] in which she moved away from the self-abnegation that Dutch Calvinism requires of its adherents and society demands of women, towards the achievement of a whole and autonomous self. However, her spiritual journey then took another course, with Engel coming to believe that "to lose the self in surrender to the unknown, is to wake up in earnest and live in joy" and that the self that she had worked so hard to achieve, despite having once been a "worthy goal," was now getting in the way of her religious path.[5]

The questioning of this dichotomy as regards spiritual practice is a major theme of Sarah Coakley's book *Powers and Submissions*. The book brings together Coakley's essays written over a number of years, through all of which runs a common thread: the assertion that, for Christian feminists, "the apparently forced choice between dependent 'vulnerability' and liberative 'power' is a false one." Coakley acknowledges the feminist critique of the valorization of submission and vulnerability in twentieth-century kenotic Christologies, concurring that such theologies may be the result of privileged male theologians "wallowing" in their own guilty social consciences. These may reinforce, in the form of doctrine, "the sexual, physical and emotional abuse that feminism seeks to expose."[6] Yet Coakley questions the assertion of feminist theologians, such as Daphne Hampson,[7] that the paradigm of Christ's self-emptying can only ever be harmful for women, suggesting that to hold up "autonomy" as "supreme good" may be the sort

---

3. Engel, "No-Self and the Calling," 144.
4. See Christ, *Diving Deep*.
5. Engel, "No-Self and the Calling," 153.
6. Coakley, *Powers and Submissions*, xv.
7. See Hampson, *Theology and Feminism*.

of mistake to which Christian feminism can offer its secular counterpart an alternative.[8] Like that of Engel, Coakley's critique of the post-Saiving valorization of autonomy is distinguished by an emphasis that, while politically informed, is more spiritual than social. Her interest lies in the paradox of experiencing empowerment in the vulnerability inherent in contemplative prayer. Coakley describes wordless prayer as the making of "the 'space' in which non-coercive divine power manifests itself."[9] As such, it is a form of vulnerability that is not an invitation to suffering or to the abnegation of the self, but rather "the place of the self's transformation and expansion into God."[10] Nevertheless, there is an element of risk to such self-opening to the divine, to the disarming of the self before the unconscious and before God, yet, for Coakley, this is a gamble worth making.[11]

Coakley nevertheless argues that one should only yield to the temptations of dependence as regards encounter with God. While she does recognize that it is not possible to draw a complete distinction between the spiritual and other aspects of life, she argues that feminism should differentiate between dependence in prayer and in the personal and political, if only to make one aware "how easily one fades into another, how the infinitely subtle and obscure operation of the divine on the dependent creature is entwined with the deepest hopes and fears about family relationships, about sexuality, power and death."[12] This reference to sexuality, along with the allusion to sexual practices that may be read in the title *Powers and Submissions*, contributes to the sense that the delights of opening the self up to God are somehow erotic. This is compounded by her terminology when claiming that the tension inherent in seeking submission in contemplation, while knowing it to be dangerous in relationships between persons, is "an appropriate reminder that our prayer is enfleshed."[13] Coakley writes of the yearnings of the Christian feminist who "experiences the tug of the dependent heart on the divine,"[14] making submission to the divine in prayer seem like an illicit object of desire; something that women want but feel that they ought not to want. Yet Coakley does not expand on the relationship

8. Coakley, *Powers and Submissions*, 3–5.
9. Ibid., 5.
10. Ibid., 36.
11. Ibid., 35.
12. Ibid., 57.
13. Ibid., 68.
14. Ibid., 56.

between vulnerability in sex and in spirituality, and discusses submission in prayer as something quite distinct from the interplay of power, pain and pleasure in sexual desire.

This, however, is intimated in Yvonne Sherwood's 2006 essay, "Passion—Binding—Passion," which suggests that a sadomasochistic tendency can be read in the relationship between God and humankind in the Hebrew Bible. Sherwood writes of her "discomfort" at where the essay has moved to, "somewhere between the cultural taboo about s/m, the last bastion of perversion, and the exacerbating taboo about imposing that on, of all things, the Bible." After years of feminist critique of the violence inherent in many of the biblical texts—a topic that has become almost tediously familiar, albeit necessary—Sherwood wonders if her discomfort here "is not so much about *s* but *m*?"[15] The desire to lay aside "the modern gift of autonomy, self-determination and pure subjecthood"[16] seems somehow scandalous, and yet "the more conflicted sites of crucifixion and Akedah may yet continue to exert a deeper pull on the imagination than the theologies of, say, God as a friend."[17] However, Sherwood argues that an attempt to honestly examine masochistic spiritual urges "would have to go very carefully so that it did not emerge as a nonreflective celebration of the shattering effects of danger."[18] At the same time, she agrees with Anita Phillips that "a strong, self-confident, humorous, flexible feminism can incorporate self-contradiction, where a more tremulous, immature version remains fundamentalist and univocal, even oddly self-mutilating."[19]

In this chapter, tracing the three-stranded plait of sexuality, spirituality, and self-negation in the symbolism of mysticism, the debates of feminist theologians, and the writing of Michèle Roberts and Sara Maitland, I am with Phillips in not wishing to practice a "fundamentalist" or "self-mutilating" kind of feminism that denies the complex and difficult reality of our sexual and spiritual desires. However, reading Phillips's book *A Defence of Masochism* leaves me troubled; I am not sure that fantasies of rape and dismemberment have any place in a "humorous, flexible feminism." This is not just because those self-assured, professional women with masochistic tendencies, "whom feminism has served best, whose self-assertion has mostly

15. Sherwood, "Passion," 186, emphasis in original.
16. Ibid., 186.
17. Ibid., 190.
18. Ibid., 188.
19. Phillips, *Defence of Masochism*, 55.

been achieved,"[20] should not be fantasizing about a victimization that so many women have no choice over, but also because it perpetuates a certain sort of view of the world that I consider to be morally and aesthetically horrendous. I cannot bear to make myself read even synopses of de Sade or *The Story of O*; they make me feel violated rather than merely discomforted.

Kathleen Sands notes that the "sex wars" that have so divided the feminist movement—a liberal "pro-sex" stance as opposed to the more morally and politically idealistic battle against prostitution and pornography of "radical feminism"—have been paid relatively little attention in feminist theology,[21] but I think that these "sex wars" are echoed in the debates about erotic asceticism in feminist theology. It seems much more glamorous to be on the exotic, naughty side of the fence, in which hinting about one's self-shattering experiences of contemplative prayer takes on the aura of wearing leather stiletto boots. With theologians such as Engel and Coakley talking about wanting something from prayer that feminism says they should not want—and, in Engel's case, being reprimanded by figures such as Carol Christ[22]—and if self-abnegation is the new sin, then, being transgressive, it becomes a turn-on. If eroticism and mysticism are characterized by the desire for loss of self, then good feminists should not want either. Yet some do want both—to lose the self they have worked so hard to develop, to surrender the autonomy they have fought for—and, due to radical feminist ideals, feel very ambivalent about it. Hence I find helpful the way that Michèle Roberts and Sara Maitland explore the complicated interplay of sexuality, religion, and masochism: ambiguous, self-doubting, sometimes dangerous, and sometimes hopeful.

"Deepest, Strongest, Richest": Feminist Eros

It is arguable that, in the language of feminist theology, it is wrong to speak of the yearning to lose oneself in submission to the other as 'erotic,' because 'eros' is a force for empowerment and delight, rather than self-negation. In the reclaiming of women's bodies and sexuality from misogynist demonizing, the erotic becomes synonymous with the yearning for mutuality and justice, a life-giving power, rather than the self-serving desire of Anders Nygren's characterization. One of the more influential and oft-quoted

20. Ibid.
21. Sands, "Uses of the Thea(o)logian," 9.
22. Christ, "Embodied Embedded Mysticism."

spiritual feminist appropriations of the concept of the erotic is that of Audre Lorde, in "Uses of the Erotic: The Erotic as Power." She defines it thus: "eros, the personification of love in all its aspects—born of Chaos, and personifying creative power and harmony. When I speak of the erotic, then, I speak of it as an assertion of the life force of women; of that creative energy empowered, the knowledge and use of which we are now reclaiming in our language, our history, our dancing, our loving, our work, our lives."[23] Erotic experience—found not only in sex but also in other instances of joy and connection—may be "a replenishing and provocative force to the woman who does not fear its revelation."[24] As such, "the erotic—the sensual—those physical, emotional, and psychic expressions of what is deepest and strongest and richest within each of us" creates a bridge between the spiritual and the political.[25] The knowledge of the erotic demands that one "not settle for the convenient, the shoddy, the conventionally expected, nor the merely safe."[26]

This powerful and compelling account of experience of the divine in deeply felt and shared joy has, and I think rightly, held an important place in feminist theology. So too has Lorde's vehement distinction between the erotic and the pornographic, described as "two diametrically opposed uses of the sexual."[27] The pornographic is "a direct denial of the power of the erotic, for it represents the suppression of true feeling,"[28] and it is the confusion of the two that has led women "to distrust that power which rises from our deepest and nonrational knowledge."[29]

Carter Heyward developed Lorde's concept of "the erotic as power" within a more theological, Christian, framework. This went on to have tremendous influence on other feminist theologians such as Rita Nakashima Brock and Mary Grey. Heyward's *Touching Our Strength* is a sustained attempt to "give voice to an embodied—sensual—relational movement" in which sexuality is experienced "as a liberating resource," including strength "in the struggle for justice for all."[30] As such, Heyward's construction of

23. Lorde, "Uses of the Erotic," 210.
24. Ibid., 208.
25. Ibid., 210.
26. Ibid., 211.
27. Ibid., 210.
28. Ibid., 209.
29. Ibid., 208.
30. Heyward, *Touching Our Strength*, 3.

Sex and the Sacred

the erotic is more associated with sex than is Lorde's, and also more explicitly with political struggle: "[l]ovemaking turns us simultaneously into ourselves and beyond ourselves. In experiencing the depths of our power in relation as pleasurable and good, we catch a glimpse of the power of right relation in larger, more complicated configurations of our life together. Good sex involves us more fully in the struggle for justice."[31] Heyward's thought on mutuality and right relation comes to bear on the revelatory quality of erotic experience, for it is in "our sensual and sexual yearnings" that we become open "to sacred movement between and among ourselves."[32] It is in this that "we come to know God,"[33] in "the divine Spirit's yearning, through our bodyselves, toward mutually empowering relation, which is our most fully embodied experience of God as love."[34]

This feminist theological concept of the erotic as spiritual power is a theme of Michèle Roberts's *The Wild Girl*, in which Mary Magdalene has transcendent experiences in her lovemaking with Jesus, described in just as idealized and breathy tones as Heyward's theology:

> As we drew closer and closer towards each other we entered a new place, a country of heat and sweetness and light different to the ground we had explored together before. I felt us taken upwards and transformed: I no longer knew what was inside and what was outside, where he ended and I began, only that our bones and flesh and souls were suddenly woven up together in a great melting and pouring . . . no longer an I, but part of a great whirl of light that throbbed and rang with music–for a moment, till I was pulled back by the sound of my own voice whispering words I did not understand: this is the resurrection, and the life.[35]

In Roberts and Heyward's writing, sex may dissolve the boundaries between self and other, in the midst of divine erotic that "blesses" with "transcendence and immanence."[36]

Heyward does take into account the problematic aspects of the erotic crossing and dissolving of the self's boundaries: she accepts the feminist dictate that "[w]omen have never had a socially established, religiously

---

31. Ibid., 4.
32. Ibid., 22.
33. Ibid., 94.
34. Ibid., 99.
35. *WG*, 67.
36. Heyward, *Touching Our Strength*, 113.

affirmed, physically safe, or emotionally secure sense of our own body integrity"[37] and that "[w]ithout a boundaried sense of ourselves, we are likely to experience sexual energy as a rush into which we simply get sucked and swallowed up."[38] It is the significance of boundaries that makes their dissolution so powerful and profound. As part of her relational worldview, Heyward suggests that boundaries should be established with rather than against one another: "[m]y boundaries are not simply mine. They are between us, our boundaries, just as your boundaries are also ours, in the context of our relationship. There is probably no greater relational capacity than to learn, with one another, how to negotiate our boundaries."[39]

She pays considerable attention to the issue of sadomasochistic sexuality, treating it as part of a wider "social structure of alienated power" in which "people learn to accept, as natural and even as enjoyable, possessing (sadistic) power-over or (masochistic) power-under others."[40] While this is a distortion of the true eros, in Heyward's thought there is the acknowledgement that sexual desires and relationships are complicated, that the 'good' yearning for mutuality is mixed up with the 'bad' masochistic tendencies: "[w]e cannot make ourselves 'feel mutual' in perfect, constant, or unambivalent ways in a social order fastened in alienated power." Yet in her—ultimately eschatological—worldview, there is an upward movement away from masochism and towards mutuality, "in which the energy for domination/submission is transformed erotically into power for sharing."[41] In Heyward's theology, therefore, a distinction is drawn between the masochistic urges towards loss of self, and the erotic yearnings for the blurred boundaries between self and other.

I do not believe that such distinctions can be drawn, at least not in any final sense. We may be able to evaluate particular moments as fulfilling, and others as self-destructive, but this is an ongoing process, moving back and forth rather than onwards and upwards. Three compelling articles by feminist theologians make just this point, critiquing Heyward's purist notion of the erotic: Kathleen Sands, "Uses of the Thea(o)logian: Sex and Theodicy in Religious Feminism," K. Roberts Skerrett, "When No Means Yes: The Passion of Carter Heyward," and Alyda Faber, "Eros and Violence."

37. Ibid., 25.
38. Ibid., 110.
39. Ibid., 113.
40. Ibid., 105.
41. Ibid., 106.

Kathleen Sands argues that feminist theological constructions of eros as an inherent good, an end in itself, are part of its anti-tragic direction. Eros is presented as a transcendent ideal, one that will ultimately rise above its perversions in prostitution, pornography and abuse, rather than an aspect of life whose moral good or otherwise is vulnerable to forces beyond our control. Sands suggests that feminist defense of eros often seems to take the place of theodicy in traditional theology, with eros, like God, having real existence, whereas sadomasochistic sexuality, like evil in Augustinian theodicy, is a lack and a distortion of the true eros. Sands proposes that instead what is needed is "a fine-tuned perceptiveness about the varied and sometimes opposing forces that comprise our actual sexual lives, and creative strategies for balancing or transforming those forces."[42] She writes,

> Sex, it seems to me, is best understood as an elemental power which can carry a variety of goods but which is fundamentally characterized by intensity. Cruelty, betrayal, and humiliation all evoke intense responses, and these responses are easily sexualized . . . to suppress this moral danger entirely is to deprive consciousness of the energy and illumination of elemental power. In relation to sexual theology, this means that we must honor eros as an elemental power, and recognize that precisely as such it calls for moral discernment and choice.[43]

Sands neglects the fact that sex is sometimes comic rather than tragic, characterized not so much by "intensity" as by tedium, silliness or affectionate familiarity. However, noting that sex—like prayer—can be boring or funny, as well as earth-shattering, is in line with Sands's project of attending to "our actual sexual lives," and not a transcendent ideal of eros.

This is continued in K. Roberts Skerrett's 1996 article, which places the assertion that "[i]dealizations of erotic relation prevent us from taking seriously the potential for conflict and suffering"[44] in the context of the "actual life" conflict that Carter Heyward had with her therapist, and wrote about in her 1995 book, *When Boundaries Betray Us*. It tells how Heyward believed that she and her therapist had an erotic connection, and thus wanted to pursue a friendship with her, which, on grounds of professional boundaries, the therapist declined. Heyward theorizes her therapist's repeated rejection of a relationship with her as a symbol of a "patriarchal

42. Sands, "Uses of the Thea(o)logian," 8.
43. Ibid., 14.
44. Skerrett, "When No Means Yes," 72.

social order founded on dynamics of nonmutual, fear-based control."[45] For Skerrett—and indeed for me—the way that Heyward uses her theology to justify her refusal to accept another woman's "no" calls that theology itself into question. It highlights that Heyward's view of eros as a transcendent ideal means that eros is given priority over respect for the wishes of the other, and the very notion of a woman's right to say for herself what she does and does not want is dismissed as remaining beholden to "unexamined liberal capitalist values."[46] In an ideal world, we could construct our boundaries together, as Heyward wishes, but we live in a world in which goods are often conflicting, and, in this case, the good of one person's love for another came to conflict with the good of the other's personal and professional boundaries. Skerrett argues that such a "tragic view of eros" does not entail a denial of eros, but rather "a practical wisdom"[47] that recognizes that "[r]enunciation—bearing the no of the beloved—is not antisensual asceticism: it is one of the positive disciplines of love."[48] It seems to me that Heyward's account of her relationship with her therapist shows how entwined our 'good' and 'bad' erotic and sexual yearnings are; how, even for the best-intentioned of people, the care for and sense of connection with another can become confused with violation of boundaries and power struggles.

Alyda Faber's article draws on Sands's observations on the feminist idealization of eros as 'natural,' as opposed to its 'social' patriarchal distortions, in a critique of Rita Nakashima Brock and Susan Brooks Thistlethwaite's *Casting Stones: Liberation and Prostitution in Asia and the United States*. In their examination of the horrific abuses of the sex industry, Brock and Thistlethwaite are "attentive to the suffering body" of prostitutes and other victims of the violent social order, but in their continued defense of what Faber terms "essentialist eros" they are reliant on "a kind of resurrected body awakened to its erotic splendor."[49] In Faber's analysis, the notion of eros in the theology of Heyward, Brock, and Thistlethwaite is "not socially constructed; it has profound and durable roots in the body, extending beyond the body's mortality into a mystical net of connection in process." In contrast, violent and abusive forms of sexuality are "fabrica-

45. Ibid., 78.
46. Ibid., 83.
47. Ibid., 90.
48. Ibid., 91.
49. Faber, "Eros and Violence," 332.

tions and dissimulations of what is real,"⁵⁰ what is natural and "prior to culture's impositions."⁵¹

I do not share the faith of feminist theologians, such as Heyward, Brock and Thistlethwaite, in a pre-social, transcultural eros. I think that, for good or ill, our ways of loving, of suffering, of desiring and hurting others are formed within embodied selves that are resolutely part of the cultural world we are born into and within which we become subjects. Our sexualities develop in a world that is shot through with patriarchy and violence; but some argue that this is not the only reason for the way that erotic relationships are marked by patterns of domination and submission. Rather, it goes back to the very process of becoming a subject.

"Batter My Heart": Unsafe Eros and Asceticism

Masochism and Religion

Jessica Benjamin argues that feminist analysis of women's masochism ought to seek to understand its roots, rather than take up a stance of moral condemnation, for "no political movement can give expression to our real hopes and longing if it condemns without understanding the alienated forms in which these longings have appeared."⁵² She discusses how "the fantasy of erotic domination" originates in the "earliest issues of intimacy and separation in infancy,"⁵³ in the process of differentiation and coming to recognize one's existence as a separate self and, in turn, the existence of others. Erotic masochism is rooted in the struggle for "recognition of the self by an other who alone is powerful enough to bestow this recognition."⁵⁴ The desire for the loss of self that is discernible in eroticism—undeniably so, according to Georges Bataille⁵⁵—is due to its relation to the transgressing "of the most fundamental taboo, that separating life from death," for "in death, not life, each individual is united with the rest, sunk back into the sea of nondifferentiation."⁵⁶ Benjamin relates Bataille's thought on the "psychic

50. Ibid., 340.
51. Ibid., 341.
52. Benjamin, "Master and Slave," 308.
53. Ibid., 292.
54. Ibid., 298.
55. Burrus, *Sex Lives*, 7.
56. Benjamin, "Master and Slave," 296.

death" of eroticism to the desire to return to the womb, to be reunited with the body of the mother.

Modern western culture's obsession with eroticism, and the ritualized forms of domination and submission in S/M sexual practices are read by Benjamin as being the "the heir to religious eroticism."[57] This is not just in the clichéd motifs of sexually rapacious nuns, crucifixion fantasies and Madonna's "Like a Prayer" video, but also in the sense that sadomasochistic eroticism is representative of "the same need for transference of self—the same flight from separation and discontinuity—formerly satisfied and expressed by religion."[58] In particular, the writings and practices of the mystics, especially those of a more ascetic bent, have striking parallels with masochistic eroticism.

Mysticism and Erotic Masochism

The interplay of the erotic and the ascetic has been a dominant theme in recent scholarship, although this may come as a surprise to the uninformed observer. The popular conception, as Virginia Burrus characterizes, is that "the repression of erotic desire is the hallmark of Christian sanctity: a 'sex life' is precisely what a proper saint lacks. At most, ascetic eros—encoded as yearning for God—may be seen as the residue of an imperfectly sublimated sexuality. Better yet: it is a merely metaphorical expression for a purely desexualized love. Worse still: it reflects pleasure from practices of self-denial rooted in a pathological hatred of the body."[59] To the contrary, sexual motifs abound in the mystical tradition: in analogies of the soul's loving relationship to God (thought to be allegorized in the Song of Songs), virgin nuns' marriage to Christ, and the imagery of rapture in prayer.

The influential work of Caroline Walker Bynum has done much to dispel the view that ascetic practices in the late medieval period stemmed from a dualistic hatred of the flesh. Rather, acts such as fasting and flagellating "should be interpreted more as elaborate changes rung upon the possibilities provided by fleshliness than as flights from physicality,"[60] expressive of "the *experiencing* of body more than the *controlling* of it."[61] Bynum has

57. Ibid., 307.
58. Ibid.
59. Burrus, *Sex Lives*, 1.
60. Bynum, *Holy Feast*, 6.
61. Ibid., 245, emphasis in original.

been keen to stress, however, that in high medieval piety, the focus on the body is not sexual in the way that it would be today: fleshliness was more associated with food and fecundity than with eroticism. Bynum's motivations for arguing thus are feminist as well as historical, going against the excesses of post-Freudian interpretations of mystics (in particular the female ones) as being expressive of repressed sexuality. A notable example of this is Jacques Lacan's comment on Teresa of Avila: "you only have to go look at the Bernini statue in Rome to understand immediately she's coming." Luce Irigaray makes the point that one could always read Teresa's own words on the matter, rather than go all the way to Rome to look at a statue made by a man.[62]

Bynum's argument against eroticized interpretations of medieval mysticism stands as a corrective to the first of the caricatures of ascetic eros as identified by Burrus, one that fails to take mystical women writers seriously and undermines the range and complexity of the symbols and metaphors they employ. Yet to do so, to refuse eroticism at every turn, often necessitates a very strange reading of the patently obvious:

> the insistent nuptial imagery of mystical marriage, including the semi-naked Bridegroom who offers and receives caresses, the brides who forfeit their virginity in Christ's heavenly bedchamber, and the burning love described by mystics who incorporate Christ's body. One would also have to ignore, neutralize or apologize for the innumerable beatas, nuns and female saints who report having kissed Christ on his mouth and body, who strip naked before the crucifix, who drink from Christ's wound as though it were a breast.[63]

Bynum's intentions may be implicitly feminist, but, as Karma Lochrie and Amy Hollywood have pointed out, they are also somewhat heteronormative.[64] Bynum's important work on the ways in which Christ's body was imaged as female in medieval mysticism is taken by her to preclude an erotic interpretation, and thus is a "refusal to see same-sex desire as potentially sexual."[65] For Lochrie and Hollywood, it is the feminine nature of Christ's body—as elucidated by Bynum's work—and particularly the associations

---

62. Canters and Jantzen, *Forever Fluid*, 49.
63. Graziano, *Wounds of Love*, 10.
64. Hollywood, "Sexual Desire," and Lochrie, "Mystical Acts."
65. Hollywood, "Sexual Desire," 165.

of drinking from the wound in his side, that "queers" women mystics' devotion.

In this way, the presence of same-sex desire and the fluidity of gender in the symbolism of mystic ascetic practice, has led to its enthusiastic appropriation by contemporary queer theory and theology. For example, in the introduction to his edited volume, *Queer Theology*, Gerard Loughlin writes, "Jesus: a lover who does not distinguish between the sex of his brides; who welcomes all alike. Christ is the lover of both Teresa of Avila and St John of the Cross. And he is a lover whose own sex is less than stable; since as Jesus he is man, but as Christ woman also."[66] Transgressive of dominant social mores such as heterosexism, mystical symbolism is a resource for both queer and feminist alike. The embodied nature of mystical writings and practices may be more attractive to feminist spirituality than modern theology's tendency to conceive of relation to God in immaterial, rational terms. As Loughlin writes elsewhere, "even as it surpasses the pleasures of the flesh," medieval mysticism "always returns to the body; to the meeting, biting, engulfing of lips and tongues, to that fateful opening verse from the Song of Songs that resounds throughout medieval theological erotica: 'Let him kiss me with the kisses of his mouth!'"[67] This is also the case for the more clearly dualistic attitudes of the ascetics of antiquity, in that "resistance to the temptations of "worldly" eroticism" becomes "an exuberant art of eroticism in which the negativity harbored within resistance is eclipsed by the radical affirmation of desire also conveyed in resistance."[68]

While queer theology has enthusiastically used the erotic symbolism of mystic ascetic practice, feminist analysis may be more ambivalent. The subversion of gender, both of the mystic and the divine object of their eros, may be valuable from a third wave feminist and queer perspective, but the violent imagery and extreme submission of some mystical writings are very problematic from a liberal or radical feminist standpoint. For example, it is difficult for a feminist to delight in John Donne's "Batter my Heart" sonnet, however 'queer' it may be, and the same goes for the writings of female mystics. I agree with Ann Loades that many of the metaphors of certain mystical writings are "monstrous images by which to conceive of the deity's dealings with human creatures."[69] I find horrific Bynum's quiet comment

66. Loughlin, "Introduction," 7.
67. Loughlin, *Alien Sex*, 12.
68. Burrus, *Sex Lives*, 14.
69. Loades, *Searching for Lost Coins*, 48.

that "[r]eading the lives of fourteenth- and fifteenth-century women saints greatly expands one's knowledge of Latin synonyms for whip, thong, flail, chain etc."[70] Julie Miller goes so far as to argue in her essay "Rapt by God" that mystic metaphors of God's rape of the soul have "contributed to the eroticization of dominance and subordination, and hence, to the eroticization of violence against women."[71] I would counter that it is important to distinguish between metaphors of ravishing and metaphors of rape, and in the writing of mystics such as Teresa of Avila, the description of the intense pain and pleasure of being "rapt by God" are very different indeed from testimonies of the trauma of rape. Yet they are reminiscent of that certain kind of eroticism, of passivity, submission and pain, and this is an element of sexuality which radical feminism has been vehemently opposed to. Hadewijch's description of the seventh name of divine Love—Hell—is a brilliant evocation of the torment of agonized erotic love, but not the sort of love that feminists usually approve of: "there is nothing Love does not engulf and damn, / And no one who falls into her / And whom she seizes comes out again /. . . / Forever to be in unrest / Forever assault and new persecution; / To be wholly devoured and engulfed / In her unfathomable essence, /. . . / To the deep, insurmountable darkness of Love."[72] As Lochrie writes, "[m]ystical sex is not just 'sex as we know it,' but that more troubling field of experience that strays into the realms of violence, suffering and torture."[73]

The literature of Michèle Roberts and Sara Maitland traverses this "troubling field" in an unwaveringly erotic way, but while maintaining a critical feminist voice.

Spiritual Masochism in Michèle Roberts and Sara Maitland

Michèle Roberts

Women's shame at their femaleness and sexuality is a significant theme of Roberts's earliest novels, but it is in *The Book of Mrs Noah* and *Impossible*

---

70. Bynum, *Holy Feast*, 210.
71. Miller, "Rapt by God," 235.
72. Hadewijch, *Hadewijch*, 356.
73. Lochrie, "Mystical Acts," 183.

Saints that the link between sexual shame and religious asceticism takes a central role. In the latter, the tale of Josephine, a fictional saint comparable to Teresa of Avila, is interspersed with darkly comic retellings of the lives of some of the female saints found in *The Golden Legend*. The novel as a whole is a comment on hagiography and women's place in history and storytelling, on how female saints are usually virgins who have tragic deaths; *Impossible Saints* could well be marketed with a wry comment of Virginia Burrus as its tagline: "[a] woman, it seems, must die in order to get a *Life*."[74]

This is particularly appropriate to the first of Roberts's revisionist hagiographies, that of Saint Paula, a protégé of Jerome, and of her daughters Julia Eustochium and Blesilla, based on Jerome's writing about them. When the story opens, Blessilla is a young woman who enjoys sensuality, "having her hair done, and going to the baths for the afternoon, and lying in bed making love with her young husband."[75] After she is suddenly widowed, in her grief, and under Jerome's influence, Blesilla starts to think that it is her fault that her husband died: that she tired him out with her sexual demands. She follows her mother's example and obeys Jerome's instruction, pouring her love for her husband into asceticism, wearing a hair shirt, cutting her hair, and fasting.

In the fourth-century church, the only way women could "transcend their unfortunate sexuality and free themselves from their corporeal shackles"[76] was to maintain their virginity, which came to have an obsessive significance for Fathers such as Ambrose, Jerome and Augustine. The ideal of celibacy had its origins in "a prophetic radicalism," a church with "one foot in eternity,"[77] and many women would have been liberated from the social expectations of marriage and family by the religious status of virgin. Yet by the time of Jerome it was used by men to reinforce the gender hierarchy.[78] In the novel, Jerome has told Blesilla's younger sister Eustochium that, as a virgin, she is superior to her mother and sister: "[y]our crown, my dear, will be the brightest. You are the flower of the women in your family."[79] The shame of not being a virgin torments Blesilla, and she wishes she could regain that status.

74. Burrus, *Sex Lives*, 12.
75. *IS*, 22.
76. Schulenberg, "Heroics of Virginity," 31.
77. Furlong, *Visions and Longings*, 11-12.
78. See Burrus, "Word and Flesh"; Ruether, "Asceticism and Feminism"; and Schulenberg, "Heroics of Virginity."
79. *IS*, 23.

In an inversion of her sensual past, Blesilla goes much further than her mother in the "seduction" of asceticism: "[s]he, who had been adept in the arts of love, pushed herself, day by day, to go further and further along the path of self-abnegation. Instead of loving her body she fought it. Instead of desiring to be given pleasure she rooted out that desire and wished only for pain and punishment."[80] Roberts portrays the correlation between the sexual drive and the drive to hurt oneself in anorexia or self-harm. This compulsive, seductive aspect of asceticism may be read as "the radical affirmation of desire also conveyed in resistance,"[81] but I do not believe that radical "affirmation of desire" is a good in itself, and it is not presented as such in *Impossible Saints*. In the end, Blesilla starves herself to death, dying without Jerome even noticing, "while he was still talking."[82] Of all of Roberts's 'Lives' of female saints, this is—tragically—the most true to the source tale. The historical Jerome wrote to Paula, "[w]ho can recall with dry eyes the glowing faith which induced a girl of twenty to raise the standard of the Cross, and to mourn the loss of her virginity more than the death of her husband? . . . her self-abasement was so perfect . . . Her steps tottered with weakness, her face was pale and quivering, her slender neck scarcely upheld her head."[83] As Maitland writes about Augustine, another misogynist Church Father, Jerome is unable to acknowledge the goodness of (non-virginal) women "except in sweet dying . . . in useless and painful moments."[84]

Another story within a novel with the theme of religious erotic masochism is that of an unnamed medieval nun in *The Book of Mrs Noah*, whose tale is narrated in the first person. Her asceticism has its roots in her childhood, in growing up in a church decorated with pictures of beautiful women burning in hell, and a parish priest who tells her "women's beauty evokes men's lust, and drags them down to vileness, away from their search for God," which she associates with herself: "[m]y father has told me how pretty I am."[85] Aged sixteen, she is entranced by the public display of three flagellants: "I am taken by the harsh music of the flagellants, the song of their whips . . . I believe I can hear the harmony of the black barbs as they

---

80. Ibid., 24.
81. Burrus, *Sex Lives*, 14.
82. *IS*, 9.
83. Jerome, *Letter XXXIX*.
84. *WFMW*, 81.
85. *BMN*, 105.

drag across bleeding wounds that are open like ecstatic mouths." She is haunted by this "voluptuous abandon to torture,"[86] and from then on God comes to her in the form of these three men. As she is accustomed to meditating on the suffering of the crucified Christ, it seems natural for the flagellants to lead her on "the way further in," the way of the "chosen" who are able to have faith "that God is surely at the other end."[87] The narrator joins a convent, where she finds not God but the presence of evil, "voices that hiss in my ear and whisper to me to lash myself until the blood comes."[88] The sexuality hinted at in the first description of the flagellants becomes explicit in the narrator's vision of them visiting her as she practices penitential discipline in her cell:

> One brother deftly strips me of my habit . . . then caresses my naked limbs with his cold hand. I like his touch; I shudder with pleasure, waiting for what will come after. The second brother takes me in his arms and hugs me to his breast, holding me so tenderly, making sure I cannot break free. I do not want to. I tremble in his embrace . . . Then the third brother lays on the whip . . . They know how to touch me delicately as though with tongues, until all my flesh tingles and cries out for more, more, harder, harder. . . . I grow to need them holding me down, holding me back, and I plead with them in ashamed and disgusting language that they will go on and hurt me more.[89]

Despite how the protagonist gains sexual enjoyment from these self-loathing fantasies, with her 'ascetic' practice not being in any sense spiritual but rather a sexual masochism that is the result of religious doctrine, it is condemned within the text. She recovers from and denounces such masochism once she learns of the sect of the Free Spirit and the thought of Marguerite Porete. A beguine, Porete was executed for heresy in 1310, and is one of the very few medieval writers to denounce ascetic practice, which (in Amy Hollywood's paraphrase) resulted in "a life of servitude, hellish torment, and exhaustion."[90] At the close of Roberts's story, it seems that the narrator will have the same fate as Porete, awaiting the verdict of a trial for heresy.

---

86. Ibid., 108.
87. Ibid., 111.
88. Ibid., 112.
89. Ibid., 113.
90. Hollywood, *Sensible Ecstasy*, 96.

Michèle Roberts's feminist disapproval of women's erotic masochism is depicted in the character of Catherine in *The Mistressclass*. She is the pseudonymous author of a number of masochistic erotic novels, something she has kept secret from her husband, Adam. By the end of the novel she realizes that she wrote about these fantasies as part of her having "played at being the arrogant, enraptured saint ... both angel and woman, able to bear the Saviour's wounds and be glad of them."[91] Rather than emulating the martyrs' heroism, "all she'd ended up doing was writing texts to entertain young businesswomen who believed they had to be punished for having some power."[92] This is Roberts's own view of "that kind" of erotica;[93] it is interesting that a writer for whom sex and sensuality play such a central role, and who does at times write very erotically about sadomasochism in religion and sex, ultimately says such a strong 'no' to masochistic eroticism.

Sara Maitland

Sara Maitland's novel *Virgin Territory* also draws parallels between contemporary women's masochism and that of the saints. A member of a liberal, apostolic order in South America, Anna has a nervous breakdown after the rape of a fellow nun, and is given leave to go to London to study. There, as she helps care for a brain-damaged child, Caro, and becomes friends with a lesbian feminist, Karen, Anna's anguish over religion and sexuality reaches a crescendo. She is tormented by the Fathers, the voices of patriarchal religion in her head, representing the doctrines and timeless authority of the Church Fathers, the autocratic image of the first person of the Trinity, God the Father, and the psychoanalytic concept of the 'Law of the Father.'

Sister Kitty's rape is the catalyst in Anna's breakdown because it forces her to think about her conception of her own virginity: "[i]f God was not going to protect his holy virgins, what the hell was the point of becoming one?"[94] Her understanding is that being a nun, a virgin, is to be wed to God, to belong to "Him" only. As Karen characterizes it: "[a]ll you bloody nuns, you're not virgins, you're just married to the Top Man."[95] For Anna, this 'marriage' provides protection and norms for life, but ultimately it is not a

91. *MC*, 248.
92. Ibid., 249.
93. *IGS*, 143.
94. *VT*, 96.
95. Ibid., 112.

sign of being free, not-owned by a man: instead it symbolizes being owned by God. In her dialogues with the Fathers, Anna's symbolic marriage to God, to Christ, comes to resemble a kind of spiritual domestic abuse: "God did not have to be nice to her, even if she deserved it, which she did not; that was not part of the deal."[96] As her mental disintegration worsens, she finds herself praying "I need forcing, God, I need you to force me. Make me, break me, make me good and acceptable again . . . Rape me chaste."[97] The Fathers accuse Anna of adultery in her desire for Karen, of being unfaithful to Christ, her crucified husband, saying "He is bleeding on the cross for you."[98]

As a victim, Anna is also aroused by that which torments her: when the Fathers descend "on her and took over her body and her fantasy and were without mercy" she finds pain, pleasure and shame in this: "[t]he rituals of masochism were complex, especially when carried on not with a human lover but with invisible demons."[99] Once Anna is able to challenge the Fathers, she faces up to her masochistic tendencies, and also declares that she is not to blame: "[y]es I want to be punished . . . Yes I am scared of internalised violence . . . Yes I have a deep craving, a need even for all sorts of horrible, deranged and unnameable things. Yes I am terrified to look inside myself and see what you have made there."[100] This recognition, that she has these desires and that they are the creation of patriarchy, enables Anna to recover from self-disgust and self-torment. The novel ends positively, with Anna, having silenced the Fathers, starting to take charge of her own life and her own self.

Maitland's 1987 non-fiction essay, "Passionate Prayer: Masochistic Images in Women's Experience" works as a companion piece to *Virgin Territory*, exploring many of the same themes and images. The essay grew out of Maitland's wondering what Karen would have written about St. Rose of Lima, whom she is researching in the British Library when she first meets Anna. Within the essay Maitland creates a compelling narrative out of theology and history, albeit one that relies on generalizations and contortions, written in a similar vein to feminist theology's rejection of redemptive suffering. Maitland takes Rose of Lima as her starting point, quoting from

96. Ibid., 39.
97. Ibid., 41.
98. Ibid., 170.
99. Ibid., 115.
100. Ibid., 191.

a hagiography and italicizing the following phrases: "she *appeared more glorious in the eyes of God*"; "her *ardent desire* for suffering"; "Rose represented forcibly the necessity she felt of suffering this continual martyrdom *in order to be conformable to her divine spouse.*"[101] As a saint, Rose is only really known for the pain she inflicted on herself, her extensive and bizarre punishments, resulting in her death aged thirty-three. Maitland asks what this says about saints like Rose, her hagiographers and the church that canonized her:

> Women flagellate themselves, starve themselves, lacerate themselves . . . The most highly praised mystical writings use metaphorical imagery from these acts: women speak of Christ's rape of them, they abase themselves, abuse themselves. What the hell is going on here? What can possibly lead women to believe that they are more "conformable," more loveable to the God of creation, love and mercy, bleeding, battered and self-mutilated, than they would be joyful, lovely and delighted?[102]

Maitland traces the history of such masochistic relationships with God back to the dualism of Hellenistic influence on the early church, and its inability to "accept such a simple forgiveness, such a cheap escape from guilt" offered them by Christ, which led to the shift from emphasis on the resurrection to imitation of Jesus' death.[103] This was first expressed in the desire for martyrdom, then, after Constantine's conversion, in the practice of asceticism—the making a martyr of oneself. It is even more dangerous to "seek torture and death" from "the good—the lover, the saviour, the divine" than from the hands of the bad.[104] This became more pernicious in the Middle Ages, when the individualizing of 'Bride of Christ' imagery, coupled with the influence of courtly love literature, resulted in women's erotic relationship with a Christ "who suffered for them, who suffers still because they are not good enough . . . This unresolvable paradox is a recipe for guilt, for that deep-laid unshiftable guilt that can be soothed only in the suffering, the physical suffering that is desired and deserved."[105] The especially female enthusiasm for self-torture in the name of God is due not only to women being more likely than men to literalize the idea of themselves as having a

101. *PP*, 126.
102. Ibid., 127.
103. Ibid., 129.
104. Ibid., 131–32.
105. Ibid., 135

divine husband who died for them, but also to the mythology of Eve having brought sin into the world and thus making Christ's death necessary. The lack of positive symbolism for women in Christianity, combined with the "highly charged positive value both on heterosexuality and on personal love, personal passion, for Jesus" means that women will always engage in masochism if the God they worship is imaged exclusively as male.[106]

Towards the end of the essay, Maitland switches from talking about "women," about "them" and "they," to "me," and "I." She declares that she wants to face up to "the joy-destroying masochism" that she sees in herself, no longer wanting to get her "spiritual or sexual thrills" from "fantasies of pain and humiliation." The writer is trying to correct herself—to repent—from the self-destructive aspects of her sexuality and spirituality, with "feminism [as] the cure."[107] Yet only a few years later, in another essay on Rose of Lima published in 1990, there is a profound shift. Within is the repeated refrain, "Rose of Lima did not have a problem. I may have a problem, but that is a very different matter."[108] No longer is Maitland comfortable with placing her own experience in the same category as that of women from times past and drawing theological conclusions from it. Here, as elsewhere, she argues against imposing modern categories and experience on to figures from such different times and places: that we should not force on historical women "a static universalist understanding of the personality," diagnose them with neuroses like "holy anorexia," or "write over their self-identity."[109]

In the 1990 essay, Rose is presented not as a tragic victim of internalized misogyny, but as an object of admiration. Respect for Rose was already discernible in "Passionate Prayer" and *Virgin Territory*—it is mentioned that she went against the desires of her family and confessor, and social convention—but what is different in "Rose of Lima: Some Thoughts on Purity and Penance" is that this kind of spirituality becomes admirable in its own right, not just as a means of escaping the normal restrictions on women's lives. Women inflicting suffering on themselves to atone for the sins of others is seen as part of "a deeply social, corporate and incarnational way of seeing the world,"[110] and Maitland comes to interpret Rose's religious

106. Ibid., 132.
107. Ibid., 137.
108. *RL*, 62.
109. Ibid., 63.
110. Ibid., 65.

Sex and the Sacred

experience in the way that Rose herself and her hagiographers did: that she was rewarded with a mystical union with Christ because of the pain she inflicted on herself, this striving for purity. Here Maitland means purity of intent, rather than purity from sin. What Maitland seems to admire is not so much the infliction of pain, but of the extremity of Rose's behavior, of the single-mindedness with which she pursued her God, no matter its risk to her well-being and eventually her life. As Karmen MacKendrick has noted, ascetic practices as extreme as Rose's are arrogant rather than self-effacing.[111] Rose's is the sort of masochism that Burrus refers to when she writes, "if psychoanalysis, as well as much popular culture, has tended to perceive women as (alas) merely natural masochists, hagiography radically denaturalizes the feminine as the unstable and queerly reversible site of a decidedly perverse, even effectively feminist, masochistic subjectivity that actively resists patriarchy from within the very structures of misogynistic discourse."[112]

In Maitland's re-evaluating of Rose of Lima, I do not read the notion that suffering is in itself redemptive, but rather a distaste towards any spirituality that seeks only suffering's opposite: comfort and safety. This is fully explored in Maitland's theological monograph, *A Big-Enough God*, which advocates a move away from a "safe" spirituality, and is complementary to her novels *Three Times Table* and *Home Truths*.

Three Times Table is about three generations of women—mother, daughter and granddaughter—who live in the same house but each contend alone with their private struggles. Rachel, the grandmother, is a paleontologist contemplating the crisis of publishing a paper that refutes her lifetime's work, accepting the catastrophe theory of evolution rather than the steady progression paradigm she had previously held to. Her daughter, Phoebe, has a tumor and nurses it like a secret lover rather than seek treatment. Phoebe's attitude to her cancer has parallels with Maitland's descriptions of masochistic and erotic spirituality:

> Phoebe's lover will love her body. Wildly. His passion will overwhelm her fear and shame, and she will no longer resist, no longer be forced to resist, to cut off. Phoebe's lover will bite, will bite into her breast which is his until it bleeds and she will be smeared with blood, with deeper pain. Her lover will rip into her body with claws and teeth and in the pain she will be at last able to have an

---

111. MacKendrick, *Counterpleasures*, 78–86
112. Burrus, *Sex Lives*, 12.

orgasm. Death will be what sex was always meant to be and had eluded her too long while she dug in her garden and slaved in her house.[113]

Phoebe's daughter Maggie is a teenager who refuses to leave the world of imagination and enter into adulthood. She flies over London with her companion, Fenna, a dragon. Rachel, Phoebe's mother, had at one time thought that her granddaughter's fantasy was out of solidarity with her work on dinosaurs, but she comes to realize that Fenna symbolizes the opposite of her beloved scientific models: "Fenna was the dark force of the imagination as well as its golden dancing; Fenna was chaos as well as order, and brought, on fiery dragon breath, the full danger of the chasm. Maggie could play safely with Fenna and explore the land of dark flames that lies in the pit of disorder."[114] But what has been delightful and exciting becomes dangerous and threatening, with Fenna possessing and hurting Maggie. The catastrophe theory motif plays out in the plot of the novel, with a freak incident bringing the three women together, and resulting in a catharsis for each of them: Rachel publishes her paper, Phoebe decides to seek treatment for her cancer, and Maggie says goodbye to Fenna. Yet the novel does not end with the moral lesson of leaving the dark and chaos and embracing safety and sanity: Fenna instead goes to Rachel, who has thus far lived a life of steady rationality, and should now embrace imagination and adventure.

The figure of Margaret of Antioch recurs throughout the novel, and in *Virtuous Magic*, Maitland tells her version of this one-time patron saint of childbirth, who was swallowed by a dragon but survived:

> It was true, as she knew, that dragons were huge and fierce and wild and mysterious; but it was also true, as she knew, that not everything that was huge and fierce and wild and mysterious was evil. Her God had made the dark at the same moment as the light. God had made the shadow and the wildness and the ferocity and the passion . . . In the dark, then, there were new joys, and the dragon was the same as her wild longings, her ferocious and stubborn courage, her desire to fly. Her heart soared as she knew this was just a new adventure, an adventure through fear and darkness into the greater darkness which might, just maybe, just might, be even more beautiful than the light.[115]

---

113. *3TT*, 122.
114. Ibid., 109.
115. *VM*, 290.

Sex and the Sacred

Home Truths centers on Clare, a woman recovering from an accident on a Zimbabwean mountain—which seems to have its own dangerous divinity—that resulted in the loss of her right hand and the death of her fiancé. The novel also swoops in and out of the viewpoints of the various members of her large adopted family, on holiday in their mother Hester's family estate in the Highlands. The overall theological theme of the novel is that God is encountered through risk, uncertainty, extremity and passion. In the character of Clare this is played out through her realization that she had settled for her domineering and rich fiancé because of the security he provided, which she turned to after being scared of the passion she found with another woman. Her recovered memory of her dead parents, and the circumstance of their death (which she witnessed as a young child), is crucial to this: they were pyrotechnicians, and were killed in an accident with their fireworks. Their death—caused by their placing their joy in beauty and excitement above their own safety and concern for their daughter—takes on mystical connotations: they worshipped "the huge wild gods of danger and magic. Her parents had dedicated themselves to the gods of beauty and risk. They had lit their own pyre, and laughed as they died."[116]

This theme is also explored through the character of Clare's brother, Ben, a recently disgraced Anglican priest, photographed taking part in a sadomasochistic gay orgy, to the horror of his family. Like Phoebe in *Three Times Table*, Ben seeks fulfillment in pleasure that is indistinguishable from pain. His urge for extreme sexual experience is not in opposition to his religious belief: rather his spirituality and his sexuality form a continuum, in which sex "is the place where the terrible beauty is born. It's the place, the language of risk and the place, the language of joy."[117] This is the antithesis of the solid and safe kind of Anglo-Catholicism preached to their seven children by Hester and James, himself a priest. Another sibling, Felicity, having found that her faith is not enough to sustain her in the demands of raising a deaf child and the grief of the language gap between herself and her daughter, says to her parents, "[y]ou promised me a place of safety and love and order and discipline and it was a damn lie . . . There is no place of safety. Your God has duped me."[118] Her sister Ceci, a nun, agrees, shocking the family with a speech declaring,

---

116. *HT*, 215.
117. Ibid., 265.
118. Ibid., 247.

> God doesn't say, be safe, be cosy . . . Bend and break the will, discipline and scourge the flesh, face blindly the unknown, the enormous, the terrifying. Love your life and you'll lose it. Risk it and—half blind, mangled, limbless, maimed—maybe, just, you'll totter into heaven; the place of both annihilation and total knowledge. The risk is absolute, you'll get nothing else out of it, not pleasure, not health, not affection, not comfort, and certainly not safety. Just beauty.[119]

The non-fiction companion piece to *Home Truths* is Maitland's exuberant theological manifesto, *A Big Enough God: A Feminist's Search for a Joyful Theology*, which explores the religious significance of the discoveries of the new physics, politics, feminism, and art. Therein Maitland shares her concept of a God who is not "tame" and "domestic," presiding over a religion that "can best be summed up as 'morals tinged with emotion,'" but rather,

> a huge, wild, dangerous God . . . a God of almost manic creativity, ingenuity and enthusiasm; a Big-Enough God, who is also a supremely generous and patient God; a God of beauty and chance and solidarity . . . there is no other credible God: it is a God as big and unmanageable as this or no God at all—only the whimperings of an individualist liberal humanism, or a brave but harsh stoicism in the face of crude materialism, red in tooth and nail . . .[120]

While Maitland does explore the ethical connotations of such a view of God, in her critique of demythologized, "safe" Christianity her emphasis is not a dour, rule-based approach to morality. Elsewhere, she writes that "[f]aith is not about goodness, but about holiness. It is about creating and maintaining the tiny holes and little rips in the membrane between time and eternity, between immanence and transcendence, between the divine and mortal, between God and humanity."[121]

Maitland's emphasis on holiness rather than goodness is apparent in *Virtuous Magic*, in which the hagiographies are not concerned with the good works of the female saints, rather their "readiness to go into the abyss of the self and confront the inner darkness or emptiness there."[122] Maitland and Mulford write, "[b]ecause these women have ultimately not been

---

119. Ibid., 248.
120. *BG*, 150.
121. *FF*, 154.
122. *VM*, 6.

intimidated, because they have not dodged the interior obstacles to surrendering the self, they are often the ones who can irradiate the everyday with the gleam of the extraordinary. They unmask another, uncomfortable kind of truth . . . the risky joy of the incalculable lavishing of the Self upon the Other. Saying 'yes' with a high-hearted certainty—but without any guarantee of safety—to what calls beyond."[123] The holiness of these women saints is in their "over-the-top dedication to chancing themselves in the unnamed game of disregarding reasonable selfish concerns," which, following Edith Wyschogrod,[124] Maitland and Mulford term "Radical Altruism." They acknowledge that this kind of spirituality is hard to reconcile with the feminist values of "autonomy, self-ownership and self-authentification."[125]

The inherently erotic nature of this kind of spirituality is expressed in Maitland's reimagining of the raptures of Teresa of Avila:

> she is carried she knows not where, and resistance is impossible and there is light and glory and sweetness and a yearning, a yearning to die, and pain because death is not given, but only the longing, the longing for the sweetness of God and she is crucified between heaven and earth and can gain no pleasure nor joy from either and yet pleasure and joy are perfected within her, and she resists and resistance is impossible so without consent, she consents. She consents. And she sees the face of Christ, her betrothed, her promised promise; she knows nothing, nothing, nothing except that she knows nothing.[126]

The ambivalence at the heart of Teresa's experience comes to play in a more considered, yet droll, fashion in Maitland's piece on Dorothy Day. The author addresses Day reproachfully, saying that she had hoped, researching her life and reading her words, that she would "like" her: "I thought you would be a teacher for me. I thought you would explain how to renounce the bourgeois self, how to identify with the poor, how to be a Catholic and a socialist pacifist, how to enter into a life of prayer that was grounded in radical socialist politics and genuine love."[127] Instead she found in Day's theology, "just one more medieval saint, born in the wrong time . . . an adorer of masochistic suffering as the root of the loss of self and the mys-

123. Ibid., 6.
124. Wyschogrod, *Saints and Postmodernism*, 371.
125. *VM*, 371.
126. Ibid., 356.
127. Ibid., 172.

tical dissolution into the crucified Christ."[128] In this piece, as the author addresses Day the dialogue is not between the revisionist writer and her subject, but between two voices of the author herself: one a strident feminist voice, the other more quiet, more doubtful: "I just don't like it when you say things like: 'It is only by denying the satisfaction of the flesh that we strengthen the spirit.' I don't like it because I'm afraid it might be true." The narrator says that Day goes too far; at the same time she wonders if one can really "go too far in the right direction." This twentieth-century 'saint' forces her to ask certain questions, such as "what is the strength of the self that can give itself away? Is a self without the boundaries of autonomy, that self that seeks and achieves dissolution into Christ, into the mass of the oppressed, into insanity, a self at all?" and "are those who love life and creation and the world and sex and joy, necessarily lukewarm about heaven, and therefore about justice. Will they (will I) like the Laodiceans necessarily be spewed out?" The piece closes with the words, "I feel convicted by you, and I don't like it. And I don't like it partly because I really don't know whether I am innocent or guilty; I don't know if you are."[129]

The ambivalence of Maitland's concept of sainthood, and how it problematizes feminist values, is explored in "Having Sex with a Saint," a strange, very short, almost parable-like story. The narrator, Jenny, takes home a woman[130] she has met at party, and finds that the stranger has had her breasts removed, and her womb, and her vagina sewn up "so that she could be all the sexes."[131] She also has a zip that runs across her torso; she asks Jenny to unzip her. "[s]he was open to me, completely open. I could peel back her skin, lift out her ribs one by one."[132] Jenny comments,

> One day someone won't put it all back . . . You should be more careful," I said it with a kind of agony—envy and fear together. She laughed, "I hope so," she said, "ah, strewn, tossed to the wind, everyone's everywhere. Go on. Please." . . . I held her heart in my hand and she smiled. There were no boundaries and no barriers . . . She was open, open and not broken and she gave herself to me, with total abandonment. She abandoned herself and gave herself

---

128. Ibid., 174.
129. Ibid., 178.
130. That this a lesbian encounter circumvents issues of male-female power relations in order to force questions about sainthood, sex, submission, and selfhood.
131. *BFG*, 178.
132. Ibid., 179.

Sex and the Sacred

to me with absolute trust or absolute despair and they were perhaps, nearly, maybe, almost, the same thing.[133]

After Jenny has put her back together, she leaves, and Jenny feels angry, because "no one should dare. The risk, her risk, put me at risk. Put my ego at risk. Put ego itself at risk. Me, I want to be inviolate . . . inside my skin, my boundary—and outside there is Other . . . I am shaken. Shaken by her generosity, foolhardy dangerous generosity; by her refusal to withhold her gifts, by her liminality, her strangeness."[134]

When I read some of Maitland's writing, I feel the same confused, questioning ambivalence that is expressed in *Virtuous Magic* about Dorothy Day, the same anger of the narrator of "Having Sex with a Saint." For me it is important to draw a line, to distinguish between a dangerous and risky spirituality in the search for joy, beauty, and the search for encounter with an untamed God, and the embrace of risk and self-annihilation for its own sake, or for a God who is not only wild but also cruel. I find that Maitland's writing straddles the line between the two, and as such is both alluring and frightening.

Maitland's exploration of hers and other's experience of silent living, *A Book of Silence*, has gained an amount of media and public attention, with the idea of a solitary and silent lifestyle being attractive, or at least interesting, to many people. At the same time, something so extreme, such an abandonment of what is to us, as social animals, the normal way of doing things, is rather terrifying. Maitland explains her decision, once she turned fifty and her son left home, to move to the Durham Dales and live alone and try to be silent as much as possible: "I did not want peace and quiet; I wanted to be wholly aflame. It is not chance that the words 'whole,' 'healthy' and 'holy' are all derived from the same root. I incline to excess."[135] The memoir details this "incline to excess," the quest for "more and deeper silence," and takes on erotic overtones, with silence as a lover, a consuming passion. *A Book of Silence* is, overwhelmingly, a joyful book, describing the pleasure and profound fulfillment that the author has found in silent living. Yet there are instances in this, and other of Maitland's texts, when we see the underside of this kind of spirituality of excess.

In *Virtuous Magic*'s exploration of Rose of Lima, the narrator considers the attraction of a devotion as extreme and self-destructive as Rose's:

133. Ibid., 180.
134. Ibid., 182.
135. *ABS*, 32.

"I cannot understand her will so set, so focused in its desire, so turned to the dark, to her own inner darkness. So desiring. So perverse. I do not know the heart of darkness—the huge dark God who gives her this dark joy. I do not know. I do not want to know. I do not dare to know. And in the darkness, I desire to know."[136] This dark desire has not abated in the intervening years between *Virtuous Magic* and *A Book of Silence*. Here Maitland writes of women such as Thérèse of Lisieux and Simone Weil: "[i]n the destruction of their individuality, the mortification of all desire, a brutal practice of silence and self-punishment, they were both waiting for a desert God without a name to come to them in the darkness of their own emptiness and the silence of their hearts."[137] Maitland is not repulsed by this "almost inhuman rigour" in their "courageous assault on their own egos," instead she finds it "challenging and somehow thrilling."[138]

In the Felicity and Perpetua story, the modern revisioning of an ancient figure is actually more disturbing than the historical woman's own words.[139] It is the voice of the narrator, not Perpetua, who writes:

> She is gone to a place where I want to be; where I want to be and yet which I mistrust. I want her to answer, to tell me, to embrace me, enfold me, take me there, there to the gates of heaven and hell, there where the martyrs sing the victory song. . . I envy her the sweetness of conclusion; of finding the place so far in the dark that the turning becomes inevitable, forced into the arms of Felicity and death. Beyond choices, to the place where there is only purity of blood and death.[140]

It seems that what is attractive to the narrator of this story is not merely courage, or single-mindedness, in the face of death: it is death itself. This I find deeply troubling, because I think that here a risk-taking spirituality can become not holy at all, just wanton self-destruction. I do not believe that extreme spirituality is ever worth it if you end up dead; when, like Simone Weil, one's asceticism reaches "the point from which there [can] be no return."[141]

---

136. *VM*, 112.
137. *ABS*, 215.
138. Ibid., 216.
139. See Perpetua in Dronke, *Women Writers of the Middle Ages*, 1–17.
140. *WFMW*, 85–86.
141. Loades, *Searching for Lost Coins*, 46.

Perhaps a rather less squeamish feminist than I, Virginia Burrus, like Maitland, finds in "the crucial intersection of eroticism and theology" of ascetic writings "no 'safe sex' but only risks worth taking."[142] In the "sublimely sadomasochistic eroticism" of "the painful disciplines of asceticism and the prayerful fantasies of mysticism" is an "intense yearning for erotic dissolution, which by definition puts 'selves' at risk."[143] Yet the sites of erotic dissolution are "places of emerging possibility,"[144] and to refuse access to them on ideological grounds is to "foreclose on the inherent transgressiveness of eros" and thus to "risk repressing the very potential for transformability."[145] I would not wish to deny such potential, or to insist upon the existence of an essentialist eros that will lead, in prayer and in sex, to mutuality and connection without risking the loss of selves.

Ultimately, what bothers me about the ascetic erotic drive to loss of self as discussed in this chapter is the metaphor that is employed here. As Loades writes, "life may be eaten away by metaphor, with those who employ it literally tested to destruction by it."[146] The erotic and mystic urge to loss of self is associated primarily with death. Yet what if we choose, as Jessica Benjamin suggests, to understand this death drive as originating in the desire to be reunited with the body of the mother, the silence and darkness of the womb? In the following chapter I consider the root metaphors that feminist theology has employed to describe its vision, and suggest that the metaphor of the sea provides a way of thinking about the divine that can hold together the feminine imagery of the womb with the moral ambivalence that is inherent in our world.

---

142. Burrus, *Sex Lives*, 14.
143. Burrus, "Theology and Eros," xix.
144. Ibid., xiii.
145. Ibid., xix.
146. Loades, *Searching for Lost Coins*, 57.

6

Sea

A MAJOR TASK OF feminist theology has been to rethink the symbolic system through which we conceive of ourselves and the divine: the metaphors we use and how they relate to one another.[1] In the introduction to this book, I have intimated that feminist theology cannot, and should not, aim to create and reify a harmonious symbolic system that replaces what has come before. This final chapter turns to the sea for "patterns" of theological reflection that are "severe and mysterious"[2] rather than whole and harmonious. Bringing together the theological fragments discussed throughout this book, I look to the ocean for a way of envisioning the divine, providing images that combine the feminine, a sense of darkness and terror, and the possibility of grace.

Garden, Desert, Sea

For all its critique of the mythology of Eve and the Fall, much feminist theological discourse hinges on the symbolism of Eden. The garden provides a metaphorical system that holds together allusions of flourishing, harmony, human work in partnership with nature, and a prelapsarian paradise. Mary Grey and Rosemary Radford Ruether have criticized goddess feminism, with its mythology of pre-patriarchal societies living in harmony with nature, for "allowing contemporary Western women to imagine themselves as the heirs of an original innocent goodness, projecting the cause of an evil culture of patriarchal domination of women and nature on to evil 'outsider'

---

1. See Jantzen, "Feminism and Flourishing"; Jantzen, *Becoming Divine*; McFague, *Metaphorical Theology*; and Soskice, *Kindness of God*.

2. *IS*, 3.

males."³ Grey calls this "ecofeminism's own particular brand of the myth of the lost Garden."⁴

The symbolism of Eden is also extensively employed in feminist theological discourse that is not invested in the goddess narrative. In her thesis that Christian emphasis on the symbol of the crucified Christ emerged in the context of the violence of the Crusades, Rita Nakashima Brock describes how Christian worship was focused on the imagery of resurrection, baptism and paradise, which was "depicted by various pastoral scenes: the four rivers of Eden and the Jordan, flower-dotted hills, emerald meadows, fruitladen trees, vineyards."⁵ For Brock, the symbolism of the garden is opposed to the symbolism of the cross. Grace Jantzen has argued that modern Christian dependence on the language of death and salvation may be offset by attention to biblical metaphors of "flourishing." She claims that "the contrast between salvation and flourishing is a gendered contrast; . . . the emphasis on salvation rather than flourishing discloses and perpetuates the masculinist bias of Western theology."⁶ While "salvation" is a model of rescue from an outside source, "flourishing occurs from an inner dynamic of growth, with no need for interference from the outside."⁷ She writes,

> We could then see human beings as having natural inner capacity and dynamic, able to draw on inner resources and interconnection with one another, and potential to develop into great fruitfulness. Whereas with the metaphor of salvation God is seen as the Saviour who intervenes from outside the calamitous situation to bring about a rescue, the metaphor of flourishing would lead instead to an idea of the divine source and ground, the one in whom we are "rooted and grounded in love," in whom we "live and move and have our being," the vine of whom we are the branches and can bring forth much fruit.⁸

I find helpful Jantzen's discussion of the place of metaphor in theology, and the danger of metaphors that become so "ingrained" that they "come to seem like literal theological truth."⁹ Yet it seems to me that her concept of

3. Ruether, *Gaia and God*, 105.
4. Grey, "Expelled Again," 8.
5. Brock, "Communities of the Cross," 112.
6. Jantzen, "Feminism and Flourishing," 83.
7. Ibid., 85.
8. Ibid., 87.
9. Ibid., 86.

flourishing demonstrates the weakness of feminist theology's attachment to Eden: the notion of 'original innocence,' and how the natural world is defined by harmony rather than conflict. She links the symbolic of flourishing with that of "natality," which "suggests a symbolic of flourishing, of growth and fruition from an inner creative and healthy dynamic, rather than a theology which begins from the premise that the human condition is a negative condition or crisis from which we must be rescued by an eternal saviour."[10] This link shows the modern, western, middle-class naivety of Jantzen's use of both "flourishing" and "natality." Infants do not grow like flowers from the mother's body: birth is dangerous, brutal, and painful; throughout history associated with the mortality that Jantzen wants theology to distance itself from. When Jantzen writes that "a plant left to itself in appropriate conditions will of its own nature grow and flower and bear fruit,"[11] there is no place for famine, only flourishing. She seems to envisage plants springing from the ground of Eden, rather than the cursed ground that is made to yield only by the sweat of Adam's brow (Gen 3:17–19).

Mary Grey considers feminist use of the imagery of Eden as she looks back mournfully at the undermining of the idealism of early feminist theology: "into this Garden of mutuality and connectedness came, not the Angel with the flaming sword, but the challenge of difference." Feminist emphasis on "mutuality" and "connection" was "accused of collapsing difference, and disguising privilege and power."[12] However, Grey wants to remain with "the Garden metaphor," not as a paradise in which the earth yields of its own accord, but as a "grounded way of describing our work together . . . Digging the garden is the best metaphor for appreciating diversity and difference . . . Diversity of colour and species is a source of delight and appreciation. It is where, as organisms, we discover our need for nurture: water, air, food; for relation as well as for standing alone."[13] As Grey comments, African-American womanism has been rooted in garden imagery: Alice Walker's famed collection of "womanist prose" is entitled *In Search of Our Mothers' Gardens*. Walker's memory of her mother's gardening, an artistry that was part of her daily life, is representative of black women's "ability to hold on, even in very simple ways."[14]

10. Jantzen, *Becoming Divine*, 161–62.
11. Jantzen, "Feminism and Flourishing," 85.
12. Grey, "Expelled Again," 9.
13. Ibid., 13.
14. Walker, *In Search*, 242.

Yet I wonder if, in feminist theology's need to "escape from paradise,"[15] the garden is still too close to Eden; to harmony, goodness and innocence. In Sara Maitland's spirituality that resists a domestification of God, she turns to the imagery of the desert God, a long way from the symbolic of flourishing and the domesticity of the garden (even though gardening was where this journey of Maitland's began). As part of her exploration of silence, Maitland travelled to Sinai, the place where "the Hebrew migrants experienced a harsh purification, a total dependence on their God and above all a direct and abiding encounter with the divine."[16] There, where she found "the deepest silence I have ever known,"[17] she considered the example of the ascetics who have sought God in the desert. The desert hermit undergoes a "systematic and determined attempt to break down, or thin out the boundaries of the self and become open to, participate in, the undefined, illimitable freedom of the divine," which Maitland recognizes is "hideous" to "a contemporary Western sensibility."[18] Yet she also found amidst the harshness and silence of the desert, "a vast, lovely and awestruck sense of God."[19]

The tension between feminism and the desert ideal is intimated in Heather Walton's review of David Jasper's *The Sacred Desert* (a book which has many interesting parallels with Maitland's *A Book of Silence*): "the stark beauty of the desert may hold a particular fascination for boys. The adventures it offers, the solitude, the silence, the purgation of words that Jasper finds so attractive and the transformation of the ascetic body into text are themes quite alien to the spiritual values espoused by most religious feminists. We have tended to emphasise connectedness, sacred embodiment and social action."[20] The symbolism of the desert is unattractive to feminism, especially when considering the associations of asceticism with athleticism and competition, a hair's breadth away from martial imagery. Yet I think there are perhaps ways in which "solitude," "silence" and "stark beauty" can sit more easily with religious feminism. Maitland characterizes Charles de Foucault's self-emptying in the desert as "a cosmic merging,"[21]

15. Sands, *Escape from Paradise*.
16. *ABS*, 194.
17. Ibid., 197.
18. Ibid., 221.
19. Ibid., 220.
20. Walton, Review of *Sacred Desert*, 189.
21. *ABS*, 191.

reminiscent of the yearning for connection discussed in chapter 3 of this book. The primal terror felt on the edge of wilderness, void, and silence also has ancient connotations with woman, the symbol of namelessness, chaos, and nonexistence. In *Virgin Territory* the spirituality that is opposed to the oppressive religion of the Fathers is mediated through the figure of Caro—the brain-damaged infant whose voice Anna hears in her head. Caro is not a false prophet of a safe, nurturing type of feminized spirituality: through her strange utterances she portrays a chaotic, dark, dangerous, and beautiful vision of the divine. The desert is not just for the boys: it was Hagar, a black slave-woman, who, in the wilderness, saw God and lived. This is a motif that recurs throughout *Virgin Territory*: "into that cosmic post-orgasmic hush, a new song and new sweet flowers growing, the desert blooming like a rose. And from your body new birthing; from your virgin flesh a new and joyful birth for the daughter of darkness, gestated in silence and brought to birth on wordless song."[22]

But it is not the desert wilderness towards which Anna heads, having left her order, the ownership of a possessive male God, and everything she thought she knew. In facing the darkness, the not knowing, the namelessness, she resolves to return to South America "to commit herself to the great river and float down into the dark interior"[23] in search of the Mothers, for the womb, to which she must go back "and be born again in the power of the spirit."[24] Maitland applies this feminine image of birthing, of the womb, to the opening verses of the Bible, in which the spirit of God brooded over the face of the deep: "Sophia . . . danced on the void before there were words . . . in the womb of darkness, in the place of the sounding waters. You can dance on the waters, if you know that you may drown, but you do not mind too much."[25] Maitland's writing, so resistant to the domestification of God, presents a risky spirituality through female imagery. That which is dangerous, joyful, and beautiful is signified not only by the 'masculine' desert, but also the watery depths of the sea.

The river out of Eden flows towards the sea. In the rest of this chapter, I look at how the sea may provide metaphors for feminist theology that displaces its reliance on innocence and goodness, as well as being rooted in the symbolic traditions of feminism and Christian theology.

22. *VT*, 132–33.
23. Ibid., 203.
24. Ibid., 204.
25. Ibid., 198.

Faces of the Deep

In Frederick Buechner's novel *Brendan*—which tells the story of the 6th century Irish saint, famed for his long and dangerous voyages—Brendan is told of the monks who "toss their oars and rudders over the sides altogether and left it to the winds of Heaven to puff them wherever they listed with nothing save fish to feed on or gulls' eggs when they could find them . . . There was no desert for fasting and praying in like in holy times, Erc said, so they made the sea their desert." The "red martyrs" are those who die for love of God, the "green" those who practice penitential discipline, the "white" those who relinquish home and family. The "blue martyrs" are the "curragh martyrs," with "beards of seaweed" and barnacled cheeks, "their eyes blear with salt from scouring the blue storms of the sea for the peace of God."[26] As an alternative image to the ascetics of the desert, the tales of the seafaring saints who sought God on the waves are no less *Boy's Own* adventure stories than those of the Desert Fathers. From the social and historical reality of the fishing industry, to explorers who traversed across the waters to find a new world, to the superstitious sailors who will not allow a woman on their vessel for fear of bad luck, seafaring is resolutely masculine.

Perhaps the most famous seafaring story—certainly one of the oldest and most venerable—is that of Odysseus, who rode the waves for ten years in his attempt to get home from the Trojan war, encountering all sorts of wonders and foes along the way. Adriana Cavarero takes Odysseus as paradigmatic for narrative selfhood, defined by his own story. This emplotted self that is characterized by moving ever forward, with a distinct sense of the narrator, the hero, is questioned in Margaret Atwood's "Circe/Mud" poems: "[t]here must be more for you to do / than permit yourself to be shoved / by the wind from coast / . . . / Don't you get tired of saying Onward?"[27] Catherine Keller, comparing Odysseus to his patient wife Penelope, describes him thus: "[a]s he intrudes, escapes and seduces his way through time and space, he creates an ego of epic independence, positing it over and against a world of dangerous opponents. Enemies and elements, monsters and magical ladies exist only to strengthen his self-identity and to test the powers of his autonomy."[28] I loved *The Odyssey* when I read it as a teenager, but, like Cixous's adolescent experience of reading the classics—"[w]hat is

---

26. Buechner, *Brendan*, 86.
27. Atwood, *Selected Poems*, 206.
28. Keller, *Broken Web*, 7.

my place if I am a woman? I look for myself throughout the centuries and don't see myself anywhere"[29]—I did not know with whom to identify. These seafaring heroes are not women. In *The Odyssey*, women are the witches, the sirens, the sea monsters Scylla and Charybdis.

Mermaids and Monsters

It is not just in Homer that women are monsters rather than heroes. Aristotle defines woman as "the beginning of the category of monster. She is a deviant from the generic human type."[30] Catherine Keller contends that women should reclaim their ancient and mythical identification as the monster—"a fabulous being compounded from elements of various human or animal forms"[31]—because, as "beings composed of Others,"[32] they undercut the indivisible ego of the masculine heroic self: "if we wish no longer to participate in the heroic myth, which almost every institution in our civilization ritually enacts daily, then we can only join in what the monster commemorates by commemorating the monster. We can thus subvert the hero myth without ever forgetting how irascibly it persists among us."[33]

The sea-dwelling monster *par excellence* is the mermaid: a composite creature, enemy of the masculine, which both fears and desires her. The image of the mermaid undulates throughout Michèle Roberts's novel *The Looking Glass*. Moving from an orphanage in the city to a seaside town to work as a maid, Genevieve is told stories of mermaids by her employer, Madame Patin:

> The mermaid had long golden hair, green eyes, and cold white arms. She was half-woman, and half-fish, a beauty who was also a monster. She seemed to promise men pleasure and then turned dangerous ... Her song, in a high sweet voice, coiled about you, a snare of enchantment, a net to lure you into her watery world, to plunge like a dolphin down into the translucent green waves, following her, lost to reason. You wouldn't call it drowning. You'd call it bliss. Only when you were lying trapped in the cold waving arms

---

29. Cixous and Clement, *Newly Born Woman*, 75.
30. Keller, *Broken Web*, 48.
31. Ibid., 50.
32. Ibid., 69.
33. Ibid., 67.

of the seaweed on the deep seabed would you realise that you were capsized and dying and would never come home again.[34]

Keller refers to Bram Dijkstra's analysis of the proliferation of mermaids and water nymphs in the art and literature of the late Victorian period as representative of "the specter of the whirling, dissipative, watery femininity" of the feminism of the New Woman: "[l]iving under clouds and surf that seem like steam rising from the boiling cauldron of the elemental sea, these women represent that unabashed independence and elemental sense of freedom the men of 1900 feared, and found most fascinating, in the viragoes of their day."[35]

The most well-known story of a mermaid, however, is from some decades earlier and far less threatening to patriarchal sensibilities. Hans Christian Andersen's 1836 story, *The Little Mermaid*, can be subjected to a psychoanalytic reading, in which the mermaid rejects the underwater matriarchal world represented by her grandmother, in exchange for the patriarchal world on land and her love for the prince. She seeks the help of the sea witch, who enables her to walk on land, but wants her tongue in exchange: "the sea witch represents the ambivalent mother, who on the one hand wishes to promote her daughter's separation, but on the other desires to keep her close. For, while the sea witch 'helps' the little mermaid in her quest to be human, it is the very nature of her assistance that in fact prevents the success of the mermaid's quest. Without language she cannot be her own effective agent in the symbolic order."[36] In the end, the little mermaid is unable to secure her prince, but she refuses to kill him in order to save herself. Her virtue saves her from the fate of dissolving into sea foam: she is transformed into one of the daughters of the air, who strive to gain for themselves an immortal soul through giving assistance to the world of men.

Hans Christian Andersen's was not the version I grew up with, however. The mermaid of my childhood imagination was that of the 1989 Disney film. If Hans Christian Andersen took a sea monster feared by men, and made her into a sanitized innocent whose purpose in life is to help mankind, then Disney took this even further by removing any trace of the 'good mother.' The sea is ruled by a powerful father, whose authority the little mermaid defies in seeking the love of another man. The 'bad mother,'

---

34. *LG*, 24-25.
35. Keller, *Face of the Deep*, 31.
36. Soracco, "Six Views," 408.

the sea witch, encourages her sexual rebellion, although she tries to thwart her happiness, but is ultimately destroyed by the wrathful but benevolent father. In the end, he consents to giving away his daughter to the human world, to the possession of another man in marriage. All the symbolism is obvious now, but I cannot quite bring myself to revile that film that I loved so much since I was seven years old. I watched another animated version once, more faithful to the Andersen tale, which ends with her dying and her soul going to heaven, the final scene the image of the mermaid sculpture in Copenhagen harbor. I hated this sad version: I would not have my mermaid stuck on a rock, forever still and staring. But nor did I like the Disney ending, the thought of her on land, two legs like a horrible mutilation. What I loved about the film was the beginning and the middle—her playing underwater, exploring; followed by the hope and joy of being in love.

To return to Michèle Roberts's novel *The Looking Glass*, Madame Patin's story of the mermaid ends with even worse consequences for the mermaid than does Hans Christian Andersen's. One of her prey, a sailor, manages to escape and she follows him on land, slowly and clumsily hauling herself along with her arms. His friends catch her in a net and cut her throat, then string her up on the church porch, where her corpse turns into a hank of seaweed. Genevieve wonders "if men fear mermaids because of drowning or because they couldn't make love to them? Or both?"[37] She is frightened by the mermaid story, "because I thought I knew what it meant, and also I didn't know. My body seemed to know, in silence, but not in any words that ever came easily into my mouth. The mermaid could not speak and neither could I."[38]

A. S. Byatt's novel *Possession* also utilizes the half-woman, half-sea-creature as symbolic of female sexual power and men's fear of it. A complex, multi-layered novel, *Possession* narrates the discovery by two present-day academics of a love affair between the two Victorian poets. Christabel LaMotte, the female poet whose work is uncelebrated other than by feminist scholars, is the author of an epic poem about the fairy princess Melusina. A recurrent figure in European—particularly Celtic—folklore, Melusina has the body of a serpent (or fish) from the waist down, a secret until her husband spies her bathing: "[t]he sinuous muscle of her monster tail / . . . / How lovely-white her skin her Lord well knew / . . . / But could not see the

---

37. *LG*, 25.
38. Ibid., 26.

beauty in the sheen / Of argent scale and slate-blue coiling fin."[39] Male horror at female sexuality is also suggested in the lines, "let power take a female form / And 'tis the Power is punished." Of the Sphinx, Christabel writes, "when they found it out they spilt her blood / For her presumption and her Monstrous shape."[40] Another poem of Christabel's concerns the City of Is, the drowned city of Breton legend, ruled by Queen Dahud and inhabited by translucent women. Under the water, female passion is not hidden: "red blood flows beneath their skin."[41] Christabel's cousin Sabine comments on her own version of the story that she had intended for the city of Dahud to be "an embodiment . . . of our desire for freedom, for autonomy, for our own proper passion, which women have, and which it seems, men fear." She notes that "this strange legend" combines "these three desires and these three great fears of man": "Paganism, woman and the Ocean."[42]

A. S. Byatt sometimes uses the association of women and water to skillfully parody the excesses of poststructuralist feminist literary criticism, for example the character Leonora Stern's interpretation of Christabel's writing: "Melusine's fountain has a female wetness, trickling out from its pool rather than rising confidently, thus mirroring those female secretions which are not inscribed in our daily use of language."[43] At other times Byatt writes of this association in way that seems to take it seriously. Randolph Henry Ash, the renowned poet who is Christabel's lover, reflects on their lovemaking: "[i]t was like holding Proteus, he thought at one point, as though she was liquid moving through his grasping fingers, as though she was waves of the sea rising all round him. How many men have had that thought, he told himself . . . all supposing themselves swimmers in salt seas, with the waves rising."[44]

Another work of fiction in which sea monsters represent the masculine ego's fear of the elemental power of female sexuality is Sara Maitland's retelling of Ovid's tale of Perseus and Andromeda. In Maitland's version, this story inscribes the heroic ideal's oppression of female agency and desire. Written in the first person, the Ethiopian princess Andromeda tells how she hates her husband Perseus, who "believes that I admire him,

39. Byatt, *Possession*, 121.
40. Ibid., 292.
41. Ibid., 134.
42. Ibid., 349.
43. Ibid., 245.
44. Ibid., 283.

because he totally believes that he is admirable."[45] He 'rescued' her from sacrificing herself to the sea monster, which for her was an act of love for her city, to appease Poseidon's rage at her mother's pride. Andromeda interprets Perseus's motivation in rescuing her as being jealousy that "someone else, not him, had laid claim to a moment of history."[46] Catherine Keller gives a similar reading of the story, pointing out that "no one asks Andromeda whether she might prefer to take her chances with the monster than face life with a well-muscled braggard." For Keller, the way that the mother's crime is to blame for the sea-monster "suggests a displacement of the mother's own womb-watery monstrosity onto the sea creature."[47] Sea monsters are readily identified with the maternal, "at least from the vantage point of an insecure ego still attempting to separate itself from her swelling, devouring, disappearing saltwatery womb." Perseus's winning of the maiden through slaying the monster speaks to "the masculine fear that his passive princess . . . will turn back into the overpowering Mother he only just escaped."[48] Keller follows Eric Neumann and Robert Graves in reading this story alongside the account of Tiamat and Marduk in the Babylonian epic *Enuma Elish*, as masculine consciousness asserting itself through the murder of the monstrous mother.

Tiamat is the "First Mother," "the primeval waters, the precreation chaos, the salt waters, the ocean";[49] from her union with the "fresh waters" of Apsu come forth the gods. The gods in her belly are restless and warring, and eventually Marduk, the "Babylonian culture hero," brings peace by slaying Tiamat (who by now "appears as a huge serpentine monster") and creates the universe with the pieces of her dismembered body.[50] From Marduk's victory come farming, language, and cities, whereas Tiamat's is the realm of terror and tempests, in which nothing has a name. The old gods of chaos being defeated by the younger gods of culture is a recurrent trope in classical myth, but it is the story of Tiamat which has for feminists been particularly symbolic of the "matriphobia" of patriarchy.[51] In this schema, Tiamat exemplifies how patriarchy's ambivalent fear of mermaids

45. *TT*, 95.
46. Ibid., 97.
47. Keller, *Broken Web*, 70.
48. Ibid., 72.
49. Ibid., 73.
50. Ibid., 74.
51. Ibid., 75; see also Christ, *Rebirth of the Goddess*, 62–67.

and sea-monsters flows from the fear of the mother and of female sexuality, of undifferentiated union and fluid ego boundaries. As such, she represents an alternative ready to be reclaimed in the feminist search for a selfhood that is not defined by separation: "serpentine, stormy and profoundly fluid, a dangerous and demonic deviant: does the gynomorphic dragon portend an alternative to the monolithic ego? She combines in herself the cosmogonic elements, the traces of all that has been, the infinite influx of the other, the others, the influent world into which she herself flows freely, fiercely and de-formingly."[52]

Original Tehom

Catherine Keller's 2003 work, *The Face of the Deep*, continues to explore a theme originally discussed in *From a Broken Web*, which links Tiamat with *tehom*, the Hebrew "deep" of the first Genesis creation account. Like the Babylonian Marduk, the Elohim of the Israelites forms the cosmos through the separation and ordering of a watery chaos. This *tehom* is not personified, but for Keller, as for many interpreters, it still bears on its waves the traces of Tiamat. She quotes John A. Philips: "[s]omewhere in the back of the minds of the writers of Genesis is the Tiamat world of dark and storm, and the story of the masculine warrior-god who creates the cosmos from out of chaos, splitting the dragon-mother's corpse as the first act of creation. The transparent image of Marduk is thus superimposed upon Yahweh."[53] Keller reads in Christian theology the same violence of Marduk's dismembering of Tiamat: a disremembering, in which the doctrine of creation *ex nihilo* "systematically sought to erase the chaos of creation"[54] in forgetting the second verse of Genesis:

> A churning, complicated darkness was wedged right between the two verses which everyone knows with indelible certainty: between *"In the beginning God created the heaven and the earth"* and *"God said: let there be light . . ."* This interstitial darkness refuses to disappear . . . It gapes open in the text: *"and the earth was tohu vabohu and darkness was upon the face of tehom and the ruach elohim was vibrating upon the face of the mayim . . ."* This void evinces fullness, its waters, viscosity. It is no wonder that this verse

---

52. Keller, *Broken Web*, 89.
53. Ibid., 83.
54. Keller, *Face of the Deep*, xvi.

got systematically forgotten, its own flood drowned out by the amplification of the first verse.[55]

Keller argues that, rather than persist in the *ex nihilo* that Christian theology has "created at the cost of its own depth," we should "cease to fight" the darkness and the deep, and "let the undertow draw us toward the depths."[56]

This is partly a response to a patriarchal theism which has no place for the female and the mother is notable by her absence, "a specter of a flushed-out femininity" amidst a theology in which the Father is "the one *unsubstitutable* name of the Creator." Keller claims that this doctrine relies upon the establishment of the Father's "capacity to create without a Mother." As such, "the *tehom* had first and always again to be sterilized," yet the word "Father" cannot be uttered without "instantly summoning its own ghost of a Womb."[57] Yet to remember *tehom* is not simply a matter of gendered nouns. It may help theology to ride another current, one that does not depend on the patriarchal ideals of separation, dominance and immutability. To reclaim the divinity of the depths provides a symbolic of "the generative tensions of order and disorder, form and formlessness . . . the multidimensionality of a bottomless Deep: the matrix in which the creation *becomes*."[58] The process theology of A. N. Whitehead, which has been so influential on Keller's thought, may be imaged by the endless movement of the waves, of the sea's great power and, despite this, its essential immanence. Thinking about how the symbolic of the ocean may help in moving away from theology's static certainties, I am reminded of the words of Jeanette Winterson's lighthouse keeper: "the sea is never still, she's always changing. I've never lived on land and I can't say what's this or that. I can only say what's becoming."[59]

Water, Womb, Words

The watery depths of *tehom* provide an image that undercuts theology's idealization of separation as well as immutability. The sea can image multiplicity and unity: in the water we are held together, our boundaries are not dissolved entirely; the ego and its will are not washed away, but they ride on

---

55. Ibid., 9.
56. Ibid., xvi.
57. Ibid., 19, emphasis in original.
58. Ibid., 12, emphasis in original.
59. Winterson, *Lighthousekeeping*, 48.

a different power. Hélène Cixous uses the language of the water to describe the act of giving birth, itself a metaphor for an alternative way of life:

> I've always taken pleasure in watching a woman give birth. Giving birth "well." Leading her act, her passion, letting herself be led by it, pushing as one thinks, half carried away, half commanding the contraction, she merges herself with the uncontrollable, which she makes her own. Then, her glorious strength! Giving birth as one swims, exploiting the resistance of the flesh, of the sea, the work of the breath in which the notion of "mastery" is annulled, body after her own body. [60]

Roger Deakin, a writer and environmentalist, recorded his experience of a year spent swimming the rivers and lakes of the British Isles. Of being in water, he writes, "[w]hen you swim, you feel your body for what it mostly is—water—and it begins to move with the water around it. No wonder we feel such sympathy for beached whales; we are beached at birth ourselves. To swim is to experience how it was before you were born."[61]

Keller is careful to insist that the watery chaos of *tehom*, in which the ego is not self-contained, does not romanticize "the peculiar cruelties of the Dionysian dissolution . . . a Great Mother of masculine projection and feminine essentialism; or with dispersal and indecision, the feminine sin diagnosed in early feminist theology," by distinguishing between "chaosmos" and chaos," "connection" and "fusion."[62] Thus, in the attempt to "subvert Freud's description of the "primary narcissism" of continuity with the mother as "oceanic feeling,"[63] it is important to go carefully in associating the depths of the sea and primordial, chaotic connection with the mother's womb. Aside from issues of biological essentialism or the reinscription of a misogynist symbolic, we should be wary of a valorization of the drive to dissolution that leads to overidentification with others in personal relationships, as discussed in chapter 3, or the erotic and mystic urge to self-destruction, as discussed in chapter 5. Yet the sea can also be used to image the tension between the desire for connection and the necessity of separation, particularly as regards the role of language in poststructuralist psychoanalytic accounts of the acquisition of selfhood.

60. Cixous, *Coming to Writing*, 30.
61. Deakin, *Waterlog*, 3.
62. Keller, *Face of the Deep*, 87.
63. Keller, *Broken Web*, 93.

Julia Kristeva describes the experience of "the loss of identity in jouissance" in reading the Semiotic language of avant-garde poetry as an "underwater, undermaternal dive." But it is necessary to go back up to the surface, to a social existence that is dependent upon Symbolic language: she compares herself to "a diver who was mischievous enough to bring back a few trophies" and yet feels "uncomfortable" upon her "return."[64] Cixous writes in a similar vein: "not a single word ever returns from the luminous depths where our truth lives. The few words that come close are turned into sighs—so, the truth which only lives sheltered by silence, is forced to appear, and then she is like a fish out of water, thinking in a final convulsion of the sea, then, the end."[65] In Michèle Roberts's writing, the sea is associated with the "true language" of the maternal and the unconscious. In *Daughters of the House*, in crossing the Channel/La Manche, at the point between her two Symbolic languages, English and French, Léonie experiences a moment of Semiotic language:

> as they left England so they left the English language behind. Familiar words dissolved, into wind and salt spray, ploughed back into foam, the cold dark sea in whose bottomless depths monsters swam, of no known nationality. Halfway across, as the Channel became La Manche, language reassembled itself, rose from the waves and became French . . . in the very centre of the Channel, precisely equidistant from both shores, the walls of water and of words met, embraced wetly and closely, became each other, composed of each other's sounds. For that moment true language was restored to her.[66]

Roberts explains to Jenny Newman her association of the sea with the language of the connection between mother and child, as "this great mouth and tongue and lips . . . lapping and speaking."[67] In *The Looking Glass*, which abounds with imagery of the sea, the connection between language and the sea is more ambivalent: the liquid ideas and emotions that have not been ordered into meaning are a form of silence: "[t]he mermaid could not speak and neither could I."[68]

64. Kristeva, *Revolution in Poetic Language*, 164.
65. Cixous in Sellers, *Writing Differences*, 50–51.
66. *DH*, 35.
67. *IJN*.
68. *LG*, 26.

Sara Maitland explores the silence of the sea in her 2008 short story, "Afterlife." It is told from the perspective of Saint Cuthbert, after his death, weighed down by Durham Cathedral and longing to be released from his incorrupt body. Images of the sea are woven through the story, highly evocative of Lindisfarne and the North East. The dead Cuthbert feels the "storm woman" calling to him: "[h]e wants her; he wants to go out to her across the breaking waves."[69] Once Cuthbert's body is placed into an ordinary grave "[h]e can go now" and as he heads towards dissolution "he can hear the waters rushing . . . pulling him towards the sea." He joins "the great nothing" and is held by the storm woman; "[t]here is silence." Using the symbolism of the sea, Cuthbert's ending is associated with his beginning:

> There is no narrative in silence. The interfolded, intwining, intricate lines of life maze round and over and under and through. They do not end, they come back to the beginning and the end is the beginning is the end. The sea deep is the spume of the waves is the foam in the wind is the billow of clouds is the rain on the crops is the stillness of the well is spilled on the ground is flowing back into the depths of the sea.
> The words drop away
> into the ocean
> of silence[70]

Although I am wary of the risks of valorization of kenotic silence, let alone the drive towards death, I find in this story a way of figuring the yearning of erotic dissolution that understands its relation to the primal connection of the womb, without the idealization of Grace Jantzen's notion of "natality." In Maitland's story, birth and death are continuous, not one opposed to the other. Cuthbert's "storm woman," "on the far side of destruction," with "bloodstained laughter" and "dark joy,"[71] may also represent the bloody destruction of our experience of the world and the divine, which feminist theology has resisted, and thus failed to attend to tragic realities.

Darkness, Tempest, and Terror

Catherine Keller explores theological implications of "darkness on the face of the deep," arguing that western Christianity's valorization of light and

69. *FN*, 69.
70. Ibid., 74.
71. Ibid., 69.

rejection of the dark has contributed to a racist symbolic: "unless Christianity unblocks the dark depths it froze in itself long before 'racism' existed, the subliminal habits of whiteness—engrained in liberalism as well as in reaction—will persist."[72] She claims that theology should embrace the darkness, placing the second verse of Genesis in the context of the *via negativa* and the 'unknowing' of the mystical tradition. In Pseudo-Dionysius's image of the divine "luminous darkness," "light and dark are not opposites," nor "a sort of gray," but "a black incandescence."[73] Here the oscillating light and dark of the ocean's waves provide an image for resisting theology's bright, solid certainties: "[t]he logos of a becoming-in-relation will here fold continuously in and out of the chaos, producing the complications of a light shining *in* the dark: neither of a new nonbeing, a mere absence, a worship of disorder, nor of a delusional solidity of Presence. What appears first as formless, a dense shadow shot through with spectral afterimages, may be incubating the form you need. Brood a while longer."[74]

Despite Keller's emphasis on "bearing with the chaos,"[75] it is significant that a book that explores the theological symbolism of "the deep" of Genesis 1:2, including a discussion of *tehom*'s guises elsewhere in the Bible,[76] never mentions that other watery Genesis text: the flood (Gen 6–9). Although Keller wants to use the symbolism of ocean depths as an alternative to theology's tendency to separate light from dark, order from chaos, being from non-being, good from evil, she avoids a narrative in which the elemental powers of water are used to destroy and renew. No matter how interested Keller is in "the great deep," she is silent on the matter of "all its fountains bursting forth" (Gen 7:11), "the waters swelling mightily on the earth" (Gen 7:19) in order to blot out "every living thing that was on the face of the ground, human beings and animals and creeping things and birds of the air" (Gen 7:23). Keller's work may represent an attempt to circumvent what Kathleen Sands names the "ongoing theological suppression of tragic multiplicity, which cannot but divide reality into the ideal and the nonideal,"[77] but her moral sensibilities prevent her from exploring the theological implications of "the face of the deep" as a means of annihilation. This is part

---

72. Keller, *Face of the Deep*, 201.
73. Ibid., 202.
74. Ibid., 40, emphasis in original.
75. Ibid., 29.
76. Ibid., 103–40.
77. Sands, *Escape from Paradise*, 90.

of a general tendency of religious feminism, which ascribes divinity to the powers of nature, but refuses to acknowledge its terrible cruelty.

In its reclaiming of embodiment and the natural world from the demonizing of patriarchal thought, religious feminist discourse has tended to portray 'nature' as an untarnished ideal. For Christian feminist theologians such as Rosemary Radford Ruether or Mary Grey, the interdependence of nature gives a vision of goodness, but it is incomplete, distorted, not here yet.[78] The natural world awaits renewal along with humanity, "creation groaning as in labor" (Rom 8:22). This eschatological outlook means that the horrors of the natural world are named as such, but nature is still held to be essentially good, yet unfinished. Sands writes that Christian feminist theology "has not been able to give up its faith in a pure, inclusive and invulnerable good. Even though it has recognized that the world is a place of innocent fault, guilty power and conflicting goods, it has insisted that precisely as such, the fallen world is *not to be believed in* as the original or ultimate truth."[79]

Goddess feminism, in contrast, has no place for eschatology or transcendence—the divine is wholly immanent in the world. The Goddess is good, and the evil that does exist is social, human, patriarchal. Carol Christ writes that, "[o]nce we realize, as our ancestors did, that life does not exist only for us, we can begin to see that hurricanes, floods, fires, earthquakes and volcanic eruptions are not evil. They are one of the ways the earth body renews herself."[80] Yet Christ's conception of the Goddess is not amoral, but "the power of intelligent embodied love that is the ground of all being";[81] her body is the innocent victim of patriarchal subjugation. These moral categories of love, harmony, and victimhood flounder in the face of the very real cruelty of the natural world. Recent years have seen so much destruction from earthquakes and floods in the Pacific region: these natural forces may not be "evil," but they are terrible. So much destruction cannot be conceived in terms of "the earth body renewing herself" while at the same time maintaining a conception of the divine as *good*.

Michèle Roberts presents the flood and the Ark as a feminine image throughout *The Book of Mrs Noah*. Noah's wife has a dream of the earth "as a woman groaning and arching in labor": "her belly shakes, threatening

78. Grey, *Sacred Longings*; Ruether, *Gaia and God*.
79. Sands, *Escape from Paradise*, 90.
80. Christ, *Rebirth of the Goddess*, 129.
81. Ibid., xv.

earthquakes. Her waters breaking are a great flood. For nine months she has carried the seed of new life safely inside her, letting it float on her waters. Now it rushes out on a flood-tide of water and blood, while she heaves and shouts. And then the waters subside, and the waves are stilled, and the new child lies on her breast."[82] The destruction of the flood is linked with the creativity of birth, yet this is not an image of purity. When the flood comes, Noah's wife "think[s] of my neighbours with the water first creeping into their mouths and then filling them up. They are below us now, sinking down onto a cold bed. We have not heard their cries in the night."[83] The renewal of the earth is tainted by tragedy: "[t]he waters, ebbing and receding from the mountain, have left a trail of litter . . . Here there are the corpses of men and animals, bloated and stinking, whose rotting flesh has turned all manner of bright colours, as though it reflected the arc of light above." The rainbow is envisioned as the umbilical cord, but "[t]he earth is a hard mother . . . we've been born onto this mountain for good or ill."[84]

Sara Maitland's theological writing also intertwines creation and destruction, with her notion of God who is "huge, wild, dangerous" and "unmanageable."[85] This echoes a trope that both Kathleen Sands and Susan Thistlethwaite have noted in the literature of black women. They argue that, lacking the security and comfort of white middle-class feminists, black women's 'closeness to nature' may be even more ambivalent than that of white women, and their literature explores how nature is divine and yet terrible and cruel, and have found this a source of theological creativity: "[a]ccording to many womanists, however, the creation is fallen, sin and evil are stunningly real and there is no (easy?) access to harmony . . . I have heard many womanists say that to know the evil of the creation is to know it more fully and that this mixed knowledge is creative."[86] The divinity in the terrible power of nature is a theme of Zora Neale Hurston's *Their Eyes Were Watching God*. The novel describes an African-American community's experience of a hurricane, lacking the protection held by "the people in the big houses"[87]: "[t]hey sat in company with the others in other shanties, their eyes straining against crude walls and their souls asking if He meant

82. *BMN*, 74.
83. Ibid., 79.
84. Ibid., 84.
85. *BG*, 150.
86. Thistlethwaite, *Sex, Race and God*, 61.
87. Hurston, *Their Eyes*, 210.

to measure their puny might against His. They seemed to be staring at the dark, but their eyes were watching God . . . the wind and waves and had given life to lots of things that folk think of as dead and given death to so much that had been living things."[88]

The ambivalence of the awe-full sacredness of the sea is a major theme of Caribbean literature, in the image of the sea as that which holds and bears witness to the history of slavery. Fiona Darroch has discussed how writers such as Derek Walcott, David Dabydeen and Fred D'Aguiar have symbolized the sea, on which slaves were brought from Africa to the Caribbean, as "a cathedral filled with the decadent and perverse treasures of a shameful past; it is also an enforced place of worship, the sacred site of a history only half told." Derek Walcott and David Dabydeen use Christian narrative and imagery in describing the violence of the Middle Passage and the sacredness of the sea, thus confronting "the Christian literary canon and its participation in slavery," subverting "Western imaginings of sacrality and sanctity . . . while simultaneously presenting a re-imagining of the sacred that recognizes the necessity of such tensions."[89] As such, the ocean carries the destructive forces of nature, but also the social evil of the human crime of the slave trade. The sea's divinity is a cruel one, but is "also a symbol of survival, of resurfacing in 'strange lands' and still being able to 'dream, surmise, invent.'"[90]

Grace

I have been confronted by the paradoxical character of the sacredness of the sea when encountering the elemental powers of wind and wave in the Hebrides and Northumberland. It was on the vast beaches of Holy Island that I first experienced a sense of a particular place as infused with the divine; the prayers of generations lapping against the North Sea's shore. On the Isle of Lewis, the Atlantic Ocean is so huge and beautiful, so frightening and exhilarating, that sometimes I can't look at it; I focus on the rock pools, or the jewel-like pebbles in my hand, or the shapes the waves have carved into the sand. Lewis is a harsh place, where islanders are buried by the sea, but women are not allowed at the burial services. Their religion is demanding and unforgiving, like their landscape, and their history. *Iolaire*, the ship

88. Ibid., 213.
89. Darroch, "Re-Imagining the Sacred," 105.
90. Ibid.

that carried across the Minch soldiers returning from the battles of the First World War, was wrecked a mile away from harbor, and three-quarters of the passengers were killed. Any divinity that I find in these waters is unutterably cruel, as well as magnificent.

These northern seas are different to the sea I grew up with. I was raised on the coast, and have always lived with sense of the sea's power and beauty; the stories borne on its waves; how the sea has formed this town, as so many others of this small island nation. But, compared with the north Atlantic or the North Sea, the water is never as cold, the wind never as strong, and on a clear day you can see across to Southend-on-Sea; over the waters and down a bit is France. The sea is that which connects, a means of communication between peoples. Thus it always seemed strange to me that in Revelation's new earth "there will no longer be any sea" (21:1), even when it was explained to me that here the sea represents separation. For the sea is the source of so many moments of communion. When I was a child our church would march along the promenade singing praise songs and waving banners, and baptism services were often held on the beach. Sitting on the pebbles watching people being immersed into the sea, it seemed like there was little more than a fishing net between us and Jesus on the banks of the Jordan. In the Gospels, it was by the sea that thousands were fed with loaves and fishes, on the waves that the disciples witnessed Jesus walking on water and calming the storm.

All these miracles simultaneously use and go against the power and gifts of the sea. And when I was little, it was the sea's gifts that most represented to me the grace of God. My family's car bore a sticker fish symbol, to demonstrate our Christianity, and I understood God's love through fishes—undeserved gifts—rather than the sacrificial love of the cross. In Maitland's *Virgin Territory*, Anna gets a tattoo of a fish, rather than the cross, as a symbol of God's grace: "[t]hey are there, they are certainly there, free food and wholly fleeting. You can see them if you want to, catch them if you can."[91]

I no longer have my childhood faith in God's generosity, in good gifts freely given, but it comes back to me sometimes, for brief moments. Leaving the Isle of Iona after a few days stay, a mistake about ferry times meant I had to spend a few extra hours there. It was windswept, rain-spattered morning; the island felt empty without all the tourists that had been there the previous afternoon; in the wet weather it had an austere kind of beauty

---

91. *VT*, 177.

that felt more real than the sunny calm of yesterday. Walking up the coast, back in the direction of the hostel where I had felt at home and made a friend, I was no longer annoyed about the planning mistake. It was a pleasure unwanted and unexpected, to see the White Strand of the Monks once more. I had time for an upmarket lunch in The Argyle. Looking out at Ronan's Bay, drinking tea and eating quiche, I saw dolphins in the wild for the first time in my life. Out of the undulating waves fins darting, then the odd flash of the curving form twisting up out of the water. The waiter told me that they hadn't seen them for about a year, and that when there's a few of them swimming round and leaping up like this, they're not catching fish, they're playing. Each time one leapt up I cried out in delight. If I'd caught the right ferry I would not have seen them. This was something so precious and unexpected. A gift.

Yet for me the sea's gifts are not always so unsullied. They tend to be flotsam and jetsam, washed up by the tide, broken and dirty, but, sometimes, still beautiful. Gathering driftwood and oyster shells along the seaside I grew up on, I pause to look at the stony beach and its groynes, the Isle of Sheppey across the water, the lines of beach huts along the grassy slopes. Views that I know so well I could draw them with my eyes shut. I think of Michèle Roberts using the flotsam and jetsam along the French beach of her childhood as a metaphor for memory and life-writing:

> My childhood in France is vanishing, a tide going out . . . The absent sea scrawls a memoir behind itself along the tideline, written in seaweed, driftwood, dead starfish, broken glass bottles, fragments of cork. I want to collect up this debris, decipher it, before the sea returns and obliterates it . . . to walk along the tideline and re-examine these mysterious traces, this line of fluid script, this low-water mark dividing the pebbles from the shingle; to reselect and rearrange.[92]

I am embarking on a similar endeavor, collecting the materials for making ornaments to hang in my bedroom. Except that it will not be my bedroom anymore. The room is being rearranged and repainted and, when finished, will no longer contain any traces of my teenage self. The redecoration will make it a nice room for me, and other guests, to sleep in, but it will also perhaps increase the house's attractiveness to any prospective buyers. When the house is sold it will be a terrible loss, not only because this house has always been home, but also because it will represent with great finality the

---

92. *UG*, 41.

end of our family in the form that it took when my siblings and I were still children and when our parents were still married to each other. I am redecorating the room with a theme appropriate to the house's seaside location, the size of the room (tiny), and that most marketable aspect of Whitstable and Tankerton: beach huts, sailing, oysters, and so on. But it is also a way of managing the emotions stirred by the passing away of my old bedroom: in decorating the room in a manner particular to where it is, and with a child-like design theme, I am commemorating my childhood on this beach, my growing up, my moving on; recreating and mourning at the same time. Trudging over the pebbles to pick up each interestingly shaped or pleasantly smooth piece of driftwood, each mottled pink and purple oyster shell, I feel terribly sad, and a little silly. But when, in the freshly-decorated bedroom, I hang up the driftwood and shells I have drilled holes in and threaded on a piece of twine, alongside pictures of boats and fish and sea gulls, the ritual is a satisfying one.

Walking along the north beach of Holy Island, I look at the tremendous amount of debris—fishing nets, tires, plastic bottles—deposited by the North Sea and I resent it. The human world, and its waste, has intruded on my solitary time with the wind, waves, and seagulls. Then I come across a tiny building that someone has erected from the beach's stones and boulders, the entrance supported by planks of driftwood. When I stoop down and peer inside, I see that it is a grotto adorned by the gifts that the tide has brought in. Driftwood frames a window from which there is a lovely view of the sea, and a bench has been formed from large slabs of rock. I imagine that this is the secret dwelling of a sea witch, and I am the only person ever to have stumbled across it. It seems like something from one of Sara Maitland's short stories. Lodged between the stones are pieces of sea glass and translucent plastic sandals; they fill the inside of the hut with colored light, even on this cloudy morning. Hanging from the ceiling, on makeshift shelves, in the walls and on the floor, are shells, battered dolls, sandcastle buckets, plastic flowers, lost bits of clothing. These items of rubbish strewn along the beach have been transformed into treasured ornaments.

These "moments of grace"[93] have been shaped in part by my relation to the literature of Michèle Roberts and Sara Maitland. I have wanted my theological reflection to be the gathering together of fragments, but into a bone collage, not a harmonious system. A collage born out of women's communal work, but also loss and conflict. Yet, unlike Adrienne Rich, I have

---

93. Duffy, *Mean Time*, 26.

not needed to dive down into the wreckage to find the shards of "treasures that prevail."[94] Sometimes, unbidden, the sea brings its gifts to our feet as we walk along the tideline. These gifts are "fragile and finite,"[95] tattered, dirty and broken, but can be formed into new strange shapes, which give no easy answers, but are beautiful nonetheless.

94. Rich, *Poetry and Prose*, 54.
95. Sands, *Escape from Paradise*, 167.

Bibliography

Alexander, Flora. *Contemporary Women Novelists*. London: Edward Arnold, 1989.

Althaus-Reid, Marcella. *From Feminist Theology to Indecent Theology: Readings on Poverty, Sexual Identity and God*. London: SCM, 2004.

———. *Indecent Theology: Theological Perversions in Sex, Gender and Politics*. London: Routledge, 2000.

———. *The Queer God*. London: Routledge, 2003.

Andolsen, Barbara Hilkert. "Agape in Feminist Ethics." *Journal of Religious Ethics* 9/1 (1981) 69–83.

Arendt, Hannah. *The Human Condition*. Chicago: University of Chicago Press, 1958.

Atwood, Margaret. *Selected Poems, 1965–1975*. Boston: Houghton Mifflin, 1976.

Bacchilega, Cristina. "Cracking the Mirror: Three Re-Visions of 'Snow White.'" *boundary 2* 15/3 (1988) 1–25.

Bal, Mieke. *Loving Yusuf: Conceptual Travels from Present to Past*. Chicago: University of Chicago Press, 2008.

Barthes, Roland. "Theory of the Text." In *Untying the Text: A Post-Structuralist Reader*, edited by R. Young, 31–47. London: Routledge, 1981.

Beattie, Tina. "Sexuality and the Resurrection of the Body: Reflections in a Hall of Mirrors." In *Resurrection Reconsidered*, edited by Gavin D'Costa, 135–49. Oxford: Oneworld, 1996.

Benjamin, Jessica. "Master and Slave: The Fantasy of Erotic Domination." In *Desire: The Politics of Sexuality*, edited by Ann Snitow, Christine Stansell, and Sharon Thompson, 292–311. London: Virago, 1984.

Bettenhausen, Elizabeth. Foreword to *Christianity, Patriarchy and Abuse: A Feminist Critique*, edited by Joanne Carlson Brown, Haskell M. Miller, and Carole R. Bohn, xi–xii. New York: Pilgrim, 1989.

Blaug, Astra, et al. *Cutlasses and Earrings*. London: Playbooks, 1977.

Booth, Wayne C. *The Company We Keep: An Ethics of Fiction*. Berkeley: University of California Press, 1988.

———. "'The Way I Loved George Eliot': Friendship with Books as a Neglected Critical Metaphor." *The Kenyon Review* 2/2 (1980) 4–27.

Boston Women's Health Book Collective. *Our Bodies, Ourselves*. Boston: Boston Women's Health Book Collective, 1971.

Brenner, Athalya. *I Am . . . Biblical Women Tell Their Own Stories*. Minneapolis: Fortress, 2005.

Brock, Rita Nakashima. "Communities of the Cross: Christa and the Communal Nature of Redemption." *Feminist Theology* 14/1 (2005) 109–25.

———. *Journeys by Heart: A Christology of Erotic Power*. New York: Crossroad, 1988.

Bibliography

Brock, Rita Nakashima, and Rebecca Ann Parker. *Proverbs of Ashes: Violence, Redemptive Suffering and the Search for What Saves Us.* Boston: Beacon, 2001.

Brock, Rita Nakashima, and Susan Brooks Thistlethwaite. *Casting Stones: Prostitution and Liberation in Asia and the United States.* Minneapolis: Fortress, 1996.

Brodzki, Bella, and Celeste Schenck. Introduction to *Life/Lines: Theorizing Women's Autobiography*, edited by Bella Brodzki and Celeste Schenck, 1–15. Ithaca: Cornell University Press, 1988.

Brown, Joanne Carlson, Haskell M. Miller, and Carole R. Bohn, eds. *Christianity, Patriarchy and Abuse: A Feminist Critique.* New York: Pilgrim, 1989.

Brown, Joanne Carlson, and Rebecca Parker. "For God So Loved the World?" In *Christianity, Patriarchy and Abuse: A Feminist Critique*, edited by Joanne Carlson Brown, Haskell M. Miller, and Carole R. Bohn, 1–30. New York: Pilgrim, 1989.

Brownmiller, Susan. *In Our Time: Memoir of a Revolution.* New York: Delta, 2000.

Brunner, José. *Freud and the Politics of Psychoanalysis.* Oxford: Blackwell, 2001.

Buechner, Frederick. *Brendan: A Novel.* New York: HarperCollins, 1998.

Burrus, Virginia. "Introduction: Theology and Eros After Nygren." In *Towards a Theology of Eros: Transfiguring Passion at the Limits of Discipline*, edited by Virginia Burrus and Catherine Keller, xiii–xxi. New York: Fordham University Press, 2006.

———. *The Sex Lives of Saints: An Erotics of Ancient Hagiography.* Philadelphia: University of Pennsylvania Press, 2004.

———. "Word and Flesh: The Bodies and Sexuality of Ascetic Women in Christian Antiquity." *Journal of Feminist Studies in Religion* 10/1 (1994) 27–51.

Byatt, A. S. "Choices: The Writing of *Possession*." *The Threepenny Review* 63 (1995) 17.

———. *Possession: A Romance.* London: Vintage, 1990.

Bynum, Caroline Walker. *Holy Feast and Holy Fast: The Religious Significance of Food to Medieval Women.* Berkeley: University of California Press, 1987.

Canters, Hanneke, and Grace Jantzen. *Forever Fluid: A Reading of Luce Irigaray's Elemental Passions.* Manchester: Manchester University Press, 2005.

Carmichael, Kay. *Sin and Forgiveness: New Responses in a Changing World.* London: Ashgate, 2003.

Carter, Angela. Introduction to *Wayward Girls and Wicked Women*. Edited by Angela Carter, ix–xii. London: Virago, 1986.

Cavarero, Adriana. *Relating Narratives: Storytelling and Selfhood.* Translated by Paul A. Kottman. London: Routledge, 2000.

Chodorow, Nancy J. *The Reproduction of Mothering: Psychoanalysis and the Sociology of Gender.* 2nd ed. Berkeley: University of California Press, 1999.

Chopp, Rebecca S. *Saving Work: Feminist Practices of Theological Education.* Louisville, KY: Westminister John Knox, 1995.

Christ, Carol P. *Diving Deep and Surfacing: Women Writers on Spiritual Quest.* 2nd ed. Boston: Beacon, 1995.

———. "Ecofeminism and Process Philosophy." *Feminist Theology* 14/3 (2006) 289–310.

———. "Embodied Embedded Mysticism: Affirming the Self and Others in a Radically Interdependent World." *Journal of Feminist Studies in Religion* 24/2 (2008) 159–67.

———. *Rebirth of the Goddess: Finding Meaning in Feminist Spirituality.* New York: Routledge, 1997.

———. *She Who Changes: Re-Imagining the Divine in the World.* New York: Palgrave Macmillan, 2003.

———. "Why Women Need the Goddess: Phenomenological, Psychological, and Political Reflections." In *Womanspirit Rising: A Feminist Reader in Religion*, edited by Carol P. Christ and Judith Plaskow, 273–87. San Francisco: Harper & Row, 1979.

Cixous, Hélène. *Coming to Writing and Other Essays*. Translated by Sarah Cornell, Deborah Jenson, Ann Liddle, and Susan Sellers. Cambridge, MA: Harvard University Press. 1991.

———. *Three Steps on the Ladder of Writing*. Translated by Sarah Cornell and Susan Sellers. New York: Columbia University Press, 1993.

Cixous, Hélène, and Catherine Clément. *The Newly Born Woman*. Translated by Betsy Wing. London: I. B. Tauris, 1996.

Clague, Julie. "The Christa: Symbolizing My Humanity and My Pain." *Feminist Theology* 14/1 (2005) 83–108.

Coakley, Sarah. *Powers and Submissions: Spirituality, Philosophy and Gender*. Oxford: Blackwell, 2002.

Daly, Mary. *Beyond God the Father: Towards a Philosophy of Women's Liberation*. 2nd ed. London: The Women's Press, 1986.

Darroch, Fiona. "Re-Imagining the Sacred in Caribbean Literature." In *Literature and Theology: New Interdisciplinary Spaces*, edited by Heather Walton, 99–110. Surrey: Ashgate, 2011.

Deakin, Roger. *Waterlog: A Swimmer's Journey Through Britain*. London: Vintage, 2000.

Diamant, Anita. *The Red Tent*. London: Vintage, 1997.

Diski, Jenny. *After These Things*. London: Virago, 2001.

Dronke, Peter. *Women Writers of the Middle Ages: A Critical Study of Texts from Perpetua to Marguerite Porete*. Cambridge: Cambridge University Press, 1984.

Duffy, Carol Ann. *Mean Time*. Anvil Press Poetry, 1993.

Duncker, Patricia. *Sisters and Strangers: An Introduction to Contemporary Feminist Fiction*. Oxford: Blackwell, 1992.

Engel, Mary Potter. "Evil, Sin and Violation of the Vulnerable." In *Lift Every Voice: Constructing Christian Theologies from the Underside*, edited by Susan Brooks Thistlethwaite and Mary Potter Engel, 152–64. New York: HarperCollins, 1990.

———. "No-Self and the Calling Given to Anyone: The Challenge of Mysticism." *Journal of Feminist Studies in Religion* 24/2 (2008) 143–59.

Faber, Alyda. "Eros and Violence." *Feminist Theology* 12/3 (2004) 319–42.

———. "Wounds: Theories of Violence in Theological Discourse." PhD diss., McGill University, Montreal, 2001.

Fairbairns, Zoë. Introduction to *Tales I Tell My Mother: A Collection of Feminist Short Stories*. By Zoë Fairbairns et al., 1–3. London: Journeyman, 1978.

Falcus, Sarah. *Michèle Roberts: Myths, Mothers and Memories*. Oxford: Peter Lang, 2007.

Farley, Margaret A. "Feminist Consciousness and the Interpretation of Scripture." In *Feminist Interpretation of the Bible*, edited by Letty M. Russell, 41–52. Philadelphia: Westminster John Knox, 1985.

Fell, Alison, ed. *Licking the Bed Clean*. London: Teeth, 1978.

———, ed. *Seven Cardinal Virtues*. London: Serpent's Tail, 1990.

———, ed. *Seven Deadly Sins*. London: Serpent's Tail, 1988.

———, ed. *Smile Smile Smile Smile*. London: Sheba Feminist, 1980.

Figes, Eva. *Patriarchal Attitudes: Women in Society*. London: Faber, 1970.

Fine, Cordelia. *Delusions of Gender: How Our Minds, Society, and Neurosexism Create Difference*. New York: Norton, 2010.

Bibliography

Fisk, Anna. "'To Make, and Make Again': Feminism, Craft and Spirituality." *Feminist Theology* 20/2 (2012) 160–74.

Freedman, Diane P., Olivia Frey, and Frances Murphy Zauhar. *The Intimate Critique: Autobiographical Literary Criticism*. Durham, NC: Duke University Press, 1993.

Frei, Hans. *The Eclipse of Biblical Narrative: A Study in Eighteenth and Nineteenth Century Hermeneutics*. New Haven, CT: Yale University Press, 1974.

Friday, Nancy. *My Mother My Self*. 2nd ed. London: Fontana, 1988.

Friedan, Betty. *The Feminine Mystique*. London: Gollancz, 1963.

Fulkerson, Mary McClintock. *Changing the Subject: Women's Discourses and Feminist Theology*. Minneapolis: Fortress, 1994.

———. "Sexism as Original Sin: Developing a Theacentric Discourse." *Journal of the American Academy of Religion* 59/4 (1991) 653–75.

Furlong, Monica. *Visions and Longings: Medieval Women Mystics*. London: Mowbray, 1996.

García Sánchez, M. Soraya. "Michèle Roberts's Protagonists: Catholicism and Sexuality." *Feminist Theology* 17/2 (2009) 229–45.

Gilbert, Sandra M. "Life Studies, or, Speech after Long Silence: Feminist Critics Today." *College English* 40/8 (1978) 849–63.

Gilbert, Sandra M., and Susan Gubar. *The Madwoman in the Attic: The Woman Writer and the Nineteenth-Century Literary Imagination*. New Haven, CT: Yale University Press, 1979.

Gilligan, Carol. *In a Different Voice*. Cambridge, MA: Harvard University Press, 1982.

Graham, Elaine. *Making the Difference: Gender, Personhood and Theology*. London: Mowbray, 1995.

Graziano, Frank. *Wounds of Love: The Mystical Marriage of Saint Rose of Lima*. Oxford: Oxford University Press, 2004.

Grey, Mary C. "'Expelled Again from Eden': Facing Difference through Connection." *Feminist Theology* 7 (1999) 8–20.

———. *Redeeming the Dream*. London: SCPK, 1989.

———. *Sacred Longings: The Ecological Spirit and Global Culture*. Minneapolis: Fortress, 2004.

Griffin, Susan. *Woman and Nature: The Roaring Inside Her*. London: The Women's Press, 1984.

Haase, Donald, "Feminist Fairy-Tale Scholarship." In *Fairy Tales and Feminism: New Approaches*, edited by Donald Haase, 1–36. Detroit: Wayne State University Press, 2004.

Hadewijch. *Hadewijch: Complete Works*. Translated by Columba Hart. London: SPCK, 1980.

Hampson, Daphne. *Theology and Feminism*. Oxford: Blackwell, 1990.

Harbord, Janet. "Platitudes of Everyday Life?" In *Temporalities, Autobiography and Everyday Life*, edited by Jan Campbell and Janet Harbord, 21–34. Manchester: Manchester University Press, 2002.

Harries, Elizabeth Wanning. *Twice Upon a Time: Women Writers and the History of the Fairy Tale*. Princeton: Princeton University Press, 2003.

Harrison, Beverly Wildung. *Making the Connections: Essays in Feminist Social Ethics*. Boston: Beacon, 1985.

Hartsock, Nancy. *The Feminist Standpoint Revisited and Other Essays*. Boulder, CO: Westview, 1998.

Hauerwas, Stanley. *The Peaceable Kingdom: A Primer in Christian Ethics*. London: SCM, 1983.

Henderson, Mae. Introduction to *Borders, Boundaries and Frames: Cultural Criticism and Cultural Studies*. Edited by Mae Henderson, 1–30. New York: Routledge, 1995.

Heyward, Carter. *The Redemption of God: A Theology of Mutual Relation*. New York: University Press of America, 1982.

———. *Touching Our Strength: The Erotic as Power and the Love of God*. San Francisco: Harper & Row, 1989.

———. *When Boundaries Betray Us: Beyond Illusions of What is Ethical in Therapy and Life*. San Francisco: Harper & Row, 1995.

Hollywood, Amy. *Sensible Ecstasy: Mysticism, Sexual Difference, and the Demands of History*. Chicago: University of Chicago Press, 2002.

———. "Sexual Desire, Divine Desire; Or, Queering the Beguines." In *Queer Theology: Rethinking the Western Body*, edited by Gerard Loughlin, 163–75. Oxford: Blackwell, 2006.

Hurston, Zora Neale. *Their Eyes Were Watching God*. London: Virago, 2007.

Isherwood, Lisa. *Introducing Feminist Christologies*. London: Sheffield Academic, 2001.

Jantzen, Grace. *Becoming Divine: Towards a Feminist Philosophy of Religion*. Manchester: Manchester University Press, 1998.

———. "Feminism and Flourishing: Gender and Metaphor." *Feminist Theology* 4 (1995) 81–101.

Jasper, David. *The Sacred Desert: Religion, Literature, Art, and Culture*. Oxford: Blackwell, 2004.

———. "The Study of Literature and Theology." In *The Oxford Handbook of English Literature and Theology*, edited by Andrew Hass, David Jasper, and Elizabeth Jay, 15–33. Oxford: Oxford University Press, 2007.

Jeanrond, Werner. *A Theology of Love*. London: T. & T. Clark, 2010.

Jerome. *Letter XXXIX. To Paula. Principle Works of St. Jerome*. No pages. Online: http://www.ccel.org/ccel/schaff/npnf206.v.XXXIX.html.

Johnson, Elizabeth. *She Who Is: The Mystery of God in Feminist Theological Discourse*. New York: Crossroad, 1993.

Jolly, Margaretta. "Speaking Personally, Academically." *Feminist Theory* 6/2 (2005) 213–20.

Joseph, Alison, ed. *Through the Devil's Gateway*. London: SPCK, 1990.

Kazantzis, Judith, Michèle Roberts, and Michelene Wandor. *Touch Papers*. London: Allison & Busby, 1982.

Kearney, Richard. *On Stories*. Thinking in Action. London: Routledge, 2006.

Keller, Catherine. *The Face of the Deep: A Theology of Becoming*. London: Routledge, 2003.

———. *From a Broken Web: Separation, Sexism and Self*. Boston: Beacon, 1986.

Kennard, Jean E. "Personally Speaking: Feminist Critics and the Community of Readers." *College English* 43/2 (1981) 140–45.

King, Jeanette. *Women and the Word: Contemporary Women Novelists and the Bible*. Basingstoke: MacMillan, 2000.

Kitzberger, Ingrid Rosa, ed. *Autobiographical Biblical Criticism: Between Text and Self*. Leiden: Deo, 2002.

———, ed. *The Personal Voice in Biblical Interpretation*. London: Routledge, 1999.

Kristeva, Julia. *Desire in Language: A Semiotic Approach to Literature and Art*. Translated by Leon S. Roudiez. New York: Columbia University Press, 1980.

Bibliography

———. *Powers of Horror: An Essay on Abjection*. Translated by Leon S. Roudiez. New York: Columbia University Press, 1982.

———. *Revolution in Poetic Language*. Translated by Leon S. Roudiez. New York: Columbia University Press, 1984.

———. *Tales of Love*. Translated by Leon S. Roudiez. New York: Columbia University Press, 1987.

Lewis, C. S. *The Lion, the Witch and the Wardrobe*. London: HarperCollins, 2001.

Lewis, Paul. "UK Riots: Paul Lewis's Five-Day Journey." *The Guardian*, August 12, 2011. No pages. Online: http://www.theguardian.com/uk/2011/aug/12/uk-riots-paul-lewis-five-day-journey.

Llewellyn, Dawn. "Women's Spiritual Reading as a Third Wave Feminist Practice." PhD diss., Lancaster University, 2010.

Loades, Ann. *Searching For Lost Coins: Explorations in Christianity and Feminism*. London: SPCK, 1987.

Lochrie, Karma. "Mystical Acts, Queer Tendencies." In *Constructing Medieval Sexuality*, edited by Karma Lochrie, Peggy McCracken, and James Alfred Schultz, 180–200. Minneapolis: University of Minnesota Press, 1997.

Lorde, Audre. "Uses of the Erotic: The Erotic as Power." In *Weaving the Visions: New Patterns in Feminist Spirituality*, edited by Judith Plaskow and Carol P. Christ, 208–13. San Francisco: Harper & Row, 1989.

Loughlin, Gerard. *Alien Sex: The Body and Desire in Cinema and Theology*. Oxford: Blackwell, 2004.

———. "Introduction: The End of Sex." In *Queer Theology: Rethinking the Western Body*, edited by Gerard Loughlin, 1–34. Oxford: Blackwell, 2006.

———. *Telling God's Story: Bible, Church and Narrative Theology*. Cambridge: Cambridge University Press, 1996.

MacKendrick, Karmen. *Counterpleasures*. SUNY Series in Postmodern Culture. Albany: State University of New York Press, 1999.

McCallum, Nema. "Anonymity Desirable, Bibliography Not Required: A Journey from Psychiatry to Theology." *Theology and Sexuality* 14 (2007) 29–52.

McDougall, Joy Ann. "Sin—No More? A Feminist Re-Visioning of a Christian Theology of Sin." *Anglican Theological Review* 88/2 (2006) 215–35.

McFague, Sallie. *The Body of God: An Ecological Theology*. Minneapolis: Fortress, 1993.

———. *Metaphorical Theology: Models of God in Religious Language*. Philadelphia: Fortress, 1982.

McReynolds, Sally Ann, and Ann O'Hara Graff. "Sin: When Women are the Context." In *In the Embrace of God: Feminist Approaches to Theological Anthropology*, edited by Ann O'Hara Graff, 161–72. Maryknoll: Orbis, 1995.

Miller, Julie B. "Rapt by God: Eroticized Violence in Medieval Women's Literature and Law." In *The Subjective Eye: Essays in Culture, Religion and Gender in Honor of Margaret R. Miles*, edited by Richard Valantasis, 235–53. Eugene, OR: Pickwick, 2006.

Miller, Nancy K. *Getting Personal: Feminist Occasions and Other Autobiographical Acts*. London: Routledge, 1991.

Millett, Kate. *Sexual Politics*. London: Virago, 1970.

Mitchell, Juliet. *Psychoanalysis and Feminism*. London: Penguin, 1974.

Moltmann, Jürgen. *The Crucified God: The Cross of Christ as the Foundation and Criticism of Christian Theology*. London: SCM, 1974.

Montefiore, Jan. *Feminism and Poetry: Language, Experience, Identity in Women's Writing.* London: HarperCollins, 1987.

Morley, Janet. *All Desires Known.* 2nd ed. London: SPCK, 2005.

———. "I Desire Her with My Whole Heart." In *Feminist Theology: A Reader*, edited by Ann Loades, 158–63. London: SPCK, 1990.

Morton, Nelle. *The Journey is Home.* Boston: Beacon, 1985.

Newton, Melanie. "The 'Accidental Rudeness' of the British." *Stabroek News*, August 15, 2011. No pages. Online: http://www.stabroeknews.com/2011/features/in-the-diaspora/08/15/the-'accidental-rudeness'-of-the-british.

Nygren, Anders. *Agape and Eros.* London: SPCK, 1953.

Ortner, Sherry B. "Is Female to Male as Nature Is to Culture?" *Feminist Studies* 1 (1974) 5–31.

Ostriker, Alicia Suskin. *Feminist Revision and the Bible.* Bucknell Lectures in Literary Theory. Oxford: Blackwell, 1993.

———. *The Nakedness of the Fathers: Biblical Visions and Revisions.* New Brunswick, NJ: Rutgers University Press, 1994.

———. *Stealing the Language: The Emergence of Women's Poetry in America.* London: The Women's Press, 1986.

Owen, Ursula, ed. *Fathers: Reflections by Daughters.* London: Virago, 1986.

Parsons, Susan Frank, ed. *Challenging Women's Orthodoxies in the Context of Faith.* Aldershot: Ashgate, 2000.

Pattison, Stephen. *Shame: Theory, Therapy, Theology.* Cambridge: Cambridge University Press, 2000.

———. "Suffer Little Children: The Challenge of Child Abuse and Neglect to Theology." *Theology and Sexuality* 5/9 (1998) 36–58.

Pearce, Lynne. *Feminism and the Politics of Reading.* London: Arnold, 1997.

Phillips, Anita. *A Defence of Masochism.* London: Faber & Faber, 1998.

Plaskow, Judith. *Sex, Sin and Grace: Women's Experience and the Theologies of Reinhold Niebhur and Paul Tillich.* Washington DC: University Press of America, 1980.

Plaskow, Judith, and Carol P. Christ. Introduction to *Weaving the Visions: New Patterns in Feminist Spirituality.* Edited by Judith Plaskow and Carol P. Christ, 1–13. San Francisco: Harper & Row, 1989.

Probyn, Elspeth. *Sexing the Self: Gendered Positions in Cultural Studies.* London: Routledge, 1993.

———. "This Body Which Is Not One: Speaking an Embodied Self." *Hypatia* 6/3 (1991) 111–24.

Ramsey, Kerry. "Losing One's Life for Others: Self-Sacrifice Revisited." In *Challenging Women's Orthodoxies in the Context of Faith*, edited by Susan Frank Parsons, 121–34. Aldershot: Ashgate, 2000.

Renshaw, Sal. *The Subject of Love: Hélène Cixous and the Feminine Divine.* Manchester: Manchester University Press, 2009.

Rich, Adrienne. *Adrienne Rich's Poetry and Prose.* Edited by Barbara Charlesworth Gelpi and Albert Gelpi. New York: Norton, 1993.

———. *Blood, Bread and Poetry: Selected Prose, 1979–1985.* London: Virago, 1987.

———. "When We Dead Awaken: Writing as Re-Vision." In *The Poetry of Adrienne Rich*, edited by Barbara Charlesworth Gelpi and Albert Gelpi, 90–98. New York: Norton, 1975.

Bibliography

Ricoeur, Paul. *A Ricoeur Reader: Reflection and Imagination*. Edited by Mario J. Valdés. Hemel Hempstead: Harvester Wheatsheaf, 1991.

Ringe, Sharon H. *Luke*. Westminster Bible Companion. Louisville, KY: Westminster John Knox, 1995.

Rowland, Susan. "Michèle Roberts' Virgins: Contesting Gender in Fictions, Re-Writing Jungian Theory and Christian Myth." *Journal of Gender Studies* 8/1 (1999) 35–42.

Rudy, Kathy. "Subjectivity and Belief." In *Queer Theology: Rethinking the Western Body*, edited by Gerard Loughlin, 37–49. Oxford: Blackwell, 2006.

Ruether, Rosemary Radford. "Asceticism and Feminism: Strange Bedmates?" In *Sex and God: Some Varieties of Women's Religious Experience*, edited by Linda Hurcome, 229–50. London: Routledge and Kegan Paul, 1987.

———. "Dualism and the Nature of Evil in Feminist Theology." *Studies in Christian Ethics* 5 (1992) 26–39.

———. *Gaia and God: An Ecofeminist Theology of Earth Healing*. London: SCM, 1992.

———. *Introducing Redemption in Christian Feminism*. Sheffield: Sheffield Academic, 1998.

———. Review of *Deadly Innocence: Feminism and the Mythology of Sin* by Angela West. *Feminist Theology* 5 (1997) 126–28.

———. *Sexism and God-Talk: Towards a Feminist Theology*. London: SCM, 1983.

———. *To Change the World*. New York: Crossroad, 1981.

———. "Women and Sin: A Response to Mary Lowe." *Dialog: A Journal of Theology* 39/3 (2000) 233–35.

Saiving Goldstein, Valerie. "The Human Situation: A Feminine View." *Journal of Religion* 40/2 (1960) 100–112.

Sanders, Julie. *Adaption and Appropriation*. New Critical Idiom. London: Routledge, 2006.

Sands, Kathleen M. *Escape from Paradise: Evil and Tragedy in Feminist Theology*. Minneapolis: Augsburg Fortress, 1994.

———. "Uses of the Thea(o)logian: Sex and Theodicy in Religious Feminism." *Journal of Feminist Studies in Religion* 8/1 (1992) 7–33.

Schaberg, Jane. *The Resurrection of Mary Magdalene: Legends, Apocrypha, and the Christian Testament*. New York: Continuum, 2002.

Schneiders, Sandra M. "The Footwashing (John 13:1–20) An Experiment in Hermeneutics." *The Catholic Biblical Quarterly* 43/1 (1981) 76–92.

Schulenberg, Jane Tibbetts. "The Heroics of Virginity: Brides of Christ and Sacrifical Mutilation." In *Women in the Middle Ages and the Renaissance: Literary and Historical Perspectives*, edited by Mary Beth Rose, 29–72. Syracuse: Syracuse University Press, 1986.

Schüssler Fiorenza, Elisabeth. *In Memory of Her: A Feminist Theological Reconstruction of Christian Origins*. London: SCM, 1983.

Sellers, Susan. *Myth and Fairy Tale in Contemporary Women's Fiction*. Basingstoke: Palgrave, 2001.

———, ed. *Writing Differences: Readings from the Seminar of Hélène Cixous*. Milton Keynes: Open University Press, 1988.

Sherwood, Yvonne. "Passion—Binding—Passion." In *Towards a Theology of Eros: Transfiguring Passion at the Limits of Discipline*, edited by Virginia Burrus and Catherine Keller, 169–93. New York: Fordham University Press, 2006.

Skerrett, K. Roberts. "When No Means Yes: The Passion of Carter Heyward." *Journal of Feminist Studies in Religion* 12/1 (1996) 71–92.

Slee, Nicola. *Praying Like a Woman*. London: SPCK, 2004.
Smith, Sidonie. "Performativity, Autobiographical Practice, Resistance." In *Women, Autobiography, Theory: A Reader*, edited by Sidonie Smith and Julia Watson, 108–15. Madison: The University of Wisconsin Press, 1998.
———. *A Poetics of Women's Autobiography: Marginality and the Fictions of Self-Representation*. Bloomington: University of Indianapolis Press, 1987.
Soracco, Sabrina. "Six Views of The Little Mermaid: A Psychoanalytic Approach." *Scandinavian Studies* 60 (1990) 403–29.
Soskice, Janet Martin. *The Kindness of God: Metaphor, Gender and Religious Language*. Oxford: Oxford University Press, 2007.
———. "Turning the Symbols." In *Swallowing a Fishbone? Feminist Theologians Debate Christianity*, edited by Daphne Hampson, 17–32. London: SPCK, 1996.
Stacey, Jackie. "Heroes." In *Temporalities, Autobiography and Everyday Life*, edited by Jan Campbell and Janet Harbord, 75–108. Manchester: Manchester University Press, 2002.
Stanley, Liz. *The Auto/Biographical I: The Theory and Practice of Feminist Auto/Biography*. Manchester Manchester University Press, 1992.
Starhawk. *The Earth Path: Grounding Your Spirit in the Rhythms of Nature*. San Francisco: HarperSanFrancisco, 2004.
———. *The Spiral Dance: A Rebirth of the Ancient Religion of the Great Goddess*. San Francisco: HarperSanFrancisco, 1979.
———. *Webs of Power: Notes from the Global Uprising*. Victoria, BC: New Society, 2002.
Stuart, Elizabeth. *Spitting at Dragons: Towards a Feminist Theology of Sainthood*. London: Mowbray, 1996.
Suchocki, Marjorie Hewitt. *The Fall to Violence: Original Sin in Relational Theology*. New York: Continuum, 1995.
Thistlethwaite, Susan. *Sex, Race and God: Christian Feminism in Black and White*. London: Geoffrey Chapman, 1990.
Tompkins, Jane. "Me and My Shadow." *New Literary History* 19/1 (1987) 169–78.
Torrance, Iain. "A Response to Professor Rosemary Radford Ruether's 'Dualism and the Nature of Evil in Feminist Ethics.'" *Studies in Christian Ethics* 5 (1992) 40–43.
Trible, Phyllis. *Texts of Terror: Literary-Feminist Readings of Biblical Narratives*. London: SCM, 1984.
Veeser, H. Aram. "Introduction: The Case for Confessional Criticism." In *Confessions of the Critics*, edited by H. Aram Veeser, ix–xxvii. New York: Routledge, 1996.
Walker, Alice. *In Search of Our Mothers' Gardens: Womanist Prose*. London: The Women's Press, 1984.
Walton, Heather. *Imagining Theology: Women, Writing and God*. London: T. & T. Clark, 2007.
———, ed. *Literature and Theology: New Interdisciplinary Spaces*. Surrey: Ashgate, 2011.
———. *Literature, Theology and Feminism*. Manchester: Manchester University Press, 2007.
———. Review of *The Sacred Desert: Religion, Literature, Art, and Culture*, by David Jasper. *Literature and Theology* 19/2 (2005) 188–90.
Warner, Marina. *From the Beast to the Blonde: On Fairy Tales and Their Tellers*. London: Random House, 1994.
West, Angela. *Deadly Innocence: Feminism and the Mythology of Sin*. London: Cassell, 1995.

Bibliography

White, Rosie. "Visions and Re-Visions: Women and Time in Michèle Roberts's *In the Red Kitchen*." *Women: A Cultural Review* 15/2 (2004) 180–91.

Winterson, Jeanette. *Lighthousekeeping*. London: Vintage, 2004.

Wittig, Monique. *Les Guerilleres*. Translated by David Levay. New York: Viking, 1971.

Wyschogrod, Edith. *Saints and Postmodernism*. Chicago: University of Chicago Press, 1990.